SECONDARY CURRICULUM DESIGN AND DELIVERY

SECONDARY CURRICULUM DESIGN AND DELIVERY

Glynis Frater

1 Oliver's Yard
55 City Road
London EC1Y 1SP

2455 Teller Road
Thousand Oaks
California 91320

Unit No 323-333, Third Floor, F-Block
International Trade Tower, Nehru Place
New Delhi 110 019

8 Marina View Suite 43-053
Asia Square Tower 1
Singapore 018960

British Library Cataloguing in Publication data

A catalogue record for this book is available from the British Library

Editor: James Clark
Assitant Editor: Esosa Otabor
Production editor: Nicola Marshall
Copyeditor: Ritika Sharma
Proofreader: Girish Sharma
Indexer: TNQ Tech Pvt. Ltd.
Marketing manager: Dilhara Attygalle
Cover design: Bhairvi Vyas
Typeset by: TNQ Tech Pvt. Ltd.
Printed and bound by CPI Group (UK) Ltd
Croydon, CR0 4YY

ISBN 978-1-5296-6812-4
ISBN 978-1-5296-6811-7 (pbk)

CONTENTS

ABOUT THE AUTHOR

Following several years teaching in schools in the West Midlands and Shropshire, **Glynis's** professional journey then led her through several different incarnations of policy change in relation to curriculum design and delivery. She was a part of the introduction of the Key Skills Support Programme and led on building a strategy in Wales for the embedding of key skills into the curriculum in key stages 2 and 3. She was a Programme Director working with the Specialist Schools and Academies Trust developing a CPD strategy for schools across England and Wales as part of a rethinking of the curriculum before 2010. In 2010, she founded Learning Cultures Limited, an organisation dedicated to developing high-quality CPD for school and subject leaders, teachers and others in education. She has been an integral part of the design and delivery of high-profile curriculum and coaching programmes and training courses for primary and secondary audiences across the UK and internationally. She is also a qualified coach. Coaching is an essential element of creating a high-quality and deeply collaborative CPD strategy in any organisation and Glynis continues to weave the principles of coaching into all her work. She is the author of *Primary Curriculum Design and Delivery* (Sage, 2023) and several business studies textbooks, has written for educational journals and creates a weekly news-post for the education profession through Learning Cultures' website. Glynis lives in Shropshire with her husband and Toby the dog.

ACKNOWLEDGEMENTS

Once again, I have been given the space and the time to write this second book about the secondary curriculum with the love, help and support of my family and close friends. I would like to thank all those who have been with me on this journey and who have patiently accepted that I am sometimes elsewhere thinking about or actually writing the content. I am especially grateful to Graham, my husband who has been patient and supportive throughout.

Thanks go to my colleagues, especially Sandra, Stansfield, Lee Taylor, John Price and Joanne Lawrence, who have a wealth of knowledge and experience of education and are always there to keep me informed about change as it occurs for all of us who work with schools and colleges. They have become friends as well as colleagues and my own understanding of the education landscape would be diminished without their continued support. As always, my closest friend Geralyn Wilson has always been there to question my assumptions and beliefs and be a true support in all sorts of ways.

Working with secondary schools across the UK has given me a valuable insight into what schools need in terms of how they develop and deliver a cohesive and high-quality curriculum offer to their pupils. I would especially like to thank Lady Maria Satchwell, the headteacher at The Madeley Academy and her Assistant Head, Kate Barnes, who gave me access to the excellent curriculum offered across the school.

Also, I would like to thank Louise Maris Assistant Head at Holy Catholic Family school in Walthamstow for giving me the opportunity to work with her and groups of subject leaders and teachers who were learning how to use instructional coaching to support their whole school curriculum improvement agenda. A third outstanding professional I would like to acknowledge here is Emma Harvey at Featherstone High School in Ealing. Emma has been a leading light at Learning Cultures in her quest to introduce a coaching model into her school which has undoubtedly had a powerful impact on curriculum delivery and teaching and learning in the school. There are many others too numerous to mention in person, but my thanks go out to all those schools who we have supported us and are building strong curriculum content along with powerful pedagogy across England and beyond.

Thanks go with gratitude to James Clark at Sage who has edited my text with great skill. He has taught me a lot about my own writing style and verbosity. Also, to Esosa Otabor who has been there to support the editing and development of this book.

Finally, this book is for my family, my daughter Rebecca and to hers and Thomas's children, Alfred and Flora. Also, to my stepsons James and William and Catherine and William's children Harry and Roxie. It is family that are the rock that steadies us all and education that enriches us. Here, in particular, this is for Alfred and Flora and Harry and Roxie as they continue to learn and grow towards their own secondary school education.

1

MAKING SENSE OF A QUARTER OF A CENTURY OF CHANGE

Contents

- An axis of two quite different ideologies over 25 years of change
- The emergence of a new approach to curriculum 2000–2010
- Key stage 3 and 4 reform in the 2000s
- The 14–19 agenda – a blend of academic and vocational opportunity
- Curriculum 2000, the start of a reform of A levels
- A change of regime in 2010 and a new knowledge-emphasised curriculum
- A new knowledge-focused curriculum model
- A change of thinking about assessment
- A radical change for key stage 4 and the qualification outcomes for pupils
- The influence of Ofsted from 2017 in shaping the curriculum as pivotal to the quality of education
- The 2020s, a pandemic and a continued focus on powerful knowledge

AN AXIS OF TWO QUITE DIFFERENT IDEOLOGIES OVER 25 YEARS OF CHANGE

> The curriculum should be treasured. There should be real pride in "our" curriculum: the learning that the nation has decided it should set before its young. Teachers, parents, the wider education community, the media and the public at large should all see the curriculum as something that they embrace, support and celebrate. Most of all, young people should relish the opportunity for discovery and achievement that the curriculum offers to them. (Waters 2008)

For all of us with an interest in the secondary school curriculum, there is a dilemma that continues to create a lively conversation about what should be taught and how best to create the spark that leads to life-long learning; capturing the learning from the primary school and continuing to ignite a passion for learning from year 7 to year 11 in readiness for adulthood.

The secondary curriculum covers both key stages 3 and 4 and, in some schools, key stage 5 and is pivotal in shaping the life chances of pupils from age 11, at the end of their primary school journey and as they enter year 7. Key stage 3 lies between the primary years and the all-important, 14–19 stages, where examinations shape the curriculum agenda. Key stage 3, as we will see as we look at the history of this period, is often the poor relation as the sceptre of key stage 4 is dominated by a prescription of awarding body specifications and their associated high-stakes testing. The structure of these key stages has not changed over the past 25 or so years, but the ideology about what the National Curriculum should contain and how it should be taught has.

During the first ten years of this century, education reform was shaped by the Labour leader Tony Blair who became Prime Minister in 1997. He made it clear through his much-quoted priority from when he became leader of the Labour party, 'education, education, education' that systems change within education was inevitable. His own political views were more towards the centre ground in his reforming manifesto and his concept of 'New Labour' as opposed to old socialist principles were what he wanted to leave behind. Initially, he set about change to the structures and systems within the education system with less focus on the curriculum.

His new government had a vision to create much greater independence across the education landscape, reforming the comprehensive system and ensuring that any change would focus on the needs of the individual pupil.

> "Let me spell it out," Mr Blair told the 1999 labour party conference, "In education, we need to move to the post-comprehensive era, where schools keep the comprehensive principle of equality of opportunity but where we open up the system to new and different ways of education, built round the needs of the individual child." (Blair 2002)

The Blair/Brown governments that shaped policy in the early part of this century focused on skills and on their belief that education is about how learners develop as citizens with the skills they will need for life and work. Their 14–19 strategy brought about a radical change to a well-established system of academic subjects by introducing new vocational style qualifications that learners could choose from the age of 14 at the beginning of year 10 as an alternative to some of the traditional optional foundation subjects. The introduction of Key Skills as an alternative to GCSEs for pupils who had not managed to obtain a Level 2 pass in GCSE as part of the post 16 pathway and the development of a suite of generic learning skills, the personal, thinking and learning skills (PLTs) all reinforced the belief that skills were the essential ingredient in ensuring pupils would achieve their potential as positive and responsible citizens.

THE EMERGENCE OF A NEW APPROACH TO CURRICULUM 2000–2010

The emphasis over the whole of the first decade of the new century was to ensure that all children achieve irrespective of their background be it race, gender, culture or otherwise. The Every Child Matters (ECM) initiative set out their priorities with five overarching principles for every child from birth to age 19.

- Being healthy
- Staying safe
- Enjoying and achieving
- Making a positive contribution
- Economic well-being

DfES (2003)

In 2004, Mike Tomlinson carried out a review entitled '14–19 Curriculum reforms', the document set out its priorities for this age group to have the knowledge, skills and attitudes needed for adulthood. It also emphasised the need to ensure that the choice of pathway was linked to an entitlement framework that gave pupils access to a wide range of learning opportunities suited to their own interests, aptitudes and ambitions.

To support schools with the introduction of the reforms that would dominate education change over the decade, a new organisation emerged called The National Strategies. They provided a wealth of supporting documentation and materials for early years, and key stages 1–3. Their work and what they produced was always to a high standard and extremely useful for all those, including myself, who were involved in the far-reaching changes that were being introduced. Their remit was to create:

- detailed frameworks for each of English, mathematics, science and information computer technology (ICT);
- generic pedagogic guidance for the foundation subjects;
- guidance on related whole-school issues, including behaviour, attendance and well-being.

KEY STAGES 3 AND 4 CURRICULUM REFORM IN THE 2000S

A new key stage 3 national strategy was launched in 2001. Its principal aim was to ensure that gains in the literacy and numeracy priorities in primary schools continued into the secondary school.

> *A major objective of our key stage 3 strategy is* to ensure that secondary teachers are well placed to take forward the work already done in primary schools. There are many excellent teachers and many examples of good practice, but we all know that there is a long way to go before we have made the progress we need. That is why, earlier this year we announced the introduction of a new strategy at key stage 3 to raise standards for all 11–14-year-olds. (Morris 2001)

The strategy was based on four main principles of expectation, progression, engagement and transformation. There were five subject strands of English, maths, science and ICT and the foundation subjects. Its main aim was to transform achievement of 11- to 14-year-olds (Knight et al. 2004).

Following consultation, a revised *National Curriculum Handbook* for schools for key stage 3 and 4 was published in 2004 by the Qualification and Curriculum Authority (QCA) which set out the following aims.

The curriculum should enable young people to become:

- successful learners who enjoy learning, make progress and achieve;
- confident individuals who can live safe, healthy and fulfilling lives;
- responsible citizens who make a positive contribution to society.

For each of these headings, there were around 10 statements, including, for example, statements on learning how to learn, having secure values and beliefs and sustaining and improving the environment.

Alongside this, a White Paper published in 2004 set out a vision for change to the 14–19 agenda for schools and colleges. The emphasis was on ensuring all learners left school with the basic skills of reading, writing and ICT and the personal skills associated with ensuring successful learners, confident individuals and responsible citizens. There was to be a much greater vocational provision with the introduction of vocational diplomas designed in consultation with business and their sector skills councils (SSC).

> The new secondary curriculum (2008) places greater emphasis on pupils' understanding of the concepts, ideas and processes of subjects, on cross-curricular themes and on pupils' development of life skills. (Waters 2009)

The changes to the key stage 3 curriculum were intended to reduce the statutory curriculum requirements and give teachers more freedom and flexibility to determine what should be taught and how it should be taught.

Whilst still focusing on the development of a core of English, maths and ICT, there was an imperative to create cross-curricular elements in ways that would promote the development of learning skills that would transcend subject specific learning.

These generic skills were prescribed as the personal, learning and thinking skills (PLTs) of:

- team working;
- independent enquiry;
- self-management;
- reflective learning;
- effective participation;
- creative thinking skills.

Each of the PLTs listed above was amplified within a National Strategies document that went into detail as to what each entailed for the teacher to incorporate them into their teaching within all the National Curriculum subjects.

The revised key stage 3 curriculum also required a focus on the development of cross-curricular thematic work ensuring pupils extended their learning across a range of subjects. There was reduced curriculum content, but the requirement to see where subject-specific concepts, themes and knowledge where prevalent elsewhere in other subjects was a change from the original national curriculum first introduced in 1988 that focused very much on individual subject content.

The final piece of this curriculum jigsaw was the introduction of a suite of seven non-statutory ‘curriculum dimensions’, these were described as:

- identity and cultural diversity;
- healthy lifestyles;
- community participation;
- enterprise;
- global dimension and sustainable development;
- technology and the media;
- creativity and critical thinking.

Several commentators were critical of the lack of attention being paid to key stage 3 as the priority was clearly to focus on the 14–19 agenda including the introduction of a completely new set of diploma qualifications.

A report by Ofsted in 2009, Planning for change: the impact of the new Key Stage 3 curriculum suggests that many schools continued to deliver the curriculum much has they had done previously paying some attention to the ideas around cross curricular themes and a much greater emphasis on the skills for learning, but the focus was still on subject learning with the greatest emphasis on the 14–19 agenda and still some criticism about positive strategies for academic transition.

THE 14–19 AGENDA – A BLEND OF ACADEMIC AND VOCATIONAL OPPORTUNITY

The 14–19 reforms seemed to be the priority for the governments of the first decade of the 21st century. They were undoubtedly linked to the vision for economic prosperity and the skills agenda that was a policy priority.

The rationale was set out in a report of the working group on 14–19 reform chaired by Mike Tomlinson, a former Chief Inspector of Ofsted, as listed below:

- Raise participation and achievement.
- Get the basics right.
- Strengthen vocational routes.
- Provide greater stretch and challenge.
- Reduce the assessment burden for learners, teachers, institutions and the system as a whole.
- Make the system more transparent.

This new approach to 14–19 education was first announced in 2005 and was to include 14 different qualification routes offered at National Qualification Framework levels 1–3. The first five were Information Technology, Society, Health and Development, Construction and the Built Environment, Engineering and Creative and Media. A further five for roll out at a slightly later date were Land-based and Environmental, Manufacturing, Hair and Beauty and Business Administration and Finance. A further four were introduced for the following year, Public Services, Sport and Leisure, Retail and Travel and Tourism.

There were plans to introduce three additional Diploma qualifications in Science, Languages and the Humanities to bring general qualifications into the Diploma stable, but this never happened.

The Diploma qualifications were designed to meet SSC guidelines as to what they would lead to in terms of outcomes and potential next steps for those learners who chose to follow this route. They were unique in creating a composite opportunity for learners to mix vocational learning with academic study of English, maths, science and another additional or specialist qualification.

They were widely criticised as a middle track, neither academic nor vocational. They had to compete with the existing system of GCSEs and A Levels and they were difficult to manage within the school system which was not equipped with the resources or staff expertise to run them.

In 2007, the then Department of Education and Skills (DfES) became two different departments, Department for Children, Schools and Families (DCSF) and the Department for Innovation, Universities and Skills (DIUS).

CURRICULUM 2000, THE START OF A REFORM OF A LEVELS

Post-16 education was one of the first areas of reform for Tony Blair's New Labour government. A review concluded that the post-16 curriculum in England was too narrow, not inclusive and was inflexible (Tomlinson 2002). It was felt that young people studying beyond the age of 16 were at a disadvantage with their European counterparts and unable to compete because of the lack of a wider range of post-16 qualifications and outcomes.

The subsequent changes that were introduced to address this were part of what were known as the 'Qualifying for Success' reforms which were introduced in September 2000. The aim was to provide an opportunity for students to study more subjects and to combine academic and vocational study.

Included in these reforms was the requirement for students to also demonstrate their competence in the key skills of communication, application of number and information technology. A Levels would remain in the same format for some alongside some 'world class tests' to stretch the more able. Introduced alongside the A Level was a new GCE advanced subsidiary (AS) qualification that embraces the first half of a full A Level worth 50% of the assessment grade.

New vocational qualifications were also introduced; the new advanced vocational certificate of education (AVCE) replaced the advanced general national vocational qualification (GNVQ). The AVCE was equivalent in size and demand as that of an A level and had the same grade structure on a similar A–E scale, there was also an AS equivalent available in some subjects.

The key skills of Communication, Application of Number and IT also became qualifications which in turn became Functional Skills and a statutory requirement for all those in post-16 education who did not have a GCSE in Maths and English.

These reforms were broadly welcomed by those in the profession who taught in a post-16 environment. However, the workload was more difficult to manage. For some teachers, the fact that year 12 was now a year of AS examinations was also seen as being hard on students who were not able to use year 12 to adapt to the inevitable leap from GCSE to advanced level study.

A CHANGE OF REGIME IN 2010 AND A NEW KNOWLEDGE-EMPHASISED CURRICULUM

The Diploma qualification structure, National Strategies, Every Child Matters, the A2 as part of A level reform were all wiped away following the election of a new coalition government in 2010 consisting of the Conservative and the Liberal Democrat parties.

In December 2011, the Department of Education (DfE) newly named from the previous Department of Children Schools and Families published its first report from the expert panel on The Framework for the National Curriculum. Their remit was to:

- review evidence of the efficacy of current curriculum provision;
- explore structural issues concerning future curriculum design;
- consider the views of subject and sector specialists and analyse calls for evidence as to what to include in relation to subjects.

The debate about skills and or knowledge was highlighted throughout this document,

> All learning has content, including skills, and this content is usually quite specific. Whilst generic forms of skill and capability are important, these cannot be taught in isolation. They must be taught in a context with content, and only then do the more generic aspects of learning become available for reflection and development. (DfE 2011: p15)

The key principles for the review were defined as:

- developed in line with the principles of freedom, responsibility and fairness;
- ensuring schools are given more freedom over the curriculum they plan and implement;
- setting out essential knowledge (facts, concepts, principles and fundamental operations);
- reflecting the collective wisdom we have about how children learn and what they should know;
- embodying rigour and exacting standards and having the opportunity to acquire a core of knowledge in key subject disciplines;
- stressing the importance of the incorporation of the national curriculum into the wider whole school curriculum which should be developed at school level;
- ensuring the curriculum is a national benchmark of excellence for all schools not just maintained schools.

A further report in 2013 analysed some of the concerns voiced by different interest groups such as those representing special needs and specific subject specialists or associations. This report was entitled Reform of the National Curriculum: Equalities Impact Assessment.

A NEW KNOWLEDGE-FOCUSED CURRICULUM MODEL

The new National Curriculum was confirmed in October 2013. The aims outlined in DfE's Curriculum Framework document published in 2014 have a much greater emphasis on knowledge and state at the beginning of the document,

> The national curriculum provides pupils with an introduction to the essential knowledge that they need to be educated citizens. It introduces pupils to the best

> that has been thought and said; and helps engender an appreciation of human creativity and achievement.
>
> The national curriculum provides an outline of core knowledge around which teachers can develop exciting and stimulating lessons to promote the development of pupils' knowledge, understanding and skills as part of the wider school curriculum. (DfE 2014)

The curriculum that came into being as part of the coalition reforms in 2014 (DfE 2014) emphasised the knowledge-rich nature of each of the statutory subjects in key stages 1, 2 and 3 and focused on what pupils should learn about as opposed to how the subjects should be taught in relation to the pedagogy and associated skills essential for learning.

The programmes of study for English, maths and science in key stages 1 and 2 are prescriptive and build a set of age-related standards for each year from year 1 to year 6. The key stage 3 and 4 core curricula are not divided into individual years, creating a freedom for those who plan to decide what to teach when. All the foundation subjects are set out to provide an outline of what to teach over the duration of the key stage. The sequencing of the learning and intertwining of concepts, topics and themes is the domain of the teacher and their subject leads.

At the beginning of the development phase of designing the new curriculum there was a debate as to the merits of key stage 3 being two years, therefore creating a three-year key stage 4. The lack of prescription as to what to teach meant that the decision about the length of these two key stages was in the hands of the school.

However, it was clear throughout the introduction of the new curriculum that Ofsted as a major player in judging the quality of a school's curriculum was in favour of a three-year key stage 3. At one briefing that I attended, one of their representatives said that Ofsted would not advise on either preference, but it was their belief that GCSEs were designed to be taught and assessed over two years and the key stage 3 curriculum should be delivered over three years which does suggest that they did indeed have a preference.

A review of key stage 3 in 2015, 'Key stage 3: The wasted years?' published by Ofsted certainly explains their concerns as to the continued lack of attention paid to this important key stage (Ofsted 2015).

A CHANGE IN THINKING ABOUT ASSESSMENT OF THE NATIONAL CURRICULUM

At the same time as the development of the new curriculum, it was also decided to reform assessment. The National Curriculum levels 1–8 that represented age and ability-related points of achievement were abandoned. Nothing was to replace them. The rationale for this was to give schools more freedom in how they assessed learning linked to the age-related standards and subject content within the core curriculum and to some extent in the foundation subjects.

A Commission on 'Assessment without Levels' was set up to define the changes and to offer advice on how to create the assessment processes that could replace the levels.

This commission produced a final report in 2015 named, Commission on Assessment without Levels (DfE 2015). The policy remains to leave it up to schools to define their approach to assessing pupils progress, knowledge acquisition and skills competence.

The reasons given for abandoning the levels were that they were not accurate enough, they were difficult to understand and often became labels for children. I am not sure expecting each school to create their own assessment processes are any easier or more accurate. Without a clear process of highly interactive and collaborative professional development and ongoing opportunities for moderation, the new approaches will not be any more accurate or fair.

Assessment is no longer prescriptive as it was when the levels existed, but the aims and the purpose of study do provide some prescription as to what pupils should know and be able to do by the end of each of the key stages. There is also the careful analysis of the mark schemes that are an essential element of study towards GCSE that could form the basis of structured assessment criteria within key stage 3.

In their original advice, the Commission on Assessment without Levels cited the work of Anderson and Krathwhol who revised Bloom's taxonomy that had been in existence since 1956. They changed Bloom's nouns into verbs as part of their more progressive taxonomy. Essentially, moving from subject matter (the noun) to cognitive processes (the verb).

The introduction into this later taxonomy of the verb remembering is linked to four knowledge dimensions, Bloom only included three. These were factual (basic knowledge), conceptual (the interrelationship between basic elements of knowledge) and procedural (the 'how to' part of knowledge). Anderson and Krathwohl (2002) introduced a fourth knowledge dimension, the metacognitive (knowledge of cognition and awareness of one's own thinking processes). These changes can be seen to mirror the changes to curriculum policy and the emphasis on knowledge, how it is decided upon and how it is learnt and remembered over time. This is explored in more detail in Chapter 12 (Table 1.1).

Table 1.1 Comparing Bloom's and the Anderson & Krathwhol taxonomies

Bloom's taxonomy	Anderson and Krathwohl's taxonomy
Knowledge: Learner's ability to recall information	**Remembering:** Learner's ability to recall information
Comprehension: Learner's ability to understand information	**Understanding:** Learner's ability to understand information
Application: Learner's ability to use information in a new way	**Applying:** Learner's ability to use information in a new way
Analysis: Learner's ability to break down information into its essential parts	**Analysing:** Learner's ability to break down information into its essential parts
Synthesis: Learner's ability to create something new from different elements of information	**Evaluating:** Learner's ability to judge or criticise information
Evaluation: Learner's ability to judge or criticise information	**Creating:** Learner's ability to create something new from different elements of information

A RADICAL CHANGE FOR KEY STAGE 4 AND THE QUALIFICATION OUTCOMES FOR PUPILS

One of the major changes to the secondary curriculum was the return to linear GCSEs and A levels. There was concern that the modular approach led to over assessment for some pupils and that ensuring the assessment was always at the end of the two-year course would be preferable. The modular approach did provide some pupils with the opportunity to resit part of a GCSE and improve their grades or to finish their GCSE course earlier.

The introduction of what became known as the English Baccalaureate defined what pupils had to study and what they could choose to study. The prescription for pupils continues to require that pupils take GCSEs in both English Literature and English Language, Mathematics and either GCSE combined science which is equivalent to two GCSEs, or three single sciences chosen from physics, chemistry, biology and computer science. They must choose either geography or history, although to study both, they can choose one or the other from the list of optional subjects. They also must take an ancient or modern foreign language.

What turns a suite of GCSE qualifications into an 'English Baccalaureate' is the adding up of points linked to the grade system that was changed from A* - G into 1-9 with 9 being the top grade so that points could be added together to ascertain how well the school has performed. The baccalaureate is not a qualification outcome for the pupil.

In terms of baccalaureate points, it was not in a school's best interest to offer vocational qualifications as they would not count. However, some do remain. A pupil can study Business, ICT, Computer Science, Engineering and Electronics.

Many subjects that had been a part of the offer prior to the introduction of the new curriculum were no longer available to pupils and the subjects available for study at key stage 4 were academic especially in the compulsory subjects that were necessary within the confines of the English Baccalaureate. The opportunity for pupils to study a range of vocational options, to take functional skills instead of GCSE English, maths and ICT was no longer an option.

One notable casualty of the new reforms was the ASDAN qualification, 'The Certificate of Personal Effectiveness (CoPE)' (CoPE 2020). This had been a GCSE equivalent and was very popular as a way of delivering the personal, learning and thinking skills and other extra-curricular activities associated with aspects of citizenship, PSHE or Duke of Edinburgh awards. Many schools do still use CoPE to accredit their non-academic studies and as evidence of breadth and depth.

THE INFLUENCE OF OFSTED FROM 2017 IN SHAPING THE CURRICULUM AS PIVOTAL TO THE QUALITY OF EDUCATION

Ofsted acquired a new chief inspector in 2017. Amanda Spielman came into office following her tenure as chair of Ofqual. In one of her speeches following her appointment, she emphasises her quest for the curriculum, the substance of education, as she calls it, to take centre stage,

> I am announcing today that I have chosen the curriculum to be the focus of the first big thematic Ofsted review of my tenure. From early years, through to primary, secondary, sixth form and FE colleges, this will explore the real substance of education.
>
> We will look at how schools are interpreting the national curriculum or using their academy freedoms to build new curricula of their own and what this means for children's school experience. We will look at what makes a really good curriculum. And we will also look at the problems, such as curriculum narrowing, and what we can do to tackle them. (Spielman, ASCL Annual Conference March 2017)

Ofsted published three phases of research spanning 2017 to 2019 to inform their revised *Inspection Handbook* and framework. Some of the findings from these research phases will be explored in more detail in other chapters of this book; so for this chapter, we are simply recording the history and the focus of curriculum as the substance and structure of education.

The first phase of the research was a small open-ended exploratory look at the curriculum in 40 schools across the distinct phases of education, the findings in a nutshell suggested: (Ofsted 2017).

- There is little or no debate or reflection about the curriculum.
- There was a greater emphasis on the timetable, which though acknowledged as important is not the curriculum.
- There were very few tangible reference points to get to grips with the complex business of curriculum planning.
- There was a lack of clarity around the language of the curriculum.
- There was a weak theoretical understanding of what is meant by the curriculum.
- There was no training in the theory of curriculum for leaders, teachers and trainee teachers.
- There were serious concerns about the narrowing of key stage 3.
- Pupils with SEND did not receive parity in terms of the curriculum.

The second phase of Ofsted's research looked to identify positive influences on curriculum design (Ofsted 2018). They identified 23 schools where leaders were 'particularly invested in curriculum design'.

The researchers asked these questions:

- How do curriculum managers perceive knowledge within their curriculum?
- What do curriculum managers do when designing, implementing and evaluating the curriculum?
- How have curriculum managers developed the curriculum over time?
- Is there a common conceptual language employed by curriculum managers?

Their findings suggested that the schools fell into three distinct categories linked to their approach to what they intended to deliver as a curriculum strategy:

- **Knowledge led** - the mastery of a body of subject-specific knowledge defined by the school. Skills were seen as an outcome of the curriculum not its purpose
- **Knowledge engaged** - knowledge remains a focus and enables the application of skill.
- **Skills led** - the curriculum is designed around skills, learning behaviours and 'generic knowledge'.

The research suggested that there were strengths and weaknesses in each of the above approaches to curriculum design (Spielman 2018). Most of the schools provided strong links with their curriculum for pupils from disadvantaged backgrounds and made reading a priority. They also agreed that designing the curriculum should be a reflective process with regular updates after discussions between senior and subject leaders. There was also a tacit understanding that to learn pupils needed intelligent repetition and recall of content and that formative and summative assessment were essential to ascertain that pupils were making good progress.

The third piece of research introduced a set of curriculum indicators drawn up following their phase 2 research (Ofsted 2018). The purpose of this piece of research was to look at whether these 25 indicators would accurately test whether it was possible to assess curriculum quality across a range of schools.

These indicators were used to authenticate the process of inspection. The purpose was to check the accuracy of inspection judgements about how curriculum intent translated into the implementation across different subjects within the school and to inform the soon to be published new handbook that came into being in September 2019. They make a useful contribution to any discussion about curriculum and will be discussed in more detail in Chapter 2.

A final piece of research (Ofsted 2019a) was published in the summer of 2019 that once again focused on the accuracy of inspection judgements and an opportunity to demonstrate how Ofsted were moderating their approaches to ensuring there was parity with the judgements they were making about the quality of education across the distinct phases and types of schools (Ofsted 2019c).

They looked at pedagogy and lesson observation and created 18 indicators of what they wanted to see when they visited lessons. The indicators focus on curriculum implementation, the quality of teaching and the behaviour of pupils. They provide a useful tool for setting the parameters for what observers see and what teachers aspire to achieve (Ofsted 2019b).

The research also looked at 'workbook scrutiny' which is in inverted commas here because I feel it is most definitely the wrong title. Demonstrating learning and progression is not just found in books, pupils draw, paint, perform, present, play sport, make models all of which provide a benchmark of how well they are doing (Ofsted 2019a).

Alongside their focus on what was happening in the classroom and what was being produced by pupils, there was an emphasis on the professional conversations that inspectors would undertake with senior and subject leaders, teachers and pupils. It was the consistency of message and the understanding of how curriculum intent translated into curriculum implementation that was at stake for the school.

The *Inspection Handbook* has been revised several times since 2019, the latest at the time of writing was September 2024 (Ofsted 2024). The focus continues to be the curriculum and its role in judging the quality of education across the whole school.

THE 2020S, BREXIT, A PANDEMIC AND A CONTINUED FOCUS ON KNOWLEDGE

We have now reached an interesting time in a post-Brexit world and in the aftermath of a pandemic where ideology in relation to education is likely to be tested by a new government. There is undoubtedly a shortage of skills across a range of professions and businesses. The rise of the internet provides us with all the knowledge we could ever want, albeit superficial and makes the teacher's job difficult in inspiring their learners to want to learn from them. Technology is changing at a pace very few of us can keep up with and most learners who leave school during the rest of this century are likely to need to learn new skills and knowledge, not yet dreamed of, for the purpose of their employment in whatever sector they choose.

In 2019, the introduction of a new *Inspection Handbook* that emphasised the curriculum as the powerful driver of quality in education set the scene for many schools to build their curriculum planning and delivery around the three I's of Intent, Implementation and Impact with a clear focus on expert subject knowledge, a sequence to the learning and an understanding of concepts within and across subject divides.

However, nobody foresaw the catastrophic change that impacted on all of us not just here in the UK but around the world: a near complete lockdown, the curtailing of freedoms and a closing of schools for most children. History will no doubt cite this event as signalling a change in how we educate, how we access and process knowledge and how we interact as part of the process of learning.

The necessity to use technology and develop strategies to support pupils to learn remotely were by and large successful. There have been many problems and many studies that suggest that pupils especially younger ones have gaps in their learning, have behavioural issues or find concentrating difficult following their return to school full time (Education Endowment Foundation 2022).

I am sure that as time progresses, technological change and strategies for a more blended approach to how we learn will prevail. Now there is a desire to return to the status quo that existed before the spring of 2020. I doubt in the longer term that this is possible and that slowly, change will create a more blended learning model for all schools.

What next is difficult to define. The skills versus knowledge debate shows no sign of abating and many of the subject reviews published by Ofsted in the past couple of years use terms like substantive and disciplinary knowledge which teachers must unpick in relation to their own subject when planning what to teach and when to teach it, to what depth and to what breadth. Substantive knowledge is the facts, the what of a subject in relation to the basic knowledge defined by subject experts. Disciplinary knowledge is effectively how the substantive knowledge is used to find out more, infer or build on knowledge to aid deeper understanding of specific concepts or ideas. We will explore these concepts in much more detail in later chapters.

Our exit from the European Union has left us as a country with a gaping skills gap for whatever reason and the policies of the past 14 years have moved us away from creating young adults who have the skills to fill the technical and specialist vacancies that continue to create problems for many businesses and industries. The apprenticeship scheme exists to address this, but the academic route many have had to follow at key stage 4 and for some into key stage 5 means their vocational learning comes too late and many are disillusioned, lack confidence and are not sure of the pathway they wish to follow.

CONCLUSION

This has been a historical journey through more than 20 years of research, review and change in relation to what we as a country think is essential content for a curriculum that will equip the next generations with what they need to be active, happy and productive citizens. There is no doubt that there is distinct divide between the first 10 years and the second. A skills agenda versus a knowledge agenda is too simplistic but will suffice for this chapter. The third decade is proving problematic for policy as the economic fallout from Brexit, the pandemic and the war in Ukraine dominate. Education policy has not been high on the agenda except for a White Paper published in March 2022 (DfE 2022).

The ideologies from both decades - the 2000s and 2010s - had one thing in common, the desire to close the gap between the advantaged and the disadvantaged. Neither have succeeded and both have been compounded by situations sometimes out of their control. Whatever happens next there is an imperative to consider the child over politics, to create an education system that is defined by the priorities our young people will have to focus on as adults; climate change, new technologies, societal change, migration, the threat of war and terrorism, food security and land use to name but a few.

Ten Top Tips

1 The National Strategies were a well-funded organisation that were producing resources that were of a high quality and extremely useful. If you can find them in the government archive, they are worth a look.

2 The personal, learning and thinking skills are a useful collection of six skills independent enquirers, team workers, effective participators, self-managers, reflective learners and creative thinkers. Each one has an amplified list of how a pupil can work towards achieving these skills, they are very useful

3 The CoPE qualification is a level 2 and 3 GCSE equivalent qualification and can be used to support pupils gather evidence against their learning in PSHE, citizenship and other extra-curricular activity

(Continued)

(Continued)

4 As a starting point, consider your policy for transition from key stages 2–3 in relation to creating a seamless curriculum that builds on prior learning.
5 Spend some time thinking about key stage 3 and the goals and ambitions you have for pupils as they journey through this stage of their education.
6 The curriculum indicators published by Ofsted following their second piece of research into the curriculum provide a useful tool for reflecting on what is going well and what you would like to change.
7 Talk to staff about their beliefs about subject specific teaching and how curriculum intent translates into what is taught and how pupils learn especially in relation to knowledge-led, knowledge-engaged or skills-led approaches.
8 Use Ofsted's 18 indicators for lesson observation as an opportunity for professional conversations about good practice in the classroom.
9 Share widely what pupils produce as evidence of how the curriculum is taught, what is in books, what is drawn, built, said, performed, debated, etc.
10 Think about your own interpretation of the quality of education, what does it mean for you and your team and how can you articulate your absolute conviction to create the highest quality outcomes for all pupils.

REFERENCES

Anderson, L. W. and Krathwohl, D. R., et al (eds.) (2001) *A Taxonomy for Learning, Teaching, and Assessing: A Revision of Bloom's Taxonomy of Educational Objectives*. Boston. MA (Pearson Education Group), Allyn & Bacon.

ASDAN (2020) *What Is CoPE? Information Leaflet*. Available online: https://www.asdan.org.uk/media/421ktma2/cope_informationleaflet_feb20.pdf (accessed 15 February 2023).

Blair, T. (2002) *Speech to the Labour Party Conference*. 1 October. Winter Gardens, Blackpool.

DfES (2003) *Every Child Matters Consultation Process*. London: DfES.

DfE (2011) *The Framework for the National Curriculum, A Report by the Expert Panel for the National Curriculum Review*. London: DfE.

DfE (2014) *National Curriculum in England: Framework for Key Stages 1 to 4* London: DfE.

DfE (2015) *Commission on Assessment without Levels – Final Report*. London: DfE.

DfE (2022) *White Paper: Opportunities for All: Strong Schools with Great Teachers for Your Child*. London: DfE.

Education Endowment Foundation (EEF) (2022) *Impact on Covid 19 on Learning: A Review of the Evidence*. London: DfE.

Knight, S., McEune, R., White, K. and Woodthorpe, A. (2004) *The Key Stage 3 National Strategy: LEA and School Perceptions*. Slough: National Foundation for Educational Research.

Ofsted (2015) *Key Stage 3: The Wasted Years?* London: Ofsted.

Ofsted (2017) *HMCI's Commentary: Recent Primary and Secondary Curriculum Research*. London: Ofsted.

Ofsted (2018) *An Investigation into How to Assess the Quality of Education through Curriculum Intent, Implementation and Impact Phase 3 Findings of Curriculum Research*. London: Ofsted.

Ofsted (2019) *Planning for Change: The Impact of the New Key Stage 3 Curriculum*. London: Ofsted.

Ofsted (2019a) *Workbook Scrutiny*. London: Ofsted.

Ofsted (2019b) *Research Commentary: Assessing the Quality of Education*. London: Ofsted.

Ofsted (2019c) *Inspecting Education Quality: Lesson Observation Report*. London: Ofsted.

Ofsted (2024) *Inspection Handbook for Schools*. London: Ofsted.

Qualification and Curriculum Authority (2004) *The National Curriculum Handbook for School: Key Stage 3 and 4*. London: QCA.

Spielman, A. (2017) *HMCI's Commentary: Recent Primary and Secondary Curriculum Research*. Available online at: https://www.gov.uk/government/speeches/hmcis-commentary-october-2017 (accessed 15 February 2023).

Spielman, A. (2018) *HMCI's Commentary: Curriculum and the New Education Inspection Framework*. Available online at: https://www.gov.uk/government/speeches/hmci-commentary-curriculum-and-the-new-education-inspection-framework (accessed 15 February 2023).

Spielman Speech Commentary at ASCL Annual Conference March 2017. London. Available online at: https://www.gov.uk/government/speeches/amanda-spielmans-speech-at-the-ascl-annual-conference

Tomlinson, M. (2002) *Interim Report into A Level Reform*. London: DfES.

Tomlinson, M. (2004) *14–19 Curriculum Reforms – Final Report of the Working Group on 14–19 Reform*. London: DfES.

Waters, M. (2008) *Memorandum Submitted by Mick Waters, Director of Curriculum, Qualifications and Curriculum Authority (QCA)*. Available online at: https://publications.parliament.uk/pa/cm200809/cmselect/cmchilsch/344/344ii.pdf (accessed 15 February 2023).

Waters, M. (2009) *The Curriculum: Progress and Opportunities*. London: QCA.

2

TRANSFORMATIONAL AND VISIONARY LEADERSHIP – DEFINING THE AMBITION AND RATIONALE FOR CURRICULUM COHESION

Contents

- Exploring the complex nature of senior leadership in the secondary school
- Focusing on generic and domain-specific leadership and the importance of both
- Shaping the curriculum vison and intent for quality, creativity and innovation
- Creating the content through the local and wider school context
- Conceptual learning in subjects and across the curriculum
- Investigating how cognitive science applies in the classroom
- Defining the concept of quality in an education setting
- Continuing professional development as an integral part of curriculum design and delivery
- Exploring depth, breadth, knowledge and skills to weave deeper and sequential learning pathways

THE COMPLEX NATURE OF SENIOR LEADERSHIP IN THE SECONDARY SCHOOL

The influence of decisions made by the headteacher or principal will have far-reaching implications for the success or otherwise of all those within their sphere of influence. Defining what we mean by leadership in a school is difficult to pin down. Senior leaders set the parameters for whole school organisation, continuous improvement and success. Decisions they make that will influence change and challenge across the whole school include:

- defining the school culture and its ethos and vision for the highest quality of education;
- articulating the rationale and ambition for the curriculum within and across subjects;
- setting parameters and boundaries in terms of behaviour and pupil voice;
- stating goals and the strategy for continuous whole school improvement;
- creating administration, financial and other systems to ensure the school runs smoothly for all stakeholders;
- embedding a system of continuous professional development to ensure all staff know their strengths and their own learning agenda to fulfil their potential;
- building quality assurance systems that ensure a collaborative approach to achieving the school vision for excellence and achievement for all.

Generic and domain-specific leadership

Although school leaders must have a generic leadership skill set much the same as those in any organisation, recent research puts a focus on domain leadership as opposed to generic leadership. This is discussed in detail in Barker and Rees (2020). In the context of this chapter and the focus on curriculum leadership, it is clear that although generic leadership skills are important, the focus on domain leadership or leadership skills that relate to the constraints and circumstances of a specific and very particular profession is essential, especially in the pursuance of high-quality teaching and learning and the design a high-quality curriculum.

Generic leadership refers to the specific skills that are pertinent to qualities of leadership and not to a specific profession, business or service. Generic leadership skills remain an essential element of the characteristics of any good leader. Such traits include being visionary and empowering others to be the same, able to communicate with clarity, manage change effectively and build quality assurance strategies that deliver time-related and goal-specific outcomes.

Domain-specific leadership is necessary for the successful implementation of a well-designed and creative curriculum that inevitably involves many middle and subject leaders who have the specific knowledge and skills to translate the vision into positive outcomes for high-quality learning and teaching (Cordingley 2015).

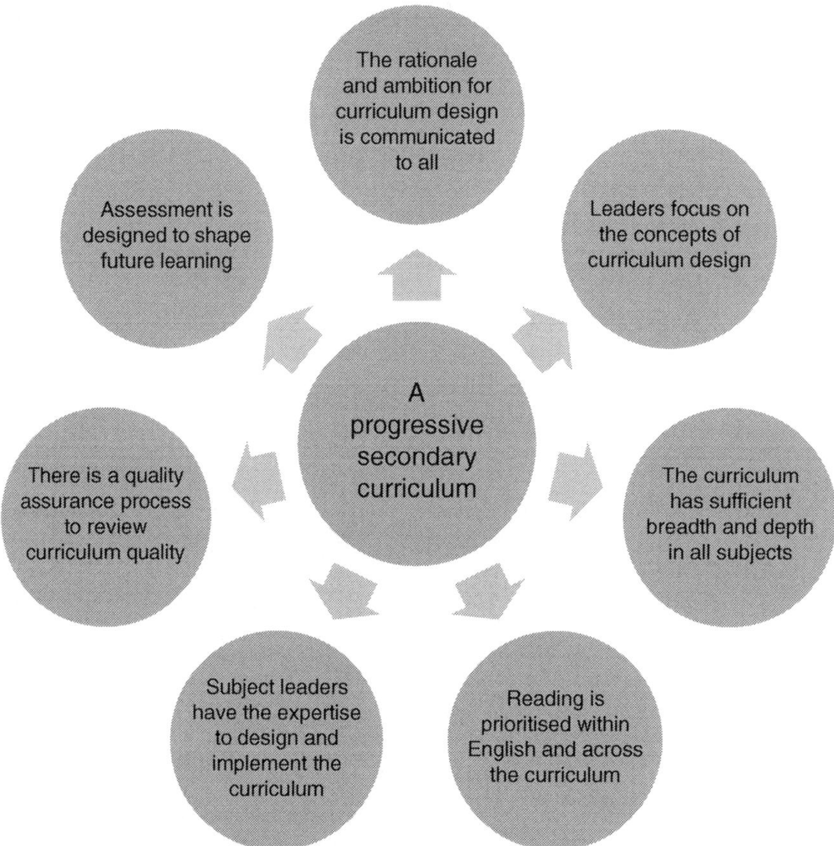

Figure 2.1 Planning a strategy for success

The diagram below outlines the essential elements of the role of the subject leader in relation to curriculum (Figure 2.1).

So, leadership in education is best seen as an embracing and not a hierarchical or dominant top-down structure. It is a distributed strategy that requires all involved to understand the rationale for decisions made, have the relevant information and resources with which to deliver and a deep conviction that they can play their part in achieving the whole school goal or vision. The senior leader must have the skills and knowledge to understand the complex nature of learning, pedagogy and curriculum but also have the skills to empower others to translate the vision into the delivery models that will lead to the highest-quality outcomes for all pupils and staff.

Leadership and the management of persistent problems

The only way to embrace the absolute concept of distributed leadership and to ensure that difficulties can be overcome, goals realised and outcomes secured is to create a culture of trust and delegated leadership especially in the pursuit of a deep and rich curriculum that delivers high-quality learning. The senior team must place faith in their subject leaders and respective teams. Equally, these leaders must be aware of the issues and persistent problems that teachers face in the pursuit of delivering pedagogy, imparting knowledge, ensuring pupils are learning and retaining an element of order and calm in the classroom.

For every one of the responsibilities and accountabilities, leaders must juggle there are potential barriers to success and difficulties that can arise. It is the role of the leader to have the self-belief and resilience to overcome difficulties by setting direction that all can follow, ensuring staff competence and ongoing professional development, orchestrating curriculum cohesion and managing behaviour, allocating resources and juggling financial priorities and constraints.

Mary Kennedy has written on the persistent problems that teachers face as they strive to deliver the curriculum that has been defined by senior leaders and set out as part of the whole school vision for change and challenge. She outlines these as:

- portraying the curriculum content in a way that is comprehensible to naïve minds;
- enlisting student participation where the captive audience is sometimes the resistant audience;
- exposing student thinking so that teachers are clear as to what students understand, do not understand and misunderstand;
- containing student behaviour to ensure students are not distracting each other or the teacher, accommodating personal needs so that teachers can address the first four persistent problems in a way that is consistent with their own personalities and needs.

(Kennedy 2016)

Successful leaders will recognise persistent problems for their leadership teams and for their teachers. They will empower deeply focused goal setting that ensures all those involved in curriculum development know their strengths and the barriers to success and can create strategies that will deliver. This is through the identification of a set of priorities, time frames and risk assessment that ensure goals will be met.

Leadership and shaping the curriculum vision and intent

With the introduction of the new curriculum in 2014, there came a distinct shift whereby the curriculum became the fulcrum for judging the quality of education in all schools inspected by Ofsted. We now have an Ofsted handbook for schools which has changed significantly (Ofsted 2024).

The Leadership and Management judgement in the most recent Ofsted handbook for Schools (Ofsted 2024) focuses on more than just the curriculum and for school leaders and their teams, a dissemination of priorities needs to be clearly drawn. For the purposes of this book, we are focused on elements linked directly to curriculum intent. Relevant Ofsted statements are listed below with some pertinent questions for senior leadership teams on how they can create consistent and cohesive plans for the school vision, rationale and ambition for curriculum implementation and the determination to deliver the highest quality of education.

Statement 1: All leaders and managers have high expectations of all pupils in the school, and the extent to which these are embodied in leaders' and staff's day-to-day interactions with pupils.

1 What does 'high expectations' mean in your school?
2 How do you communicate what you want in terms of high expectations to all staff and pupils?
3 What do you think the word 'interactions' means in the context of ensuring high expectations for all pupils?
4 What examples can you provide of leaders having high expectations?
5 What is the impact of high expectations on pupils' behaviours and attitudes to learning?

Statement 2: The extent to which leaders focus their attention on the education provided by the school. There are many demands on leaders, but a greater focus on this area is associated with better outcomes for pupils.

1 What evidence is there that there is a consensus on the education provided across all learning within the school?
2 What are your priorities for ensuring a focus on high-quality education outcomes for every learner?
3 What does high-quality education mean to you and what examples can you give?
4 What mechanisms do you have in place to measure high-quality education provision?
5 How does the term 'education' differ from the term 'curriculum'?

Statement 3: Whether continuing professional development for teachers and staff is aligned with the curriculum, and the extent to which this develops teachers' content knowledge and teaching content knowledge over time, so that they can deliver better teaching for pupils.

1 How is CPD organised in your school and how is it aligned to the curriculum intent/design and implementation/delivery?
2 How do you know CPD is having an impact on school, team and individual improvement?
3 How do you calculate the CPD needs for your teaching and other staff?
4 What are the areas of strength and areas for development in curriculum content alignment for your school?
5 How can the quality of CPD be enhanced so that it is part of the process of continuous school improvement?

Statement 4: The extent to which leaders create coherence and consistency across the school so that pupils benefit from effective teaching and consistent expectations, wherever they are in the school.

1 How do you explain the difference between 'cohesion' and 'consistency'?
2 What have you done to create coherence in relation to curriculum content across your school for all pupils?

3 How do you ensure teaching and learning is of a consistent high-quality across the curriculum?
4 What do you now need to do to improve consistency and coherence?
5 What do you do when inconsistencies arise?

Statement 5: Whether leaders seek to engage parents and their community thoughtfully and positively in a way that supports pupils' education.

1 How do you define the local community and the wider context within which your school serves?
2 How well do leaders and managers seek to engage with other stakeholders and your local community?
3 What is the evidence that your engagement with external stakeholders has been carefully thought through?
4 How do you know your engagement is having a positive impact on pupils' education?
5 What actions need to take place to improve or extend your community engagement?

Statement 6: Leaders and managers are thoughtful in drawing boundaries and resisting inappropriate attempts to influence what is taught and the day-to-day life of the school.

1 What policy parameters are in place in you school to help resist inappropriate attempts to influence what is taught?
2 How do you monitor the culture of day-to-day life in your school?
3 What do you do when attempts are made to influence boundaries you have set?
4 How are other stakeholders involved in setting boundaries and parameters?
5 What examples can you provide where other stakeholders have made positive contributions to the curriculum and the school culture?

There are four other elements here that will still have an indirect influence in relation to curriculum and do need careful consideration. These are linked to well-being, the hard to reach, pupil premium and governance.

For those working directly with the creation of a clear vision for curriculum intent and design starting with the questions above provides a framework for positive discussion and consensus. If the curriculum is to be the essence that measures the quality of education, then it must be at the forefront of clearly mapped out strategies that define how the school will plan for a vision for excellence and continuous improvement.

Shaping the curriculum framework for quality, creativity and innovation

The Ofsted handbook created the three I's, Intent, Implementation and Impact as a framework for developing a curriculum that, through the teaching of knowledge and the development of related skills, sets out the school's rationale and ambition for delivering outstanding teaching and learning and inspiring a culture of collaboration, continuity and cohesion.

Not every school is driven by Ofsted. However, much of their current advice and research is relevant in a wider context and their research and their original 25 indicators for what is deemed to define curriculum quality are useful for all schools to use as a starting point for discussion to define how the curriculum will deliver the highest quality of education (Ofsted 2018).

Alongside Ofsted's 3 I's, I would like to suggest another framework that is, I feel, less prescriptive. The '3D curriculum model' I prefer uses words that provide greater scope for creativity, innovation and a more progressive approach to defining the quality of outcome we are looking for from our pupils. So instead of Intent, Implementation, Impact, I would suggest Design, Delivery, Dissemination.

Design - allows those who shape what the curriculum should look like to their context, their cohorts, their environment and the cultural potential around them. The National Curriculum provides scope to make sure that the curriculum serves the learner both pupils and staff and will have an influence on the motivation, the learning and the life chances of its recipients.

Delivery - is a term that suggests giving, passing on, providing someone with something of worth. Implementation suggests the implementer retains the rights, not the one in receipt, of what is implemented. To deliver is to arrive and to provide a feeling of self-worth for what has been delivered. Opening a package that delivers deep knowledge, a range of essential skills and ensures parity and stretch and challenge is something every leader in education wants.

Dissemination - Impact is a harsh term synonymous with a crash, a fall, a smash. Dissemination allows the school leader, the subject leader and their team to focus on the many facets of the curriculum and learning that need to be reflected on and discussed widely.

Below is a list drawn from many conversations about the different facets that make up a 3D curriculum. Use them to take a 3D tour of how successful your curriculum is being translated from vision to pupil success (Table 2.1).

Table 2.1 The facets of a 3D curriculum

Design	Delivery	Dissemination
Ambition	Sequencing	Who knows what?
Pupils	Building on prior learning	Misconceptions
Culture	Cognitive load	Deep learning
Knowledge	Knowledge	Cross – curricular connections
Local context	Metacognition	Problem solving
Skills	Pedagogy	Questioning
Challenge	Concepts	Pupil output
Context	Shared conversations	Moderation
Cohesion	PSHE	Skills within subjects
Whole child	Citizenship	Skills that transcend subjects
Learner voice	Careers	Effort
Stakeholders	Fostering curiosity	Challenge
Community	Differentiation	Feedback
Parity	Recall	Growth mindset
Creativity	Reflection	

Words matter, they conjure images and either enhance creativity or stifle it. Where the leader is erudite with their language, is positive with their feedback and builds confidence through eloquence, others become inspired and ready for change and challenge.

The formal curriculum and the hidden curriculum

The local context where pupils can see how their learning relates to them and their lives gives meaning. It provides relevance and the context for creating opportunities to look at less familiar knowledge. The formal curriculum that is taught as part of a planned structure that defines knowledge to be learnt and skills to be mastered sits alongside the hidden curriculum that forms the rest of a learner's experiences, the gaining of knowledge and the practice of a range of skills that are absorbed as part of activities outside school. Inevitably, these are wide, either beneficial or not, but always a key element of what a pupil is learning and should not be underestimated. Senior and subject leaders should think carefully about all the diverse ways that pupils learn (Bromley 2019).

We must focus on pupil voice as part of decision-making in relation to what to include within subject specific curriculum design and delivery. Giving the pupil a voice in the process ensures a sense of belonging and ownership of their learning. Allowing pupils and teachers to work together to determine curriculum content and how it will be delivered creates a better relationship where the teacher and pupil are in a partnership looking for the same outcomes.

Through my work with learner voice (Frater 2011), I know how important it is to involve the pupil and their experiences in shaping the knowledge and skills that will ignite their desire to learn. I have seen that pupils' enjoyment of the curriculum is associated with a sense of being drawn into innovative ideas and concepts, opportunities for progression and achievement and being challenged. This is underpinned by the way pupils talk about how they are taught. They place much more emphasis on the distinctive styles of pedagogy and creative ways teachers help pupils to deepen their knowledge and understanding than on choices made about the content within the subject being taught.

This is a list compiled from a survey of our local community of secondary schools as to what pupils say they want in relation to the curriculum:

- More emphasis on learning skills and their own personal and social development
- More practical work linked to their interests of aspirations for the future
- A more obvious link with the curriculum and their real life
- More connections made across different areas of the curriculum
- A balance between academic subjects and those that are more creative, practical or vocational
- More choice especially at key stage 4
- More variety in how lessons are delivered in the classroom
- More opportunities to learn how they can improve their own work
- Becoming independent learners

Creating opportunities for pupils to be involved in discussions about their own locality and the experiences that shape their lives outside as well as inside school and then defining the curriculum content around their experience can be uplifting.

Concepts and moving from the local to the wider context

The local and wider context for curriculum planning should build on key aspects of the local environment and community. Take geography and a focus on the local community and its shape as a settlement. Why did it originally become a place to live? What are the physical features such as a river, flat land or the ready supply or raw materials? How this then relates to a wider context in the study of other countries, cities or civilisations provides an opportunity to explore the concepts that underpin the learning, in this case, these could be settlement, survival and growth.

From year 7, pupils have five years before they will be sitting externally set examinations. In this time, creating opportunities for pupils to deepen their learning and understanding of key concepts in as many contexts as possible will help them to understand how these relate to places and events they have not specifically studied and answer questions that allow them to recall their previous learning and apply their knowledge.

Within each subject, the focus is inevitably on the prize of the highest possible grades at the end of year 11. The build-up of knowledge and the development of skills continues over the five years that pupils study a range of discrete subjects.

This requires a deep focus on sequential planning within each subject that ensures pupils can build a deeper understanding over time. The focus on how we move from the local to the wider context in each subject must also include how we look at the concepts that remain constant in the pursuit of that deeper knowledge. These concepts are the threads that create meaning and allow pupils to make connections within specific subjects and where they intertwine with other subjects. For instance, in history concepts such as liberty, landscape, migration, conflict, health, welfare and society, transcend many of the topics that are included within the key stage 3 programme of study.

These concepts will also be there in the questions asked in GCSE papers and it is up to subject leaders and their subject teams to plan their sequential knowledge pathway so that pupils are able to use their conceptual knowledge and understanding even if the question does not marry exactly with their historical reference.

Alongside the specific subject planning, there needs to be a clear focus on where some of these concepts transcend subjects and provide the pupil with more opportunities to consolidate their conceptual learning. The list of history concepts above includes migration and landscape which are equally important in geography. All of this requires time and opportunities for professional conversations and the development of a curriculum tapestry that allows all senior and subject leaders and their teams to build a rich cornucopia of learning within and across a range of subjects.

The role of cognitive science in the deepening of understanding and learning

One element of current research is the emphasis placed on theories from cognitive science and how pupils learn which can make a significant difference to their ability to retain and remember knowledge over time. The Education Endowment Foundation (2021) have produced a comprehensive and thorough review of research into the role of cognitive science in the classroom.

There is an increasing interest in making sure that school staff understand the science of learning; what it is that makes us learn and retain that learning over time. For pupils to deepen their knowledge, they need to become consciously and then unconsciously competent in a range of skills. Senior leaders need to create the opportunities for collective dialogue where teachers reflect on how they impart their subject expertise to cascade meaning; how they create a classroom that reinforces what pupils are learning and supports pupils to accept challenge and deepen their learning over time.

Memory is an essential part of the learning process; we all know that. However, to remember something, we must ignite a passion that will mean that whoever is doing the learning wants to listen and pay attention to what they are expected to learn.

The key elements of cognitive science are defined in the diagram below (Figure 2.2).

- The input stimulus is important because it alerts the learner that they want to learn.
- Sensory memory is triggered when the learner is stimulated by sound, images, touch, smell and taste.
- The working memory can only store between four and seven pieces of information.
- Knowledge is processed through the working memory.
- Learning happens when knowledge is stored in the long-term memory.

All learning is incremental and requires rehearsal, reflection and retrieval. Forgetting is a natural part of the process and will happen if the working memory is overloaded or there is no opportunity to build on what is contained in the long-term memory (Figure 2.2).

Leaders need to be aware of the mechanisms that will support subject teams to create delivery strategies that will allow pupils to build on prior learning, recognise key concepts and make connections. Leaders need to ensure that subject teams are paying attention to the key skills of literacy and numeracy, the use of information technology and those meta-cognitive skills that are the secret ingredient to fostering deep learning.

It is this rich tapestry of inter-connected learning that will last in pupils' memory and stimulate a desire to learn more. The more they can consolidate and reinforce their learning in a variety of contexts that are relevant, innovative and connected, the more the learning will enter and remain in the long-term memory.

Quality systems and structures for curriculum cohesion

The leadership statements in the *Ofsted Handbook for Schools* guide inspectors in judging how well leaders have created the structures, strategies and resources that can demonstrate that

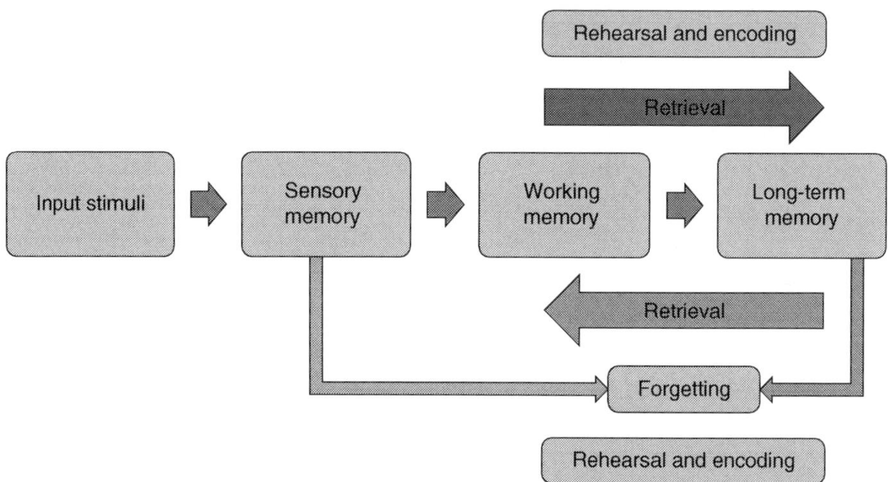

Figure 2.2 Developing an understanding of cognitive science theory into practice (Learning Cultures 2021)

the school has a positive impact on all its pupils. This focuses on the actions of leaders and how they influence the quality of education provided.

Within the Quality of Education judgement, inspectors focus on the curriculum itself. The curriculum sets out the aims of a programme of education and sets out the structure for those aims to be implemented (Ofsted 2019). Leaders need to ask themselves, what is the scope of the knowledge and skills that they want subject leaders to shape into their plans. There is an imperative to ensure that the objectives set out for what pupils will achieve at certain pre-determined end points are realised. Senior leaders need to ensure that their subject leaders have broken down the content of the curriculum into its component parts and have sequenced that content in a logical progression, systematically and explicitly (Kumari-Wood & Hadden 2021).

Quality transcends the curriculum and requires the school leader to look more widely beyond what will be taught in terms of content. They must know how it is delivered and to what level of expertise in terms of pedagogy, subject knowledge and a profound understanding of the curriculum as much more than simply a group of discrete subjects but as an interwoven tapestry that helps a learner to prepare for life and readiness for further study or the world of work.

Senior and subject leaders should have a set of parameters that will support them in defining what quality means in their subject and then create the right conditions to support cohesion and consistency over how the curriculum can deliver the highest possible quality of education.

Quality assurance is a well-established term used extensively in a business context. It is a process that ensures delivery and practice achieves the defined outcomes where there is an emphasis on 'self-review' rather than checking by a third party or inspector. School leaders must create systems where their teams have clearly defined goals and prescribed end points and can work together to create the checks and balances that will lead to the highest quality outcomes for themselves, their colleagues and the pupils. There must be a culture of self-, peer- and team evaluation that encourages innovation and carefully orchestrated risk-taking. Reflection is essential where comprehensive review leads to change and challenge and never to an admission of failure.

Leaders need to find ways to build a process-driven quality system where they have defined the outcomes they are looking for. They need to create incremental steps that will lead to a collaborative and highly effective system that can be implemented across all departments, teams and stages. Those charged with implementing or delivering the different elements of the quality system can then set the priorities that will lead to the desired quality outcomes. These priorities become a timeline for success and all those involved can plot their progress and the progress of others, celebrate success and focus on change where it is necessary.

The quality indicators that form a good starting point for a quality assurance system in an education setting are re-configured from the indicators included in the ISO9001 standards typically used for businesses looking to use a quality assurance framework. They are:

- positive and effective leadership;
- identifying the needs of all learners;
- engaging and empowering all staff;
- achieving successful learning outcomes;
- defining assessment and continuous improvement strategies;
- data and information to inform evidence-based decision-making;
- informing and engaging with the community and all stakeholders.

Leading a strategy that builds the highest quality systems can be set out as a distinct framework with three key elements:

- the learner and the characteristics that must be considered when determining a curriculum that embraces the learning needs of all pupils;
- the key elements that go into embedding the vision for the highest quality learning and teaching;
- the outcomes that we are looking to achieve, knowledge we want pupils to have, the skills they need to learn and the other skills we want to build in to deepen their learning and potential.

The curriculum as the fulcrum for continuous improvement

To create high-quality outcomes that are consistently delivered across the whole organisation, middle, subject and team leaders must be given the responsibility for developing the stated level of quality. If the curriculum is the benchmark that measures the quality of education within a school, then it is their role to dovetail quality within their planning to ensure all staff have the knowledge and skills to deliver what has been determined within its design.

To create the right conditions, the following are essential:

- Empowering teams to deliver a cohesive and high-quality curriculum
- Developing a whole school model for continuous improvement linked to curriculum implementation
- Fostering continuous professional dialogue in the pursuit of cohesive and collaborative curriculum delivery
- Celebrating success in the pursuit of high-quality pedagogy and learning

Continuing professional development (CPD) is the term that most educators are familiar with. However, recent research questions this term (Cordingley et al. 2020) and suggests that we need to include the word 'learning' so that CPD becomes CPDL. Incorporating the word 'learning' gives the school leader more scope to ensure that the training is used and practised in context and not just in the training space.

Professional development is only ever of value if it has a lasting impact on learning in the classroom and where there is a measurable impact on the experience of the pupil. Therefore, expressing the planned development of those who create and deliver the curriculum as 'learning' can strengthen an understanding of why it is such an important part of curriculum leadership.

Leaders who are defining the vision for the curriculum must include continuing professional development and learning as vital to how this will be achieved. The constraints in relation to budgets, time or staffing should not be seen as a consideration. CPDL is essential for success and is therefore a priority. This means that professional learning is embedded within a culture where there is an absolute commitment to promoting and participating in teachers' CPDL based on a clear understanding that the goal of continuing improvement is about what happens in the classroom where teachers have the opportunity to learn in the classroom, alongside their colleagues and in the presence of experts who can support their development.

Understanding the implications of curriculum delivery across all subjects

Subject leaders or Heads of Department are pivotal in the pursuance of high-quality education outcomes. It is they who must interpret the vision, ambition and rationale for the curriculum and communicate that to their teams. Successful teams are those that can work together to create the evidence that the curriculum has a profound impact on learning, aligns with the vision and embraces the needs of every pupil, the less able, the disadvantaged, those with EAL and those who need to be challenged and stretched. Use Table 2.2 as an aid to conversations about curriculum cohesion.

If the curriculum is at the heart of building successful schools, then leaders must ensure that there is sufficient time to plan for how the curriculum will be delivered in each subject, where there are connections across subjects and as part of a strategy for excellence and improvement (Myatt & Tomsett 2021).

Table 2.2 A framework for understanding education quality

Learner characteristics	Enabling inputs	Outcomes
Aptitude	Positive leadership	Knowledge
Perseverance	Curriculum design	Literacy skills
Prior knowledge	Subject specialists	Numeracy skills
Reflective	Learning time	Digital competence
Barriers to learning	Pedagogy	Wider life skills
Accept challenge	Conditions for learning	Creative skills
Embrace failure	Assessment and feedback	Emotional impact
Own interests	The wider community	Values
		Social skills

Curriculum cohesion can be developed by combining subject knowledge; literacy and numeracy skills across all subjects; thinking and metacognitive skills; concepts that apply within subjects and across the curriculum and the creativity and innovation that motivates learners to feel inspired to go beyond the familiar (see Figure 2.3).

There is a danger that curriculum planning is done in isolation where each subject leader and their team plan their own subject-specific content. In this way, wider understanding of curriculum vocabulary across subjects is lost. The table below outlines some of the key curriculum concepts that need to be part of conversations that transcend subject-specific planning. Curriculum leaders should aim to have incisive professional conversations about what they mean for all subjects and how they apply in specific contexts (Table 2.3).

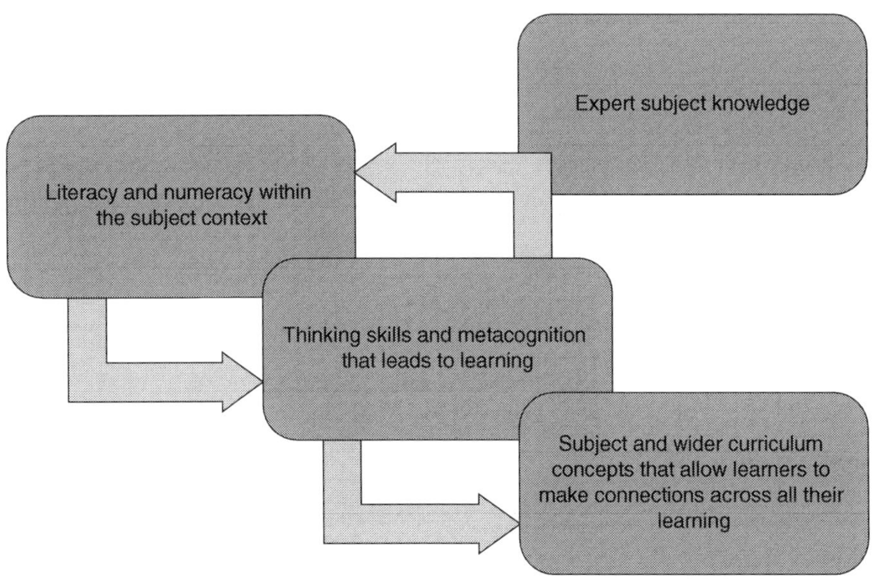

Figure 2.3 Creating the culture for curriculum cohesion

Table 2.3 Generic curriculum concepts

• Breadth across a full range of subjects • Balance of time, subject content and skills development • Relevance to learners' needs • Coherence so that content inter-relates • Interweaving of discrete subjects • Differentiation to match learning to learner attainment • Progression to extend learning, knowledge, skills and understanding • Continuity that links existing with new subject knowledge	• Knowledge linked to learning in and across subject divides • Conceptual learning applied in a variety of contexts across the curriculum • Skills development in relation to accessing learning, deepening learning and ensuring progression • Deepening understanding to enable learners to construct meaning • Attitudes to learning and attitudes about learning • Subject vocabulary understanding the complex language linked to knowledge, curriculum planning and assessment

These concepts are drawn from several conversations and commentary that senior leaders along with curriculum and subject leaders need to use as part of a dialogue about what is essential in every subject. Take, for example, 'continuity' and its allied word 'sequencing'. It is an essential element of curriculum planning in every subject that pupils build on their prior learning and that there are clear plans that demonstrate the continuity of subject content that leads to deeper learning over time.

Senior and curriculum leaders should work together to look at progress in delivering the curriculum across different subjects. The time should be diarised, there should be an agenda and the issues raised should be carefully crafted to incorporate a shared understanding of what builds curriculum quality into the planned delivery model.

The 'deep dive' questions that might support this process could include:

- How do you know that your curriculum offer is of a high quality and will have a positive impact on learning and progression?
- How is the learning sequenced so that it builds on prior learning, deepens learning over time and is designed with clearly defined end points in mind?
- What is rich knowledge in each subject and how is knowledge taught, remembered and retained?
- What key concepts will be taught within a designated period?
- How do key concepts interrelate with others already taught or that will be taught later?
- How do the concepts in one subject translate into another?
- What is the evidence that the planned content, the pedagogy and the opportunities for learning are accessible for all pupils including those with SEND?
- How are literacy and numeracy skills used to create opportunities for pupils to access knowledge and make sense of it?
- How is knowledge organised to ensure that pupils are deepening their understanding and have opportunities to reflect, review and develop the ability to use higher level thinking?
- How does assessment of the learning create opportunities to plan next steps to ensure challenge, reinforcement or an opportunity to revisit the learning?

Senior and subject leaders must know what terms like 'sequencing', 'subject concepts', 'the organisation of knowledge', 'metacognition' and 'higher-level thinking' mean in relation to their understanding of curriculum and education quality.

The key concepts of curriculum design are just one element of understanding the complex issues that make up what we want to see as a high-quality curriculum. Subject leaders and their teams of teachers need to focus on another suite of important phrases. Understanding these terms and how they apply in different subjects ensures that subject leaders and teachers have a shared vocabulary to support them in developing their curriculum from year 7 to year 11 and beyond.

Some of the vocabulary of the curriculum is contained in this list:

- The quality of education
- The substance of education
- Building on prior learning
- Working towards clearly defined end points
- Knowledge-rich content
- Breadth and depth of curriculum coverage
- Literacy, numeracy and metacognition
- Parity for all learners including those with SEND
- Consistent formative assessment
- Conceptual learning within and across subjects
- Mastery learning

Any subject specialist will tell you their subject is unique and requires its own set of parameters to work within. This is true, but there are so many opportunities to look across the curriculum to ensure that for, the pupil, meaning translates into other contexts.

The list of vocabulary above is a starting point for professional conversations that explore how different departments are designing and delivering a curriculum. Each point raises the potential for clarifying questions and creates professional development opportunities for all those with subject responsibility. Use the questions in Figure 2.4 as a framework for planning.

One of the biggest shifts in thinking since the introduction of the new curriculum in 2014 and the subsequent shift in emphasis from Ofsted is the focus on knowledge (DfE 2014).

Mentioned in chapter 1 Ofsted's research into successful curriculum design in 2018 Ofsted introduced three different approaches schools might use, knowledge-led, knowledge-engaged and skills-led (Ofsted 2018). Although it was always stressed by Ofsted that they had no preference, some leaders believed that a knowledge-led approach was favoured. The subsequent subject reviews that were published during 2021 and 2022 for the core subjects and many foundation subjects also place a great emphasis on knowledge (Ofsted 2021 and 2022).

The research review series throughout uses the terms 'substantive' and 'disciplinary' knowledge. Using the history review as an example of what is meant by these two phrases,

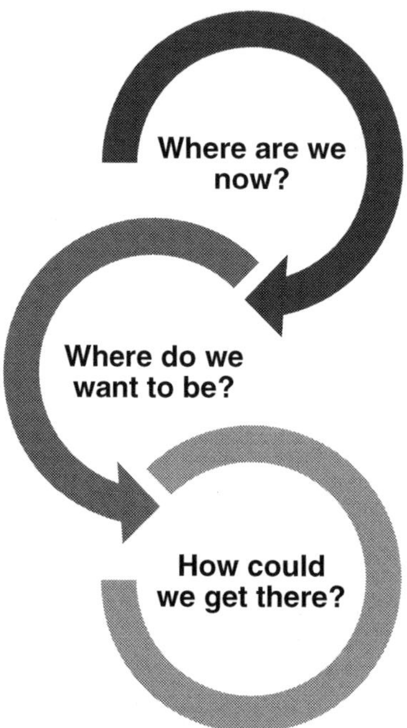

Figure 2.4 The theory of knowledge and its application to curriculum breadth and depth

Pupils make progress in history by developing:

- their knowledge about the past - substantive knowledge;
- their knowledge about how historians investigate the past, and how they construct historical claims, arguments and accounts - disciplinary knowledge.

It is interesting to look in detail at all these research reviews and I use them as part of analysis of different subjects and their similarities and differences in relation to the focus on knowledge in other chapters.

A key commentator in relation to the knowledge debate is Michael Young and his concept of powerful knowledge (Young 2014). He maintains that there are three possible 'futures' for the curriculum in his work from 2014 when the current curriculum was first introduced.

- Future 1: Knowledge is treated as given and established by tradition.
- Future 2: Knowledge is constructed in response to contexts needs and interests.

Future 3: Knowledge is not fixed but is open to change through the work of specialist subject communities linked to changes that may have happened or are happening in the world. The academic and political commentary that creates these three futures is interesting. In the context of defining what kind of curriculum best suits a particular cohort within a particular local context, a combination of futures 2 and 3 may work. We may need to consider a new future altogether that looks in more depth at the skills pupils will need to navigate the rest of the 21st century, where a knowledge-engaged model weaves together a tapestry of skills and knowledge that equip pupils with the strategies that will help them to be successful as problem solvers, creative thinkers, team players, independent enquirers and self-managers.

CONCLUSION

Leadership in schools is complex. Senior leaders need to have the command, the confidence and the skills to define a vision for whole school continuous improvement. Each school is different, requires the leader to create the right structures and systems that will allow middle, subject and other team leaders to empower their teams to design the curriculum and other strategies that will deliver the vision and ambition for the highest quality education outcomes it is aligned with.

If the curriculum is the fulcrum for defining quality, time must be given to ensuring all staff have the knowledge and skills to plan, design and deliver the threads that are explicit in some subjects and implicit in others. Planning must demonstrate a mixture of deep and increasingly complex subject knowledge and opportunities for pupils to develop the skills that will allow them to access that knowledge. Teachers must also have the pedagogical expertise to create the right conditions that allow pupils to use that knowledge to demonstrate higher level thinking, make connections and understand concepts within subjects and those that transcend subject learning.

Quality is a relative term and needs to be defined as an integral part of the school vision for continuous improvement. Embracing a system of quality assurance that involves every member of staff in the planning and delivery of a quality assurance framework has the potential to secure the highest quality outcomes that are consistent and sustainable in every element of school life.

To achieve high levels of continuing success, senior leaders must have the faith and trust in their subject and team leaders to take the baton of quality. A distributed form of leadership is essential in the pursuit of excellence.

Finally, the purpose of school is to create pathways to a successful future for all those who spend time there. Here the role of the learner and their voice is essential to ensuring that the curriculum is relevant, meaningful and fully engages them in wanting to learn.

Ten Top Tips

1 Think about what transformational leadership means in relation to your style of leadership.
2 Ensure the vision for curriculum quality is owned and embraced by those who play a part in design and delivery of its component parts.
3 Work collaboratively to define strengths and gaps that exist between subject/faculty leaders and their teams.

(Continued)

(Continued)

4. Senior, middle and subject leaders need to be able to articulate the barriers and problems that might impede progress and deter the delivery of solutions.
5. Ensure that time is set aside for curriculum planning, quality assurance and reflection.
6. Challenge subject leaders and their teams to be creative and innovative with conceptual learning, sequencing and enabling pupils to make cross-curricular connections.
7. Ensure all those with a pupil facing role are familiar with the theory of cognitive science and its application in the classroom.
8. Build quality assurance as a strategy for ensuring cohesion, consistency, excellence and improvement.
9. Professional development should be woven into the fabric of curriculum design and delivery.
10. Remember the importance of learner voice, the curriculum must be the right fit for every pupil across the school.

REFERENCES

Barker, J. and Rees, T. (2020) *Chapter 3: The ResearchED Guide to Leadership*. Woodbridge, John Catt. pp23–39.

Bromley, M. (2019) *Curriculum Design under a New Ofsted Regime: Headteacher Update*, London, MA Education Limited.

Cordingley, P. et al. (2015) *Developing Great Teaching*. London, Teacher Development Trust.

Cordingley, P. et al. (2020) *Developing Great Leadership of CPDL*. University of Nottingham, University of Durham and CUREE sponsored by Right to Succeed. Penrith, Curee.

Department of Education (2014) *National Curriculum: Programmes of Study London*. DfE.

Education Endowment Foundation (EEF) (2021) *Cognitive Science Approaches in the Classroom*. London, Education Endowment Foundation.

Frater, G. (2011) What Students and Staff Want: Taking Account of the Curriculum Choices that Matter to Them. *Curriculum Briefing*, 9(3).

ISO 9001 (2015) *Quality Assurance Standards*. Geneva, International Organisation for Standardardization: ISO.

Kennedy, M. (2016) Parsing the Practice of Teaching. *Journal of Teacher Education*, 67(1) pp6–17.

Kumari-Wood, M. and Haddon, N. (2021) *Secondary Curriculum Transformed* London Routledge.

Myatt, M. and Tomsett, J. (2021) *Huh: Curriculum Conversations between Subject and Senior Leaders*. Woodbridge, John Catt.

Ofsted (2018) *Curriculum Research: Assessing Intent, Implementation and Impact, Phase 3 Findings of Curriculum Research*. London, Ofsted.

Ofsted (2019) *Inspecting Education Quality: Lesson Observation and Workbook Scrutiny*. London: Ofsted.

Ofsted Research Reviews (2021 and 2022) *English, Maths, Science, History, Geography, Modern Foreign Languages, Design Technology, Art and Design, Computing, Physical Education.* London, Ofsted.

Ofsted (2024) *Ofsted Handbook for Schools.* London: Ofsted.

Young, M. (2014) *Knowledge and the Future School: Curriculum and Social Justice.* London, Bloomsbury.

3

CROSSING THE TRANSITION BRIDGE FROM PRIMARY TO SECONDARY SCHOOL

Contents

- Setting the scene that suggests a need for change
- A continuum of English learning across the transition bridge
- Maths concepts and the development of seamless learning from upper key stage 2 to year 7
- Thinking and working scientifically
- Reading across the divide
- Pedagogy and the skills for learning
- Assessment as an essential part of planning
- Planning for success

SETTING THE SCENE THAT SUGGESTS A NEED FOR CHANGE

Research suggests that there is an average drop in performance of pupils from the end of year 6 to the end of year 7 of anything up to 40% and that 'two out of every five pupils fail to make the expected progress in the year after the transition from Key Stage 2 to Key Stage 3' (Hargreaves and and Galton 1999).

Imagine if that statistic were to turn around to a 20% *increase* in performance over the same 12 months. I have been involved in creating positive partnerships between primary and secondary schools for over twenty years and it is with some frustration that I observe very little that has changed over that time.

Pupils spend around eight years in their primary school, even longer if they start school in the nursery section. However, it is still telling that when pupils arrive in their respective secondary school, there is often little recognition of the learning that has taken place already.

> Research from the Scottish government reinforces the clear lack of partnership working that often exists across the transition bridge (Jindal-Snape et al. 2019). Several studies focusing on how the pandemic has impacted on pupils' progress as they move from primary to secondary school conclude that there continues to be a lack of a shared understanding of how to ensure pupils continue to progress as they transfer across the transition bridge from year 6 to year 7. Many studies look closely at social, well-being and behaviour issues, few studies look specifically at academic and curriculum issues. (Bagnal et al. 2022)

The failure to create the right strategies for academic transition is a historic problem that is difficult to solve. Traditionally, we have small intimate primary schools that serve local and tightly-knit communities. Here pupils are nurtured from their early years until they are ready to go to much larger and less local secondary schools (Ofsted 2015).

Many secondary schools will question the data captured at the end of year 6, from SATs tests and other means, which often leads to testing early on in year 7 which can be demotivating and may still not provide the accurate data sought. This is especially so where SATs testing has only taken account of achievements in English, and maths and, to some extent, science through a moderation process.

Figure 3.1 below shows how learning is a continuum and requires all those involved in transition and transfer to respect what has gone before and what is being planned for over time. There remains an imperative to address the dip in performance, where it exists and make changes so that pupils' secondary experience takes prior learning into account. Their learning needs to be built into a planned approach ensuring opportunities for recall and reflection and that new learning builds on conceptual understanding.

A positive and structured strategy is one that puts the curriculum at the heart of strong partnerships between the many and varied primary schools and the secondary schools who will take on the baton of learning at the beginning of year 7.

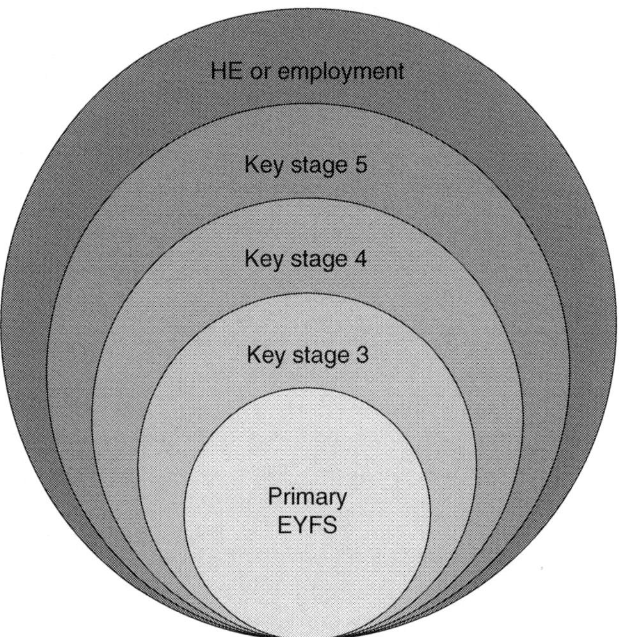

Figure 3.1 The curriculum as a fulcrum for partnership between the primary and secondary phases

I have already alluded to the difficulties of creating such partnerships that work because of the sheer number of small primaries that transfer into a large secondary school. However, there is rarely clear policy in place that defines what a partnership might look like. For many, a breakdown in understanding and perception creates a lack of trust and suspicion between the phases. This results in primary schools feeling that their secondary partners appear superior and where the secondary school does not have the inclination or the resources to create a bridge.

Where partnerships do work there are profound opportunities to make transition a positive experience for pupils, allow secondary school teachers to enhance their own knowledge of primary learning and pedagogy and for primary teachers to understand what is expected of pupils and how the expertise of the subject teacher can support learning in upper key stage 2.

Here are some examples of good practice that can make a difference to the pupil and the teacher at this important bridge.

- Opportunities for secondary teachers to observe lessons in years 5 and 6 can lead to those involved being impressed by the high-level of knowledge, the quality of teaching and the output from pupils
- Working in partnership with several primary schools to develop bridging projects where year 6 pupils start a topic agreed with the secondary school where they can take their learning with them across the transition bridge

- Science, music or art clubs where the secondary school works with pupils who want to build their knowledge and expertise by working with a secondary school expert
- Joint CPD where year 6 teachers work with year 7 teachers to plan sequential schemes of work that create seamless learning across the bridge
- English and maths teachers team teach in year 6 with their primary colleagues create deeper and broader content linked to prior learning in the primary phase
- A themed approach to learning in the last half term is agreed between the primary schools and those teaching in year 7 so that pupils work towards a cross curricular topic which pupils continue into the first term or half term of year 7
- Year 6 teachers are involved in the induction programme for pupils starting their year 7 journey
- Pupils take photographs and keep a diary of their last few weeks in primary school and what they did in the holidays and use these resources to create a newsletter about themselves in year 7

A CONTINUUM OF LEARNING IN THE CORE SKILLS ACROSS THE TRANSITION BRIDGE

For key stage 3 curriculum planners, there is a deep reservoir of knowledge and understanding of what pupils bring with them. To ignore the expertise and understanding that the primary school, their teachers and the fabulous array of writing, artwork, reading material, models, musical composition, mathematical and technical skills and abilities that has been an integral part of learning is a folly and a travesty for pupils who have had access to a rich tapestry of learning.

Teachers who are responsible for planning the English, maths or science curriculum for year 7 should start with a deep focus on what has been taught in upper key stage 2.

The key stage 1 and 2 programmes of study for English (DfE 2014a) reveal what should have been taught and what pupils should be able to confidently take forward in year 7. There is a sequential and detailed spelling appendix contained within the key stage 1 and 2 programmes of study. It provides examples of words that pupils should have learnt and are able to spell. There are word lists for years 3 and 4 and 5 and 6 and these are worth reproducing as spelling bees or low-stakes tests for pupils in year 7. They provide an opportunity to assess how well pupils can see the relationship between sounds and letters and how well they can read and spell a whole range of quite complex word structures.

The English curriculum at key stage 1 and 2 also has a sequenced appendix entitled 'Vocabulary, Grammar and Punctuation'. This lists the statutory content that must be introduced year on year. It is essential to look at what is statutory in years 5 and 6 and ensure that what is planned for year 7 builds on this detailed analysis of what pupils need to become fluent writers and to be able to read well.

Pupils will have been exposed to learning grammar terms throughout their time in primary school. Such terms as antonym, adverbial, digraph, ellipsis, homonym, phoneme, preposition, subjunctive, synonym and trigraph are all included in this glossary. It is likely that many pupils will not remember these terms, but they have been taught them and they have been expected to use them in a variety of classroom lessons and test situations to assess their ability to understand their context. How well this is taught or used to enhance the written work of pupils is dependent on the quality of teaching in each primary school, but it is certainly important that the secondary English subject team responsible for year 7 are aware of what pupils have been exposed to in relation to grammar training.

The key stage 3 programme of study for English contains the following statement:

> Teachers should build on the knowledge and skills that pupils have been taught at key stage 2. Decisions about progression should be based on the security of pupils' linguistic knowledge, skills and understanding and their readiness to progress to the next stage. Pupils whose linguistic development is more advanced should be challenged through being offered opportunities for increased breadth and depth in reading and writing. Those who are less fluent should consolidate their knowledge, understanding and skills, including through additional practice. (DfE 2014b)

There is a wealth of ways to ensure that learning is not lost.

- Giving primary partner schools the exercise books that pupils will use in their secondary English lessons to pupils to begin to use in the last term of year 6 so that year 7 teachers can assess the quality of their writing
- Ensuring secondary school planning in the English department takes account of the detailed content included in the key stage 2 programmes of study
- Providing primary partner schools with novels that pupils can read in year 6 and that form the basis of further reading in year 7
- Organising a creative writing project linked to a particular theme that pupils can work on after SATs in year 6 and then carry over into year 7
- Opportunities for joint CPD for primary and secondary English teachers to work together to look at how they teach the different facets of the English curriculum

Maths concepts and seamless learning from year 6 and into year 7 and beyond

When the new curriculum was introduced in 2014, there was a shift in depth of maths skills pupils were expected to be taught by the end of year 6. What was previously taught in year 6 was now expected to be covered in year 4, for instance. This means that when pupils arrive in year 7, they have probably been exposed to maths teaching that in previous years would have been taught in year 9. This should be common knowledge; we have had this new curriculum for ten years at the time of writing.

The maths curriculum in key stages 1 and 2 is carefully sequenced and provides teachers with a pathway to deepening pupils' mastery of maths in a variety of disciplines (DfE 2014c). The aims within the programmes of study in all the key stages, including at key stages 3 and 4, clearly state that pupils should become fluent in the fundamentals of mathematics, reason mathematically and solve problems in a variety of routine and non-routine situations.

The vocabulary and application of maths is about deepening knowledge and continuous reinforcement of concepts so that pupils become unconsciously competent in using maths as an integral part of learning. Using year 7 to consolidate pupils' learning from the primary phase will strengthen pupils' ability to develop as proficient mathematicians.

- Some examples of good practice that might help to ensure that pupils build on their prior learning and have the right platform to progress well
- Organise maths clubs and summer schools for both year 6 and year 7 pupils to attend
- Specific taster days in the secondary school for pupils from their partner primary schools to work together to focus on what they know and can do
- Design the first half term for pupils in year 7 so that maths is taught as part of a well-structured project where pupils have to find ways to use their mathematical knowledge to create something, solve a problem or produce a project on a mathematical-themed subject

NCETM suggest using the following questions as part of a discussion about the planning of year 7 maths content (NCETM 2020).

- What do we mean by 'secondary ready'?
- What aspects of knowledge, skills and understanding do we want students to have in order to be ready for our year 7 curriculum?
- How do we find out whether these aspects are in place?
- Is our year 7 curriculum structured in such a way that we build on students' existing knowledge and fill any gaps, if they exist?
    - What works well?
    - What changes might we need to make?

One good example is where an INSET day is given over to groups of year 6 and year 7 subject teams. They are tasked with creating a presentation that explains where maths is integral to their subject. The afternoon is then set aside for each subject to present. Small departments like drama and music might work together and the English department may need a bit of help, but it is a revealing and highly enlightening opportunity to really focus in on maths in context.

Read the paper from DfE (2014e) *Teaching Mathematics in Primary Schools*, it is a powerful tool to support all teachers of maths in year 7 and in key stage 3 to have the evidence that they are building on prior learning.

Thinking and working scientifically

Science is a pivotal subject in the primary phase and has undertaken a shift since the new curriculum inception in 2014. Previously, pupils were expected to 'know how science works'. They are now expected to 'think and work scientifically'. The key stage 2 programme of study lays out what is expected of pupils in their quest to demonstrate that they can work scientifically (DfE 2014d).

The table below sets out what the programme of study wants to see pupils be able to do and learn by the end of their time in their primary school. The depth within these statements is clear and those planning the key stage 3 curriculum will enrich what they set out to teach and assess if they take this into account.

The journey to secondary school can be turbulent. SATs test revision, post-SATs relaxation of formal learning, a long holiday and a vastly different approach to lessons will all take their toll. But to lose this vein of aptitude that pupils have been exposed to is a folly and all those involved in the teaching of science should celebrate what has been a part of pupil's science learning and acknowledge their potential to reignite this (Table 3.1).

Working scientifically continues to be an important feature in the key stage 3 programme of study and is broken down into four key elements of scientific attitudes, experimental skills and investigations, analysis and evaluation and measurement which build sequentially on what is found in the key stage 2 programmes of study. Working scientifically is dealt with in more detail in Chapter 7 (Table 3.2).

Where there is a collective awareness within the secondary science department as to what has been taught and touched upon in the primary phase, especially in upper key stage 2, there is the potential to build on prior learning and ignite a passion in pupils. The alternative is often that pupils simply repeat what they have already been taught and become disillusioned with their learning across the three science disciplines.

Table 3.1 Working scientifically in lower and upper key stage 2

Lower key stage 2	Upper key stage 2
• Asking relevant questions and using scientific enquiry • Setting up practical enquiries, comparative and fair tests • Making systematic and careful observation, taking accurate measurements using standard units, using a range of equipment, including thermometers and data loggers • Gathering, recording, classifying and presenting data in a variety of ways to help in answering questions • Recording findings using simple scientific language, drawings, labelled diagrams, keys, bar charts and tables • Reporting on findings from enquiries, including oral and written explanations, displays or presentations of results and conclusions • Using results to draw simple conclusions, make predictions for new values, suggest improvements and raise further questions • Identifying differences, similarities or changes related to simple scientific ideas and processes • Using straightforward scientific evidence to answer questions or to support their findings	• Planning different types of scientific enquiries to answer questions, including recognising and controlling variables where necessary • Taking measurements, using a range of scientific equipment, with increasing accuracy and precision, taking repeat readings when appropriate • Recording data and results of increasing complexity using scientific diagrams and labels, classification keys, tables, scatter graphs, bar and line graphs • Using test results to make predictions to set up further comparative and fair tests • Reporting and presenting findings from enquiries, including conclusions, causal relationships and explanations of and a degree of trust in results, in oral and written forms such as displays and other presentations

Table 3.2 Working scientifically at key stage 3

Scientific attitudes	Experimental skills and investigations
• Pay attention to objectivity and concern for accuracy, precision, repeatability and reproducibility • Understand that scientific methods and theories develop as earlier explanations are modified to take account of new evidence and ideas, together with the importance of publishing results and peer review • Evaluate risks	• Ask questions and develop a line of enquiry based on observations of the real world, alongside prior knowledge and experience • Make predictions using scientific knowledge and understanding • Select, plan and carry out the most appropriate types of scientific enquiries to test predictions, including identifying independent, dependent and control variables, where appropriate • Use appropriate techniques, apparatus and materials during fieldwork and laboratory work, paying attention to health and safety • Make and record observations and measurements using a range of methods for different investigations; and evaluate the reliability of methods and suggest possible improvements • Apply sampling techniques
Analysis and evaluation	**Measurement**
• Apply mathematical concepts and calculate results • Present observations and data using appropriate methods, including tables and graphs • Interpret observations and data, including identifying patterns and using observations, measurements and data to draw conclusions • Present reasoned explanations, including explaining data in relation to predictions and hypotheses • Evaluate data, showing awareness of potential sources of random and systematic error • Identify further questions arising from their results	• Understand and use SI units and IUPAC (International Union of Pure and Applied Chemistry) chemical nomenclature • Use and derive simple equations and carry out appropriate calculations • Undertake basic data analysis including simple statistical techniques

Some examples of how science leaders and their teams in the secondary phase can be proactive in capturing the learning are:

- A shared INSET with secondary and primary science leads working together to dovetail a scheme of work that is sequenced across years 5, 6 and 7
- Designing a collaborative bridging project that starts after SATs in the primary school and is continued in the first term of year 7.
- Year 5 and 6 teachers observe science teaching in year 7 as part of a planned CPD strategy to upskill science leads and teachers who teach in the primary phase

  Year 7 science teachers invite year 6 pupils to a fieldwork day at a science museum, river or coastal study or a scientific place of interest where pupils can take photographs, samples of materials such as pebbles, rocks or plants and answer questions.

The rich vein of knowledge in the key stage 1 and 2 programmes of study is sequenced by topic and by year. The sequence is predicated on the depth of learning and the levels of response that pupils are expected to demonstrate as part of their growing understanding of science. The verbs that define progression are clearly in evidence from early years to year 6. For instance, the study of plants and other living things has a sequential progression from early years to year 6, the verbs are sequenced here from year 1 to year 6:

- identify and name
- explore and compare
- identify functions
- recognise the differences
- describe how living things are classified

Understanding how these verbs create opportunities for the pedagogy of independent and proactive learning starts here and, if nurtured well, can be the basis for how pupils respond to higher level questioning.

There is clear progression built into this sequence, as for English and maths, and this can be adapted to create progressive learning in the foundation subjects as well. The same level of detail is not there in key stage 3, but there are opportunities to think about how what is taught can be sequenced to ensure readiness for GCSE and beyond.

Reading across the divide

Reading deserves a separate space when focusing on smooth transition from key stage 2 to 3. It is an unrelenting challenge to ensure that pupils can read fluently and comprehend what they are reading as they enter their secondary school. According to recent research from the Adult Literacy Trust: '16.4% of adults in England, or 7.1 million people, can be described as having "very poor literacy skills." They can understand short straightforward texts on familiar topics accurately and independently, and obtain information from everyday sources, but reading information from unfamiliar sources, or on unfamiliar topics, could cause problems. This is also known as being functionally illiterate' (Adult Literacy Trust 2023).

Up to 50% of those who inhabit our prisons are deemed to be illiterate or struggle to read (Shannon Trust 2023). This shocking statistic highlights the duty of our education system to ensure that no one falls through the net. Transition is a pinch point that may signal issues that can be addressed and resolved when it comes to reading and the absolute need to ensure nobody leaves school unable to read fluently.

It should be the absolute, unrelenting goal of politicians and educators to ensure that pupils do indeed learn to read. As pupils transition to secondary school that we must assess their reading age and their ability to decode the written word: 'without identification of their reading needs and targeted additional teaching, pupils who arrive in secondary school as poor readers are likely to continue to struggle. As the secondary curriculum places increasing demands on reading comprehension, older pupils who struggle with reading comprehension do not catch up' (Ofsted 2022).

There are many opportunities for teachers to work together to look in detail at how well pupils are reading by the end of year 6. Finding out the following key facts should form the basis for developing a reading strategy for year 7 and beyond:

- What novels are pupils reading as a class in years 5 and 6?
- What are the specific ways that reading is an integral part of the planning for studying maths, science and the other foundation subjects?
- Which pupils demonstrate highly competent reading skills and have the opportunity read independently?
- Which pupils are still struggling to decode words and what interventions are in place to support them?
- How is phonics used in upper key stage 2 to support pupils who have difficulty with their reading and how can secondary teachers tap into this expertise?
- How many pupils do not demonstrate that they are fluent in their reading and what support do these pupils receive as part of intervention in years 5 and 6?
- How can year 6 and 7 teachers work together to share their strategies for supporting pupils towards fluency and comprehension?
- What is the specific vocabulary that pupils have acquired in subject specific learning and in other cross-curricular contexts?

Many secondary English teachers will not have had substantial training in how to teach phonics, or any of the skills that are part of learning to read and teachers of other subjects will most definitely not have had any. Why not? This is a question that does need an answer, reading is essential to learning and is the life skill from which everything else flows. In short, if you can't read it is very unlikely that you can learn especially in our data-driven society that relies on tests and exams to measure success or otherwise (National Literacy Trust 2014).

Pedagogy and learning

Pedagogy is the science of teaching. It is pedagogy that ensures pupils learn. It is important that those involved in the process of transition know how pupils have been taught in their primary years, especially in years 5 and 6, and the similarities and differences that exist between the two phases. It is the art of instruction that builds pupils' knowledge in a range of subjects and it is the different approaches to classroom management that ensure that pupils feel safe and secure, motivated, inspired and ready to learn.

In the primary school, pupils stay predominantly in one classroom; they are taught most of the core and foundation subjects by one teacher. They are familiar with the routine and rhythm of the day and know what is expected of them. The secondary school is very different, pupils only consistency is often within their tutor or year groups where they have one teacher for the whole year. Subjects are taught by different teachers and pupils move from room to room across the day as part of five or six different lessons.

For those teaching in the secondary school, knowing why it is so important to create clear learning pathways that connect pupils' previous learning to their new learning is essential. Learning is a process which is governed by the ability of the brain to take in information into the working or short-term memory. This working memory can only manage to process between four and seven elements of learning (Lovell 2020) at any one time. In order for these elements to stick and be remembered over time, the learner needs to have opportunities to practice, revisit and refresh the knowledge they are exposed to so that it will eventually enter and remain in the long-term memory.

Skilful pedagogy leads pupils to recall and revisit their learning as part of a sequence of new learning that links to what they have already been exposed to. This requires time and opportunities for collaborative planning, with primary teachers, and with teachers within their subject or faculty domain. The detailed programmes of study from key stages 1 to 3 provide the blueprint to building a sequence of learning. Some pedagogical approaches that teachers could share are:

- Pupils working in groups with a range of pictures, phrases or diagrams linked to the subject they are learning and asking them to share what they learnt in their primary school
- Encouraging enquiry where pupils are given a set of questions and (electronic and physical) resources to answer them linked to their learning in the primary phase and what they will be doing in year 7
- Asking pupils to create mind maps using words and phrases on card or on a whiteboard linked to a topic that they should have some knowledge of that will give them a visual picture of their learning
- Creating a piece of text or providing an extract from a textbook and asking pupils to share their thoughts on what the piece is explaining. This will test their reading ability and provide some measure of understanding of knowledge in specific foundation subjects
- Providing pupils with a data set, a graph or a problem to solve to test their mathematical knowledge in different contexts
- Creating a vocabulary bank that pupils can add their own meaning alongside, with dictionaries, the internet and sharing ideas with their peers
- Giving pupils objects to feel, smell and observe in order that they can talk about their properties, origin or use
- Using a picture or a diagram to create opportunities for pupils to share what they already know about it or how it relates to their previous learning.
- Providing pupils with a problem or an idea and giving them time to come up with a presentation that explains the problem or expands on the idea linked to prior learning but also to what they will be learning next

Start with these ideas as an opportunity for professional learning with colleagues and ask for other ideas they have that have worked well.

Creating accurate assessment and the tyranny of data

Data are a snapshot in time collected to inform where pupils are in relation to others in their class or group. It is used as a measure of accountability that defines how well the school has performed against itself in previous years and against other local, regional or national schools.

Data will never give a true picture of the pupil and their abilities, attributes and understanding. It is especially difficult to interpret as pupils cross the transition bridge.

There are issues with learning, retention and memory for year 6 pupils who are trained to take the SATs tests in May. Many schools spend the whole of year 6 focusing on maths and English to prepare for tests. Science has to be given some consideration as some schools are chosen to be assessed on their science teaching and the outcomes pupils produce. The foundation subjects are often neglected. This is less likely since the new Ofsted handbook was introduced in 2018, but the temptation is still there as the stakes are high.

Following on from SATS, pupils and their teachers understandably relax and spend time on other activities such as visits or trips, sport and play and less on academic learning. There is also the long summer holiday where pupils have no formal learning. All this takes a toll on pupils' memory across the transition bridge. The data can never give an accurate picture. It is taken as a result of a narrow and contrived test on one day.

Pupils have so much to offer in terms of their knowledge, skills and their growing sense of who they are, where they belong and what they want for the future. If year 7 teams don't tap into this rich vein, they are missing out on so much learning, aptitude, potential and enthusiasm. Pupils deserve more from their new school and the opportunity exists to create a platform for learning that builds on the tacit understanding that data analysis is not and never will be a panacea.

Here are some of the best practice examples I have been privileged to be a part of (Table 3.3).

All the above requires a shared commitment and understanding from both primary and secondary schools to work together to capture exceptional work created in primary schools. In this way, there is an opportunity to learn about pupils, their needs, aspirations and abilities that is far less granular than a data set.

Formative assessment should also be a shared pedagogy. Where there is a policy to create opportunities for moderation between year 6 and year 7 teachers, a much greater understanding exists of the awareness of the rubrics that primary schools use and what standard of work is expected at each stage of assessment. For instance, if the rubric is 'emerging, achieving, exceeding' what standard of work is expected for those pupils who are emerging, what has been acted upon to move them towards achieving, what happens when a pupil is exceeding, how are they stretched and challenged?

What in the primary phase is accepted as 'achieving age-related expectations' or 'achieves the expected standard'? Creating opportunities for teachers from both phases to share examples of pupils' work and discuss their interpretations is professional development that will create a far deeper knowledge base for those responsible for ensuring there is a continuity of knowledge and skills.

Planning for success – Building strong partnerships across the transition bridge

Successful outcomes are built on strong foundations that sustain ambitious design and allow innovation and creativity to flourish. The foundation that shapes the secondary curriculum must ensure that all senior, middle and subject leaders share a common purpose in their determination to know and capture every essence of learning that has shaped the child through their primary journey.

Table 3.3 Examples of high-quality learning across the transition bridge

Pupils are given exercise books from their secondary school to use during their last term in year 6 so that secondary teachers can assess their writing, maths aptitude and other skills and knowledge they have gained. Where secondary teachers can see the quality of the work and the depth of the subject-specific teaching, they can capture more of the learning.	The secondary school asks for the best of art the pupil has produced in year 6 and puts on an exhibition of the pupils' work in the corridors or the hall so that teachers, other pupils and parents can visit. The art department can assess the aptitude of the young artists as well as the quality of art instruction that may have taken place in the primary phase.	Pupils take photographs of the last term and their holiday experiences and send them to the secondary school. They are then used by the pupils to create a collage or electronic scrapbook as part of their computer or information technology lessons. They could also use the photographs as part of their English lessons to write about themselves.
Pupils and their teachers start a history project in the last term of year 6 focusing on the second world war which they continue in year 7. They are asked to use some time in their holiday to interview a significant older person such as a grandparent to tell them about their experiences of the war and they bring their recording or notes to use in year 7 history.	Pupils build a portfolio of their work throughout year 6. They gather a sample of their work from each subject that they are studying. This should not necessarily be their best work but a sample that shows how they have progressed throughout the year. All those including form tutors have access to the work in the portfolio. It acts as an aide memoire of what pupils know and can do.	Pupils in year 7 produce a newsletter about their first term in secondary school that they can send back to the next year 6 cohort from their school. There are opportunities to give tips about what to do and not to do, the best experiences and the worst ones, photos about learning, sport or other subjects. Pupils demonstrate their English skills and their technology skills putting the newsletter together.
Pupils build wall collages that explain what they have learnt in different subjects in year 6. They can create pictures, write stories or find objects that reflect their learning and that builds a picture of their prior learning. Pupils can be encouraged to add in vocabulary of the individual subjects created on cards by their year 7 subject teachers. The collage remains in different classrooms for the first terms so that pupils have a reminder of their prior learning.	Pupils who will be joining the secondary school attend taster days where secondary school subject teachers work together across two or three subjects to provide pupils with activities that they can start in year 6 and then pick up again in year 7.	Year 6 pupils work with year 7 pupils to plan a play or a concert or some kind of exhibition that will take place at the end of the first week of the autumn term where the then year 8s and new year 7s work together to rehearse and share ideas about their production/ exhibition or concert. Pupils take on roles and responsibilities and as much as possible are only lightly supervised by teachers who can assess their ability from a distance.

Developing a transition policy that puts the curriculum as much at its core as pastoral and organisational needs will help to weave seamless learning. Where each department begins with a close analysis of the content that exists within the programmes of study for each subject, there is at least some understanding of the vocabulary, key concepts and skills that pupils have. These basic building blocks can then be used to construct a curriculum plan that defines subject content and a progression model.

Year 7 is a pivotal year in so many ways. Pupils have high expectations. They are nervous of what is to them imposing and different. They are leaving behind friendship groups, familiar teachers and routines. Their experience at the beginning of year 7 should be planned to be a positive one linked to a pursuance of learning, well-being and a deep understanding of pupils' needs, aspirations and talents (Hanewald 2013). All of this requires a determined effort to create meaningful partnerships that will support an approach to transition that delivers seamless learning.

I started this chapter with a statistic that pupils dip in performance from anything up to 40% from the end of year 6 to the end of year 7. If we focus on turning that around to a realistic 15%–20% *increase* in performance over the same period, secondary schools would be able to build towards GCSEs from a strong foundation. Where there is a curriculum map that starts in the primary school and provides a springboard for seeing year 7 as 'the first year of five', profound change happens.

There are many examples of good practice to draw on and every school is different. There are many ways to create these essential partnerships. Equally if partnership is not easy to realise considering organisational or socio-economic issues, there needs to be a determined strategy to rid the secondary school of unhelpful preconceptions about what pupils are learning and bringing with them.

Here are some examples of how change can make a significant difference to the whole of a pupil's secondary school experience.

- A joint agreement to create a steering group where individuals with responsibility for transition from larger primary schools and their partner secondary schools shape transition strategy from year 5 to year 7
- The secondary school appoints a primary specialist as Transition Coordinator who has a good understanding of the curriculum in years 5 and 6 and can build strong partnerships
- Teachers of English are also year 7 tutors and spend time observing learning in year 6 as preparation for planning the year 7 curriculum and being able to support pupils with their English in tutor time
- Similarly, all maths teachers are appointed the tutors for year 8 pupils and also have a role in planning a sequenced curriculum from year 5 to year 8 so that they can provide support for pupils
- Share schemes of work so that secondary and primary teachers are involved in the planning of a sequenced curriculum from the beginning of year 6 to the end of year 7
- Appoint a non-teaching head of year 7 who can coordinate meetings, manage data and create information structures

- Develop a programme of mutual lesson observation so that those teaching in year 6 can work with those teaching in year 7.
- Develop a strategy of cross phase moderation where teachers jointly mark and assess work from across a range of curriculum subjects
- Instead of formal testing at the beginning of year 7, plan an induction week where activities are designed to create opportunities for teachers to assess pupils' literacy and numeracy skills, their ability at problem solving, group working and enquiry.
- Give pupils a voice so that they can explain how they feel, what they would like to support them on their journey into secondary school and an opportunity to share their skills and expertise in the curriculum and in other skills for learning

CONCLUSION

Dave Harris, in his book *Transition* (2020), suggests there is an elephant in the room when it comes to discussions about policy planning for how pupils should move from primary to secondary school. There seems to be a reluctance to try to change the system even though it is clearly broken. Many schools cite the very real problem of large numbers of primary partner schools that feed into individual secondary schools. This is an issue but not insurmountable particularly with the technology that now exists to make communication with partner schools easier. The perceptions that both the primary and secondary school have of the other in relation to the curriculum and how it is taught, different classroom etiquette and behaviour management and the quality and accuracy of what is produced and assessed still create barriers that seem difficult to overcome.

The evidence is stark that pupils dip significantly in performance from the end of year 6 to the end of year 7 so it makes complete sense to see year 7 as a priority in defining curriculum intent. Doing so ensures all pupils can continue to learn from the first day they arrive in their secondary school. Pupils can experience quite traumatic change and challenge; it is a big step in their short lives. The secondary school can minimise negative experiences by creating a genuine celebration of pupils' prior learning, their abilities and attributes and their ambitions for their future. Where schools put the pupil at the heart of planning for year 7 and beyond, there is a measurable difference in performance and achievement as they move through their secondary years.

Ten Top Tips

1 Design a transition policy that focuses on the academic as well as the pastoral transfer
2 Find alternatives to testing at the beginning of year 7 such as an induction week, topic learning or a bridging project that assess pupils' ability in a low-stakes environment

3. Ensure English teachers have access to the comprehensive grammar and spelling appendix that indicates the depth of grammar and literacy skills that have been, introduced, taught and assessed that form part of the programmes of study for key stage 2
4. Create opportunities for maths teachers to review the content of the maths programmes of study for the whole of key stage 2
5. Identify in every subject the essential vocabulary that is unique to the subject and that has a similar or different meaning in other subjects
6. Create opportunities for teachers of subjects such as geography, science, design, etc., to work with the maths department to look at how the maths integral in other subjects is taught in both
7. Give time to leaders of science to analyse the key statements that focus on working scientifically in the science programmes of study in key stage 2 and 3
8. Ensure reading is an absolute priority in the quest to know which pupils are fluent readers and which still need support to develop as successful readers
9. Create opportunities for teachers from both year 6 and year 7 to observe learning and pedagogy and reflect on the similarities and differences that exist
10. Create opportunities for moderation of pupils' work and output from years 5 and 6 as part of assessing the true ability of pupils

REFERENCES

Adult Literacy Trust Website (2023) London. Available online at: https://alt.org.uk/impact-of-illiteracy/

Bagnal, C.L., Skipper, Y., Fox, C.L. (2022) Primary and Secondary Transition under Covid. *British Journal of Educational Psychology*, 92(3): pp1011–1033.

DfE (2014a) *Programmes of Study Key Stage 1 & 2*. London, DfE.

DfE (2014b) *English Key Stage 3 Programme of Study*. London, DfE.

DfE (2014c) *Maths Key Stage 1 & 2 Programme of Study*. London, DfE.

DfE (2014d) *Science Key Stage 1 & 2 Programmes of Study*. London, DfE.

DfE (2014e) *Teaching Mathematics in Primary Schools*. London, DfE.

Hanewald, R. (2013) Transition between Primary and Secondary School: Why It Is Important and How It Can Be Supported. *Australian Journal of Teacher Education*, 38(1): pp62–74.

Hargreaves, L. and Galton, M. (eds.) (1999) *Moving from the Primary Classroom: 20 Years on*, London, Routledge.

Harris, D. (2020) *Transition*. Camarthen, Independent Thinking Press.

Jindal-Snape et al. (2019) *Primary to Secondary School Transitions: Systematic Literature Review*. Dundee, Scottish government.

Lovell, O. (2020) *Cognitive Load Theory in Action*. Woodbridge, John Catt.

National Literacy Trust (2014) *Literacy Changes Lives: Anew Perspective on Health, Employment and Crime*. London, National Literacy Trust.

National Centre for the Excellence in Teaching of Mathematics (NCETM) (2020) *Shaping the Year 7 Curriculum: Building on Year 6*. London.

Ofsted (2015) *Key Stage 3: The Wasted Years?* London, Ofsted.

Ofsted (2022) *Prison Education: A Review of Reading Education in Prisons*. London, Ofsted.

Ofsted (2022) *Now the Whole School Is Reading: Supporting Struggling Readers in Secondary Schools*. London, Ofsted.

Shannon Trust (2023) *Reading Programmes for Prisons, Turning Pages*. London, Ofsted.

4

KEY STAGE 3 – A VITAL PIECE IN THE CURRICULUM JIGSAW

Contents

KEY STAGE 3: A PIVOTAL SPACE WITHIN THE SEQUENTIAL CURRICULUM

Key stage 3 nestles between pupils moving from primary school to begin their secondary journey and starting to study for GCSEs in key stage 4 which will lead them towards a suite of examinations at the end of year 11. It is these that will define their future and be the benchmark that determines how well the school is judged against other schools and by the local community, the wider public, the government and the inspectorate.

The lack of importance placed on key stage 3 manifests itself in many ways. The previous chapter focused on transition and the need to ensure that the curriculum for year 7, the first of the key stage 3 phase, builds on what the pupils have learnt in years 5 and 6. Many secondary schools timetable key stages 4 and 5 before key stage 3 to make sure that resources and expert staff are prioritised for examination classes. Sometimes this leads to teachers who have less experience, poor subject knowledge and pedagogical expertise being assigned to teach classes in key stage 3.

There is a consensus that key stage 3 should span three years, but some schools shorten this to two years (Harford, Ofsted 2015). Whatever the length of time, there is still the conundrum of what to teach, how to teach it and how to create the right springboard so that what is learnt in years 7 to 9 creates the knowledge and skills pupils need for the next stage and the rigour of preparation for examinations.

I do believe there is a case for a condensed key stage 3 curriculum which is potentially useful due to the greater demands made because of the introduction of the EBacc curriculum (Kumari-Wood and Haddon 2021).

The potential advantages of a two-year key stage 3 are:

- For pupils who are thriving and came to their secondary school with a high SATs score of, say, above 106 may well be ready for a more challenging year 9 curriculum.
- Those pupils who are deemed to have SEND, who are disadvantaged or who have gaps in their learning may benefit from three years of GCSE study to fully cover the content within their chosen subjects.
- It is likely with a concentrated key stage 3 that pupils will feel that they are simply completing work that they undertook in their primary school.
- Choosing to study less subjects in year 9 could provide valuable time for pupils to undertake enrichment activities, work-related learning, enterprise or cultural experiences.
- By having three years of study, some pupils could enhance their subject choices by adding additional supplementary GCSEs such as drama, performing arts or statistics perhaps.

PLANNING BREADTH AND DEPTH WITHIN KEY STAGE 3

Once the length of time for key stage 3 has been decided, there must be a focus on what will be taught and what pupils should know and be able to do by the end of key stage 3. This is more complex than it first appears. There is the imperative for all curriculum planners to have some understanding as to what pupils have learnt in their primary schools, what have they remembered and what is ingrained misconception.

This, as discussed in chapter 3, is often a neglected area of planning but does need to be reviewed and revisited. To simply ignore the often detailed and increasingly well-taught subject-specific learning that has been a part of upper key stage 2 is a lost opportunity to build on some basic but secure knowledge and a range of well-taught skills. It is also de-motivating for pupils who may lose interest if they have to revisit knowledge that they have previously learnt and feel that the learning they bring with them from their primary school is underappreciated by their secondary school teachers (Bromley 2017).

Within this overarching five-year strategy, key stage 3 also needs to have its own identity. Each subject is unique in relation to the knowledge that subject experts want their pupils to learn. However, there are some generic considerations that could form part of a consensus as to the whole school vision for the key stage 3 curriculum.

Use the statements Table 4.1 to make a set of cards that you can use with subject and cross-curricular teams to start a dialogue that creates the cohesion for weaving the tapestry of knowledge, skills and learning together (Table 4.1).

A DEEPER LOOK AT LITERACY

There is an imperative to look closely at literacy in every subject, not just in English. How well pupils read should be assessed when pupils arrive in year 7 and those who are not fluent in their reading will need support, otherwise they will not be able to access the depth of knowledge across the range of subjects they are studying. A study of the curriculum that has been taught in key stage 2 will reveal the vocabulary that young pupils have been exposed to. An assessment of how well they have retained an understanding of subject-specific vocabulary and how it can be used to build on the learning in years 7- 9 can form an important part of the planning mechanism.

Table 4.1 Action statements for key stage 3 curriculum planning

• Build on prior learning from key stage 2 • Create a sequential learning map across the key stage 3 landscape • Ensure equitable delivery for all pupils • Develop independent and reflective learners • Explore the potential of computer science and e-learning	• Use cognitive science theory to create deeper learning pathways • Prioritise reading in all subjects and in cross-curricular contexts • Raise awareness and use concepts that exist within subjects and across the curriculum • Define and use subject and cross-curricular vocabulary widely	• Celebrate staff expertise and knowledge • Define what knowledge will be taught in each subject • Embed literacy and numeracy as part of learning in every subject • Plan a CPD strategy to include all staff

Fluency and clarity of purpose in writing should be honed during key stage 3. Key stage 3 teachers across all subjects should have a clear understanding of how well pupils can write for purpose, audience and effect. There is an imperative to assess pupils' ability to write fluidly and with meaning as well as knowing the quality of their command of language, grammar, inference and style. Writing is a key part of GCSE success across most subjects and where pupils develop their skills in writing as they progress through key stage 3, the more they will be ready for to use higher levels of response required for GCSE study.

Key stage 3 is an ideal time for pupils to begin to understand the taxonomy of progression that ensures that they know the difference between describe and explain, how they justify an answer, compare and contrast with clarity and understand what is meant by analysis and how it is different from evaluation. Continuous assessment and consistent dialogue between teacher and pupil in English, and in other subjects where extended writing is a key element, will reap many benefits for pupils as they progress into key stage 4 and beyond.

The taxonomy below, discussed in more detail in chapter 2, provides the starting point for teachers to support their pupils to firstly demonstrate their ability to remember prior learning, add to their growing understanding and then apply that to unfamiliar and different contexts. The ability to analyse and evaluate honed in key stage 3 will equip pupils with the higher levels of response to succeed at GCSE and beyond. Pupils with the ability to show their creativity and independent thought will be able to accept challenge, take risks and find solutions when the content is difficult or complex (Figure 4.1).

Remember	Understand	Apply	Analyse	Evaluate	Create

Figure 4.1 DfE (2015) Anderson and Krathwohl Revised Bloom's taxonomy

It is also important to consider the value of highly effective speaking and listening skills that provide pupils with opportunities to develop their own presentations, share their learning with others, work in groups and with peers and articulate their understanding and deepening knowledge.

Where subject leaders from across the curriculum work together to build a consensus of how to ensure pupils are fluent as readers, have exceptional subject level and conceptual vocabulary knowledge and can write with clarity pupils will increase their potential. The opportunities for cross-curricular professional dialogue, shared approaches to teaching reading, writing and oracy skills and a structured approach to explicitly planning how literacy skills are an integral part of every subject, is powerful CPD that will benefit all departments.

Reading is a critical skill. The English team must convey to all other subject leaders where pupils may need help. Equally, those pupils that are strong readers need to be challenged to deepen their knowledge and understanding in response to mastering the complexities across all subjects.

For teachers who support those pupils who are still not fluent readers, it is important to identify gaps in phonics knowledge and try to ameliorate the problems and allow pupils to access the essential knowledge packed into a crowded key stage 3 curriculum.

The following table suggests some of the ways that teachers can support pupils who have reading difficulties as they arrive in the secondary school. Put each element of the table onto card to create opportunities for staff to share their approaches to supporting poor reading. Focus on pertinent issues that require a collaborative approach to managing the potential of each pupil (Table 4.2).

Table 4.2 Reading and fluency - Learning Cultures' training cards

Use rhyme, mnemonics and phrases	**Subject and cross - curricular vocabulary**
Use rhymes and give pupils the opportunity to say them out loud to hear the sounds Think about how to break down words that are not phonetic and that pupils find difficult to spell (friend – fri the end of your friend) (said – Sally-Ann is dizzy) Use mnemonics to build meaning out of a key word ie **magnet** **m**oving **a**ttracts **g**ravity **n**orth **e**lectricity **t**ypes and uses	Develop vocabulary lists for every subject Identify where words mean different things in different subjects Create opportunities to look at root words Be aware of common spelling mistakes and create opportunities for pupils to make their own corrections Identify where new and unfamiliar vocabulary is likely to be introduced and create opportunities for pupils to find meaning in the unfamiliar words Consider the concepts that are within each subject and that transcend subjects and ensure pupils know their meaning
Engage all the senses	**Model good reading behaviour**
Ensure pupils know the alphabet from A – Z Use multi-sensory techniques such as touching and shaping the letters, see the letters in a sequence to make a word, say the letters and the words Use wooden or plastic letters to make words, say words and speak words Create opportunities for pupils to listen to texts and discuss their meaning Have objects or pictures with labels so that pupils can link the picture to the words Use poetry, rhyme or songs to show pupils how words sound to create rhythm	When reading aloud, regulate the voice for emotion, suspense or atmosphere Encourage pupils to move their finger along the words that they are reading from left to right When asking pupils to read help them understand punctuation by asking them to count in their heads 2 for a comma, 4 for a full stop and 6 for the end of a paragraph Expose pupils to as many texts as possible both fiction and non-fiction
Fluency	**Comprehension**
Identify where pupils struggle with certain words Assess how well pupils can access the whole words in a piece of text Support pupils to decode words in their quest for ultimate fluency in their reading Encourage prosody or reading with expression to assess their understanding Remind pupils of the importance of punctuation in the quest for fluency and pace Encourage pupils to read to themselves as well as out loud	Create opportunities for discussions about what pupils have read to assess their understanding Ask pupils to tell you about the characters, the plot, the detail or the facts to test their understanding Give pupils time to think about what happens next or what surprises them about what is happening so far Encourage pupils to write a short synopsis of what they have read Let pupils be critical about what they have read and their points of view about different texts both fiction and non-fiction

Where pupils SATs scores are below 95, it is likely that they are not secondary ready because the score reveals a probable reading age of less than 10. Some of the texts pupils will be exposed to in many subjects will be beyond their capacity. All teachers need support in finding ways to help pupils develop effective comprehension skills. Ruth Miskin's *Read, Write Inc: Fresh Start* is a programme for struggling readers in secondary schools and provides a useful tool for teachers who have not been trained in phonics.

There is also the need to challenge more able pupils with high scores who have been exposed to reading texts that have allowed them to develop as confident readers beyond their chronological reading age. There is evidence to suggest that where poor readers and good readers work together to decipher texts, there is a benefit for both. The poor reader is working with someone close in age who can decode in a meaningful way and the better reader is consolidating their own learning (Education Endowment Foundation, 2021).

TEACHING ENGLISH LITERACY IN PREPARATION FOR KEY STAGE 4

Key stage 3 is a valuable time to create a lifelong love of reading, poetry, plays and stories. Here we can create opportunities to understand how the written word is shaped to make sense of the human condition and the many scenarios and mysteries that surround our consciousness and understanding of ourselves. Decisions about the texts and creative works to introduce to pupils during this phase will have a bearing on their ability to sustain a love of reading and a deepening awareness of the powerful influence of fiction.

Introducing pupils to Shakespeare in key stage 3 is an opportunity to allow time for them to become familiar with the language, the medium and themes such as identity, ambition, relationships and conflict. Well-loved plays such as A Midsummer Night's Dream, Twelfth Night and Romeo and Juliet have stories that are easy for young teenage minds to relate to and comprehend in terms of their own situation. Opportunities to build in some of the works of Charles Dickens such as A Christmas Carol and Oliver Twist also provide for links with history themes and modern-day issues such as migration, homelessness and narrowing the gap for many in society.

Where pupils have the opportunity to become familiar with the dense nature of the text and the language of Shakespeare and 19th century novels from authors, such as Dickens, they are likely to be ready to tackle more complex themes and structures in key stage 4 and beyond. Key stage 3 provides an opportunity to explore such texts in a different way, creating opportunities for pupils to build their own narrative around some of the themes, consider the plotlines and how some issues remain the same, today. One interesting area for pupils to consider is how we communicate now through phones and email as opposed to letters sent through a slow but effective postal system. The issues of family ties and the change in attitudes to relationships and familial structures is also fertile territory for discussion.

Drama is not a National Curriculum subject but where it is included as a key stage 3 subject aligned to English literature, it can create a powerful medium for expression. Free from National Curriculum constraints means that drama provides an opportunity to express meaning through performance or through other ways such as its links to design in the pursuit of creating sets, costumes or lighting. Drama and history are so intricately linked, the history of the theatre, the history behind a plot or a concept, the history of a local theatre or film and more modern streaming media.

MAKING MATHEMATICS AND NUMERACY COUNT WITHIN KEY STAGE 3

Working mathematically asks that pupils are fluent in the fundamentals of mathematics, can reason and can solve problems by applying their mathematics to a variety of routine and non-routine situations (DfE, 2014a). The subject content is set out in distinct disciplines, number, algebra, ratio, proportion and rates of change, geometry and measures, probability and statistics.

Explanations of the three aims of fluency, reasoning and problem solving are underpinned by key verbs that are evident in the content of the programme of study for maths at key stage 3. A focus on these can create a pupil-centred approach to deepening mathematical competence. Linking these verbs to the planned pedagogy creates a fluid and seamless pupil-centred key stage 3 maths curriculum that builds on prior learning from key stage 2 and ensures the security of pupils' unconscious competence in preparation for key stage 4 and beyond.

Pupils should be given as many opportunities as possible to use maths concepts in the context of learning across a range of interconnected elements of maths and in the application of maths in other subjects such as science, geography, computing, art and design and design technology. Opportunities to deepen mathematical understanding in readiness for key stage 4 and beyond should be seen as both a responsibility of the maths department but also anywhere where maths is an integral part of the learning.

Decisions as to the challenge and depth of understanding must lie with an assessment of what pupils already know and can do and how well they can make sense of concepts and then take on more sophisticated problem-solving activities. Where pupils have still to grasp the necessary elements to progress and consolidate their learning, there should be a collective and cohesive plan that ensures opportunities for further practice to build confidence and competence in readiness for key stage 4.

The possibilities are many and require a real consensus not just on the potential to enrich the curriculum for the pupil but also for teachers to create a positive dialogue that will enhance their own professional and pedagogical understanding and their approach to teaching of maths across the curriculum.

THE POTENTIAL OF SCIENCE IN THE KEY STAGE 3 CONTINUUM

Science and its three distinct disciplines are compulsory and pivotal to making sense of the world we live in. Science links with maths, and it requires essential literacy skills; it has subject content aligned to the geography curriculum and is bound up with history. It also has a very detailed programme of study that must be covered during the key stage 3 years (DfE, 2014c).

Key stage 2 science is prescriptive and provides science leads with a clear sequence with which to teach the different elements from year 1 to year 6 (Frater 2023). The problem with the key stage 2 curriculum is how it is taught. Many teachers will not be scientists or have studied science beyond year 11.

The challenge is to create a suite of learning experiences that will stretch the pupil that has had the advantage of being taught by a scientist in key stage 2 and will also enhance the learning for those pupils where there has not been an expert science teacher. Dialogue is required among the science community in school who need to ask questions such as:

- What should we teach?
- When and how will what pupils learn in key stage 3 prepare them for deeper and more complex understanding of many of the same concepts in key stage 4 as pupils prepare for their GCSEs?
- How do we sequence the learning to build and consolidate their learning over time?
- How do we create discrete learning in the three disciplines but also show their interconnectedness?
- What are the links that bind subjects together?

The science department needs to create a continuum that delivers a curriculum offer that starts with the fundamental principles of science so that pupils can build a knowledge base that over time builds deep understanding. Particles, solids, gases, in chemistry, the fundamentals in physics, forces, energy, matter and radiation and in biology reproduction, nutrition and cell structure.

HUMANITIES AND MAKING SENSE OF THE WORLD

The subjects that make up the humanities, history, geography and religious education are all subjects that might not be in a pupil's repertoire for study in key stage 4 so for these departments there is an imperative to use key stage 3 to market their subject as something worth continuing to study at GCSE and beyond. The potential for creativity in all these subjects is profound especially in relation to the local context, a focus on cultural capital and other enriching and spiritual considerations.

There is time in history to focus on the local context. Wherever the school is, there will be a rich historical perspective. It could be that your school is near to a world heritage site such as Stonehenge, or Ironbridge, it could be that war came perilously close such as in Coventry or some parts of London. There may be a history of mining, steam and railways, cotton or rope making, or rural heritage that has changed over time.

Creating opportunities to focus on concepts that transcend the three humanities subjects can build pupils' vocabulary and help them to see connections across their learning. The river is a simple concept that is such an essential asset for many settlements and explains where towns grew up and thrived. It also has a place in religions, pilgrimages and places of sanctuary. The river features in many of the stories pupils will learn in their pursuit of a historical perspective. The river Thames was an essential mode of transport in Tudor times and the proximity of the Tower of London saw many people who lost their heads take their last journey down the Thames towards their fate.

Geography in key stage 3 can be a combination of the physical and the human and provide pupils with an opportunity to build depth and breadth from year 7 by creating a sense of place where pupils can learn using local maps, photographs and technologies to look in detail at the local topography and how it has shaped the landscape and allowed people to settle and become a community. In year 8, pupils can begin to explore the economic or the wider regional environment they are part of, the nearest cities, their policy and decision makers and the proximity of their school and where they may go next to continue to learn.

Year 9, if that remains within key stage 3, can provide an opportunity to look in detail at the local and wider context in relation to global issues that affect us all such as climate change, migration and food security. Creating opportunities for debate and analysis of some of the threats we currently face can be lively and will foster the language and ability to infer, reason and form an argument that will set them in good stead at key stage 4.

Whatever the decisions made about the geography curriculum, there are threads and links within geography and the other humanities subjects. The idea of a tapestry curriculum is explored in this quote,

> To adopt a tapestry model in which we see our curriculum as being made up of many threads that weave together to reveal the big picture, the whole being greater than the sum of its parts. The tapestry model means that nothing stands in isolation' everything studied becomes relevant and powerful. (Enser 2021: p113)

Here Enser is talking about geography, but the tapestry can be even richer if it embraces a much more dynamic whole curriculum potential. Developing historical perspective, understanding the concept of the past and how it helps us to make sense of the present can all form a part of a key stage 3 narrative.

Key stage 3 is a time for pupils to consolidate their understanding of the past which, with their limited experience, is sometimes difficult to grasp. Learning that history is a collection of evidence that is flawed and open to interpretation can fascinate young minds and provide a rich vein of questioning. Open-ended enquiry questions that challenge assumptions can help pupils to see how historians come up with interpretations that have become assumed facts but can be questioned in all sorts of different ways. For example:

- What leads us to assume that?
- How do we know?
- What is the evidence that has given us that perspective?

Across the humanities curriculum is the need to ensure pupils can access both the substantive knowledge that is the bedrock of the subject and the disciplinary knowledge that creates the skills and ability of pupils to access the former. In history and religious education, evidence is a key factor at play and it is the skill of the teacher and subject expert to foster pupils' ability to develop that disciplinary knowledge to make sense of the substantive (Counsell 2011). Evidence and its efficacy in history, physical and human geographical features in geography and belief and the stories from the past in religious education all create opportunities for debate and enquiry. The use of evidence to formulate hypothesis leads to new questions that may need further investigation and helps pupils learn the essential ability to use their growing repertoire of higher-level thinking skills.

DEVELOPING CREATIVITY IN ART AND DESIGN IN KEY STAGE 3

By year 10, leaders of art departments in secondary schools tell me pupils should be able to say what they are doing and why. They should know the artistic influences that shape their work. Key stage 3 is a time to expose pupils to a variety of forms of creative expression and give them time to experiment and apply different techniques using different mediums and styles.

Giving pupils opportunities for freedom is not letting go of the actual teaching of art, but it is creating the teacher as coach, the guide on the side so that the pupil has a relationship with the teacher but is slowly moving from being a novice in their ability as artists to becoming competent in their use of certain techniques and styles.

The art curriculum could be linked to the history curriculum as pupils study artists from different periods, their subject matter and influences in relation to events and issues of their day. Also, pupils can imitate the style of artists from different periods and replicate their approach in their own work. The precision of Rembrandt or Vermeer, the impressionism of Van Cogh, Monet or Lautrec, the satire of Lowry and the abstract works by Pollock, Banksy or Perry. The more exposure pupils have to different artists in key stage 3, the more they begin to learn about their own artistic potential and see the influence art has on society today and in the past.

POSSIBILITIES IN DESIGN TECHNOLOGY IN KEY STAGE 3

Design technology in key stage 3 should provide pupils with an opportunity to experience food technology, product design and textiles. Pupils should have an opportunity to learn computer-aided design techniques and be exposed to graphics. Key stage 3 should give pupils the opportunity to develop some overarching skills in each discipline.

It should also make links with maths, science, business, enterprise, culture and the environment. Where those responsible for design technology can build relationships with their colleagues in other relevant subjects, they can strengthen an understanding of why design technology is such an important subject and can be a passport to many creative and exciting jobs.

The design technology programme of study covers a wide range of possibilities in terms of designing, producing and evaluating products and techniques. Pupils can look at the world from all sorts of perspectives through the window of design technology, looking at the history of a product, for instance, the telephone or the car. They can consider product design in relation to durability, effects on the environment or accessibility. The potential for pupils to develop a range of higher-level thinking skills that translate into other subjects is profound. This is illustrated in this extract from the aims statement for design technology, Programme of Study for key stage 3:

> All pupils develop the creative, technical and practical expertise needed to perform everyday tasks confidently and to participate in an increasingly technological world; build and apply a repertoire of knowledge, understanding and skills... critique, evaluate and test their ideas...work with others... (DfE 2014b)

DEVELOPING PUPILS AS MUSICIANS AND LOVERS OF SOUND

Music is an important part of a primary school curriculum, but it is unlikely that most pupils do much more than learn songs and develop some understanding of instruments such as the recorder, the tambourine and the triangle. Some pupils will of course have much more knowledge because of parental influence and already be fluent at reading music, playing an instrument or singing as part of a group or choir. It is, therefore, important that pupils arriving in year 7 all feel they can play their part in music lessons.

Creating opportunities for pupils to work with sound, whatever their ability is a good starting point. Also, exposing pupils to the vocabulary of music in its many forms and ensuring pupils can make the connections between meaning in a musical context and in other contexts across the curriculum is important. Take pitch, texture, rhythm, all have very definite meaning in music but can mean something entirely different across a range of other curriculum subjects.

A key stage 3 music curriculum is enriched where teachers bring into school their own musical community, the local choir, opportunities to hear local musicians. There may be talent higher up the school starting their own band or who are part of an orchestra, drama group or community group. Music has the power to bring people together. It is present throughout history, it links with science in terms of how it is created or how sound travels and it is powerful in evoking emotions linked to nature and bird song, the flow of a river the passage of the seasons, our solar system and the sounds of animals.

A key report published in 2022, A National Plan for Music Education suggests that outcomes schools should be looking to achieve by the end of key stage 3 include that pupils:

- sing or play with sufficient control to be able to perform or compose with purpose, expression and musical understanding, including when using music technology;
- perform with connection and co-ordination when making music with others;
- can use a system, for example, staff notation or tab, to learn and perform music appropriate to the instrument and musical style;
- demonstrate knowledge of Western classical music and music from a range of musical traditions and understand some of the context that brought the music to being (DfE 2022).

KEY STAGE 3 PHYSICAL EDUCATION – PARTICIPATION, SKILLS AND TALENT

The PE department faces the same dilemma as many other foundation subjects. The inconsistency in how and what pupils have been taught in key stage 2 requires some thought when designing curriculum content at key stage 3. Pupils may not have had access to the same sports facilities and the choice of which sports to focus on may be due to the preference and the skills of their primary teachers.

Participation and understanding the rules of different sports are important. Not every secondary school pupil will demonstrate sporting prowess, but developing an understanding of the different sports they will encounter through their lives should be a fundamental starting point for secondary pupils.

Sport and physical education have a part to play in helping pupils to develop some of the most important traits they will need in life, standards, competition, fitness and health, fairness and expectation. How pupils learn a variety of sports will help both those who may become elite athletes and those who find other ways to fill their leisure time. All who embark upon any sport or physical activity must learn the basics, how to throw, catch, hand-eye coordination, to run, to be alert and to hit the target or show skill and prowess.

Other powerful advantages to a rich curriculum in PE in key stage 3 are that pupils begin to learn how to work in teams, how to reflect on their contribution, accept when their team doesn't win and analyse strategy and tactics. PE is great for cognition; practice is an essential element of the processes of learning a sport. To move from the big picture, the final performance to where pupils make mistakes, keep practising until they get it right and then start to be able to demonstrate their skills are unconscious elements of the learning process.

IGNITING A PASSION FOR COMPUTER SCIENCE

The programme of study for key stage 3 talks about terms such as design, use and evaluate, use logical reasoning, solve problems and understand the fundamentals linked to information technology. It is easy to see from the language that creating the right sequential platform for pupils at key stage 3 years is about learning a range of skills that are transferrable to subjects where decomposition and abstraction are an essential element of learning.

Areas of the computer science curriculum are about making mistakes and analysing how to make the necessary changes in order to put them right. It is about trying to find solutions to problems that may be simple in years 8 and 9 but are the bedrock of the future breakthroughs that may change the world.

For senior leaders, it is worth a focus on the potential of computer science to support pupils in their ability to develop skills through pattern making, abstraction and programming. All help pupils to develop the skills they need to tackle real life issues and be ready for the technological breakthroughs of the future.

TEACHING PUPILS A SECOND OR THIRD LANGUAGE

Language teaching can be a powerful opportunity to create for pupils a place they can go to that is very different from their reality. Deciding which target language to teach is a difficult starting point for many language departments as pupils could have had some exposure to any number of languages in their primary school. Some will already be fluent in a second language or have English as their second language. Others may not have had any real exposure to another language and may still struggle to read and speak well in their mother tongue.

Language curriculum planning should align with a focus on literacy including phonics and the vocabulary that pupils need in order that they can access the language to speak, read, comprehend and write fluently. Where pupils are aware of the links to learning grammar and deepening their reading ability in English, they can begin to make connections and see similarities and differences in the conventions in their learning of another language.

Reading a case study from the Reach Academy in Feltham written by Hannah Pinkman for Huh (2021), I was struck by how different their approach is to my own experience of learning a second language. Hannah suggests that learning vocabulary in the context of a few useful phrases and sentences that can then be built on creates fluency and relevance for the learner.

Creating successful linguists takes time and a great deal of exposure to the language they are learning. The more opportunities there are in key stage 3 to relate learning to real life examples, pen friends, children's literature, comics and magazines, podcasts and programmes, the more pupils will have confidence and fluency at key stage 4. There is also the need to challenge more able pupils. They could be encouraged look towards news and current affairs and the opportunity to discuss similarities and differences in the life of those who live as citizens in the country of the target language.

KEY STAGE 3: THE WORTHWHILE YEARS

Let us rethink key stage 3 as 'the worthwhile years'. It is a bridge from key stage 2 that should be strong and durable and a springboard to key stage 4. It is a valuable time for consolidating learning, building the motivation to want to find out more and preparing pupils for key stage 4 and beyond (Figure 4.2).

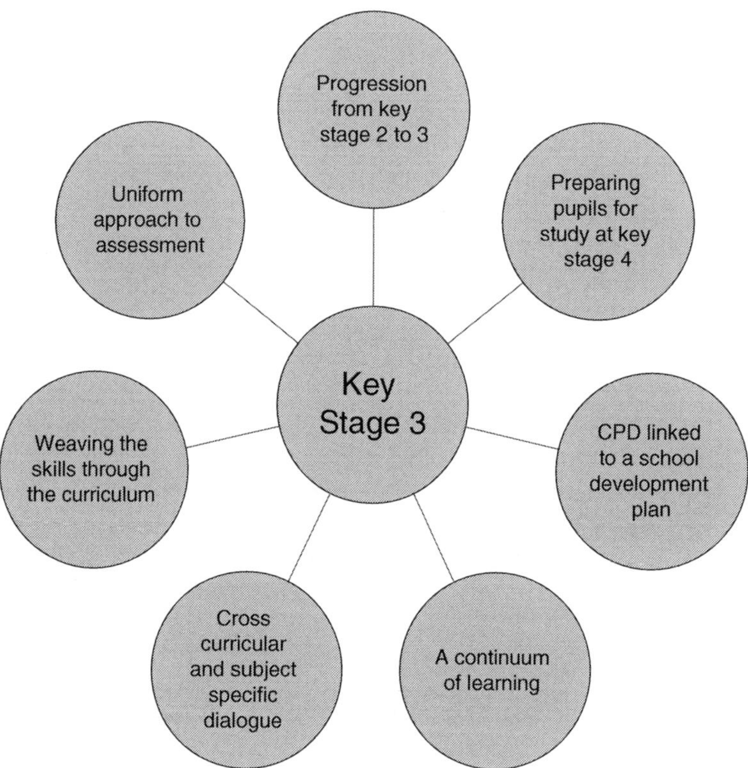

Figure 4.2 The teaching and learning opportunities at key stage 3

Key stage 4 is when data builds a picture of how well the school educates and creates well-rounded young people. However, data is a snapshot of what pupils have achieved in a suite of examinations that are the culmination of five years of study in the secondary school and at least six years study in their primary school. For senior and subject leaders, to work together to design an innovative and deeply inclusive key stage 3 curriculum will reap extraordinary benefits for the department, for the staff within it and for pupils who know that their learning across all their secondary years is important and is worth pursuing.

Each subject has its own unique focus. It can become all consuming. What to teach? When to teach it? Who can teach it? How much knowledge content do we need to include?

All of these and many more are the question that senior and subject leaders and their teams need to discuss and agree on the answers. Senior leaders need to work with their subject leads to learn what the unique and specific needs of each subject are and the resources and expertise that will deliver a rich and meaningful key stage 3 curriculum.

There are other potential additions to a key stage 3 curriculum for some pupils especially where the decision is to condense key stage 3 to two years. Some pupils may benefit from an opportunity to start on a vocational journey with three years to develop their portfolio for a T level, BTEC or OCR National that will set them up for a potential future career pathway. Another possibility is to use the ASDAN CoPE qualification for some pupils in years 9 and 10. CoPE is the Certificate of Personal Effectiveness and provides an opportunity for pupils to gain a qualification that accredits all sorts of curricular and extra-curricular activities such as voluntary work, sporting prowess, cultural experiences, fieldwork, hobbies, etc. The qualification also requires pupils to demonstrate their ability to work with others, problem solve and show that they have improved their own learning and performance (ASDAN 2003).

CONCLUSION: CREATING STRUCTURE AND SUBSTANCE

I like the term 'intellectual architecture' (Myatt and Tomsett 2021) which I believe sums up the rationale for a deep focus on key stage 3. This focus can be transformational and pivotal in building a seamless curriculum that creates opportunities for pupils to see the bigger picture that their learning provides as they begin their journey towards adulthood.

Planning the curriculum should be collaborative and create cohesion within subjects and as part of a deep focus on the cross-curricular connections that weave the learning together. The curriculum architecture, much like in the design of a building, starts with an overview of the finished structure. So, planning the key stage 3 curriculum should start with the question: What will success look like at the end of key stage 4?

The task for those involved is to look at the foundations that will strengthen the learning to ensure that it is secure and will be refreshed, recalled and remembered. It is then to look at the different elements that go into its construction, literacy and numeracy skills, thinking skills, the key concepts and the subject knowledge, themes and ideas. Each component is an essential and key part of the whole and without each being carefully considered the substance of the curriculum will have no real strength and leave pupils without the underpinning foundation they need to begin their study for GCSE and other qualifications in key stage 4 and beyond.

Equally, the ability to create the structure is bound up in the quality of the pedagogy, the expertise of subject specialists and the commitment to see key stage 3 as important, if not more important than key stage 4, where we want pupils to be developing a love of learning, a motivation to want to know more and the curiosity and creativity that leads to deep thinking and exciting potential.

Ten Top Tips

1 Make key stage 3 a priority in overarching curriculum planning
2 Know why you have made the decision in relation to the length of key stage 3. Two or three years, have your reasons carefully crafted and share them with your teams
3 Create strong partnerships with your primary partner schools and find ways to ensure you have the evidence that you are building on prior learning
4 Subject teams should work closely together to create a sequential curriculum from year 7 to year 9
5 Ensure that not only is the curriculum offer at key stage 3 broad and balanced, but that teaching is as high quality as that in key stage 4 so that pupils are challenged and ready at the beginning of year 9 or 10 for study towards examinations
6 Create better cross-phase partnerships with primary schools to ensure that Key Stage 3 teachers build on pupils' prior knowledge, understanding and skills
7 Make sure that systems and procedures for assessing and monitoring pupils' progress in key stage 3 are robust
8 Focus on the needs of disadvantaged pupils in key stage 3, including the most able, in order to close the achievement gap as quickly as possible
9 Build resilience through a deep look at the thinking skills that transcend all subjects
10 Create opportunities to ensure that literacy and numeracy are an integral part of all learning

REFERENCES

ASDAN (2003) *Certificate of Personal Effectiveness.* Bristol, ASDAN.

Bromley, MJ. (2017) *Making Key Stage 3 Count.* England, Bromley Education.

Counsell, C. (2011) Disciplinary Knowledge for All, the Secondary History Curriculum, and History Teachers' Achievement. *The Curriculum Journal,* 2(22), pp201–225.

Department of Education (DfE) (2014a) *National Curriculum in England Programmes of Study for Maths: A National Plan for Music Education.* London, Department of Education (DfE).

Department of Education (DfE) (2014b) *National Curriculum in England Programmes of Study for Design Technology.* London, Department of Education.

Department of Education (DfE) (2014c) *National Curriculum in England Programmes of Study for Science.* London, Department of Education.

Department of Education (DfE) (2015) *Commission on Assessment with Levels.* London, Department of Education.

Department of Education (DfE) (2022) *The Power of Music to Change Lives.* London, Department of Education (DfE).

Education Endowment Foundation (EEF) (2021) *Secondary Literacy.* London, Education Endowment Foundation.

Enser, M. (2021) *Powerful Geography: A Curriculum with Purpose and Practice.* Carmarthen, Crown House Publishing.

Frater, G. (2023) *Primary Curriculum Design and Delivery.* Chapter 6. London, Sage/Corwin.

Kumari-Wood, M. and Haddon, N. (2021) *Secondary Curriculum Transformed.* Abingdon, Routledge.

Miskin (2006) *Read, Write Inc: Fresh Start.* Oxford, Oxford University Press.

Myatt, M. and Tomsett, J. with Pinkman, H. (2021) *Huh: Curriculum Conversations between Subject and Senior Leaders*, pp. 178-183. Woodbridge, John Catt.

Ofsted (2015) *Key Stage 3: The Wasted Years?* London, Ofsted.

5

COMMUNICATION, LANGUAGE AND LITERATURE IN THE DIGITAL AGE

Contents

DEVELOPING A NATURAL COMPETENCE IN THE ESSENTIAL SKILLS OF READING WRITING AND ORACY

Reading, writing and the skills of listening, speaking and sharing ideas are essential to everything we do in whatever subject and in all our interactions and communications. The emphasis for schools is to ensure that the school's curriculum 'is ambitious and designed to give pupils, particularly disadvantaged pupils (including those with SEND) the knowledge they need to take advantage of opportunities, responsibilities and experiences later in life' (Ofsted 2022: p227).

We know that the aim is to ensure that the curriculum is constructed as a knowledge-rich vein of powerful learning that deepens over time. To create this, we must build the potential for pupils to be highly educated and exceptionally interesting individuals who will be successful in all their endeavours. The first essential ingredient in creating highly articulate learners is ensuring that pupils can access the knowledge we want them to learn. To do this, they must have the fluency to write well, to demonstrate that they can read fluidly and with profound understanding and can speak confidently about the knowledge they are acquiring.

Secondary English teachers need to carefully scan the content of the key stage 1 and 2 programmes of study in terms of the sequential year on year acquisition of a range of statutory requirements that is contained within them and look in detail at the spelling conventions (DfE 2013).

They should also be aware that the grammar, punctuation and vocabulary that is detailed as a glossary in the key stage 3 programme of study appears as appendix 2 in the programmes of study for key stage 1 and 2.

Creating a sequential approach to ensuring all pupils can build on the vocabulary, spelling punctuation and grammar skills must assume that pupils have strong foundations developed during their primary years. The acquisition of a growing body of knowledge is dependent on pupils becoming increasingly confident and competent in their unconscious and accurate use of the English language. GCSE examinations in every subject award marks of 20% for spelling, grammar and punctuation. This is a game changer for the pupil, all departments and the school. Using the correct conventions not only helps to prove good English language skills but can also enhance a pupil's ability to understand the question and the quality of how a question is answered.

Many secondary teachers will not have an in-depth knowledge of the terminology or where these conventions impact on the quality of pupils' written work, their appreciation and comprehension of what they read and their ability to hear intonation and speak with power and inflection. So, it is also important to build a strategy for professional development that will ensure teachers know these conventions and can support pupils to become eloquent in their use of the English language.

THE PRE-EMINENCE OF ENGLISH IN EDUCATION AND SOCIETY

The English programme of study for key stage 3 (DfE 2013) can be seen as the overarching weft that helps to create the tapestry that binds together all the other compulsory key stage 3 subjects and those that form essential EBacc study for GCSE and beyond.

It talks about the importance of the spoken language in pupils' development across the whole curriculum, cognitively, socially and linguistically. Opportunities to develop spoken language should underpin pupils' written work and their growing fluidity as readers.

Pupils should learn the conventions for discussion and debate and work well in groups so that they become adept at cooperative learning and shared understanding of their growing body of knowledge.

Pupils should read widely. What they read should be challenging and have variety and depth to the content. They should read for information as well as for pleasure. Pupils should acquire a deepening vocabulary through their reading and teachers should show pupils how to understand the relationship between words and how words can have different meaning in different contexts.

Pupils should develop their skills as writers, learning how to make drafts and refine what they have written. They should be taught to write formal and academic essays as well as writing imaginatively. In all subjects, the importance of the sentence and how it is constructed should be taught as part of Standard English. Pupils should develop their ability to write more extensively to plan their writing and develop their arguments using linguistic and literary conventions that will enhance their presentation and demonstrate their deepening knowledge and understanding.

It is easy to become embroiled in the debate on whether the focus here is about teaching the skills of reading, writing and speaking and listening or that somehow, we can develop these essentials through the acquisition of a growing body of knowledge. The current curriculum is knowledge-centric and requires pupils to deepen their knowledge over time in readiness for the high stakes systems that test that pupils have acquired sufficient knowledge at given points along their learning journey.

However, it is difficult to argue against the fact that these skills must be taught, they must be practised and they must form a part of a deepening awareness of their fundamental importance in how pupils acquire knowledge.

EVERYONE A READER, EVERYWHERE AND ALL THE TIME

Reading is the skill that isolates a pupil who is not a good reader by the time they reach secondary school. We have all met someone who goes to great lengths to hide their lack of reading ability and who has the most amazing strategies to hide their lack of competence. One of the most affecting examples for me was watching the film *The Reader* adapted from the book of the same name and written by Bernhard Schlink (2011). It tells the story of a woman caught up in the Holocaust and who is imprisoned for something she is clearly not guilty of because she cannot admit to being unable to read. Reading is the skill we start to learn from the day we are born (Quigley 2020).

We can read colours, see faces, patterns and shapes in our earliest encounters with the world around us. Fabric books and picture books, pop up books and books with textures and sounds can all help the child to begin to comprehend and connect their understanding of words and the pictures they convey.

Pupils arriving in their secondary school are a polarised mix of learners. There are those who can read as adults enjoying 'chapter' books and building their hidden knowledge to add to the knowledge they are gaining in school. There are those who have not had the same exposure to a rich literary and textual heritage but who may have grasped the building blocks and can read reasonably well. The last of the groups that we may encounter and that often fall through the net are those that struggle with word recognition and cannot concentrate on the dense text that other pupils find accessible.

The English language is difficult and more complex than many. It has three times as many words as German and six times as many as French. Many English words have more than one meaning, different spelling patterns and an array of grammar conventions that all need to be mastered in order that we can be adept readers and potential scholars of whichever branch of knowledge we choose to follow.

In terms of reading, a secondary school strategy must focus on ensuring that all teachers, not just in the English department, understand how the ability to read fluently is at the top of the school improvement agenda in every subject.

SUPPORTING PUPILS WHO STILL STRUGGLE TO DECODE OR ARE STILL NOT FLUENT READERS

Secondary teachers are unlikely to have the same exposure to professional development in phonics teaching or developing reading as a basic skill as their primary counterparts. The SENCO or a teacher appointed as a specialist may have and it will be they who will support struggling readers.

In 2016, a research review of reading intervention reported that 22% of students did not have secure age-appropriate reading skills on entering secondary school (White Rose Research 2016). For whatever reason, and there will be several, some pupils will have fallen behind their peers. A year 7 pupil who comes to secondary school with a reading age of 8 or less needs specialist support; otherwise, they will not be able to cope with the increasingly complex fiction and non-fiction texts they will encounter.

Support and intervention are essential and here the well-structured use of teaching assistants (EEF 2021) can be invaluable if their role complements the teacher and allows the learning, whether whole-class or in smaller groups, to align with what the teacher has planned. Interventions that focus on the reteaching of phonics, reading comprehension skills and peer tutoring all score highly in the EEF Teaching and Learning Toolkit as interventions that work (Blatchford 2018) (Figure 5.1).

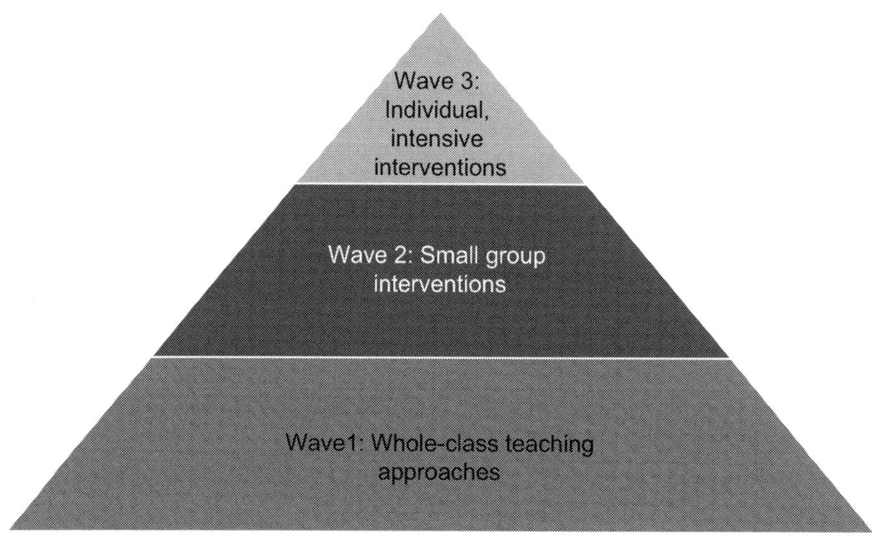

Figure 5.1 The response to intervention model
Source: Based on Burns et al. (2005).

The Response to Intervention model (Burns et al. 2005) provides us with a structure to use when planning how to create the right pathways for pupils who are struggling with reading. Having these three approaches gives the subject leader, the SENCO the teacher and the teaching assistant the opportunity to work together with a framework to decide on the intervention that will serve individual pupils best.

The starting point must be to know the pupil and to try to ascertain what it is that is causing them to find reading difficult. Is it decoding, where an appropriate phonics programme might be the starting point? Is it a lack of ability to comprehend dense text, or does a limited vocabulary mean they cannot access complex word structures they encounter?

Try out some of these strategies early on in year 7 where there are pupils who have been identified as low ability readers.

- Provide pictures that represent the text that is associated with the learning topic for less able pupils to use as prompts
- Simplify the text by drawing out the key words and phrases that a Teaching Assistant can use to share ideas about the topic being studied
- Create cards with unfamiliar and subject-specific words that can be presented to pupils as part of learning new topics or revisiting related topics
- Use graphic organisers that integrate text and visuals so that pupils can see where there are connections and a sequence to the learning

- Create opportunities for the teacher or a Teaching Assistant to read the text where it is also placed on a whiteboard so that pupils can follow the spoken and written word together
- Use other mental models such as Venn diagrams, fishbones concept maps to scaffold the knowledge that is hidden in dense text
- Invest in an age-related phonics programme such as Key Stage 3 Phonics (2019), three workbooks and a Teachers' Guide (2019) or Ruth Miskin's Fresh Start (2017)

EVERYONE IS A TEACHER OF READING

There is a necessary focus on those pupils who are not secondary-ready when they arrive in their secondary school. However, all pupils can dip in performance as they move across the transition bridge. This is well documented and forms a part of chapter 3 of this book. Textbooks become more complex often written to the subject and rarely take account of the reading age of the pupil. It is important that great care is taken to ensure that pupils can understand what they are reading, can read fluently and can use the information they gain from their reading and apply it to a variety of outcomes that lead to learning.

Creating profound opportunities for teachers from across the subject divides to come together to look at what they intend to teach, what vocabulary is necessary to the learning, the concepts that are essential within subject learning and that can transcend subjects, needs careful consideration. Where pupils encounter words, they don't understand and have not seen before they will stop learning. We have all sat through a lecture or training session and heard an acronym that is new and incomprehensible. We look around, no one asks, others look as if they know what it means or stands for and everyone that is at a loss has stopped learning.

Where teachers work within subject-specific teams, there are opportunities to think about how best to introduce new vocabulary, recall existing vocabulary and ensure pupils can make sense of what they are reading to add meaning to their growing knowledge.

Deliberately building a programme of continuous professional learning around vocabulary will reap considerable benefits. Here are some ideas where explicit time is spent on ensuring teachers have the words so that the pupils they work with will grasp their meaning and fly to the knowledge moon.

The first is to consider the three tiers of vocabulary Beck and McKeown (2013) and is a good starting point for a lively discussion about what to include and why, when defining the words that pupils need to learn and comprehend within their reading of complex fiction and non-fiction texts.

Within each of the three tiers are words that pupils will encounter, either very frequently in all subjects or infrequently in subject-specific domains. Many will apply across the curriculum and give teachers and pupils opportunities to make connections across their learning.

Tier one words - This is a starting point, the most basic words that pupils have been exposed to for a long time. Normally these are early reading words such as book, girl, boy, run, dog, or cat.

Tier two words - High-frequency words that occur across a variety of domains. That is, these words occur often in mature language situations such as adult conversations and literature, and therefore strongly influence speaking and reading.

Tier three words - Consist of low-frequency words that occur in specific curriculum and cross-curricular contexts. We use these words as part of a deepening understanding of specific subjects and topics. There are over 400,000 words in the English language so there is plenty of opportunity to find new and challenging three tier words.

Where each subject leader and their teams create their own table of one-, two- and three-tier words, they have a growing bank of vocabulary to support pupils to deepen their own learning potential.

Another useful visual support for helping secondary subject teachers to think about comprehension and how pupils learn to read well is Scarborough's reading rope (2001) which takes the teacher or learner through the sequence that looks at the steps towards fluent reading. Starting with word recognition that is possible because the pupil has learnt the relationship between the sounds (the phenome) of letters (the graphene) and the alphabetical code those sounds relate they can turn those sounds and recognition of the squiggles to make words. The visual rope is easy to access, but the sequence below provides a very useful set of steps for a focus on ensuring pupils are moving towards language comprehension and ultimately verbal reasoning.

Word Recognition

- **Literacy Knowledge** - It sounds obvious, but it is important for child readers to understand concepts of printed text such as reading from left to right and top to bottom, how to hold a book, and that full stops complete one sentence (unit of meaning) before the text moves on. These things do not work in the same way in other languages, so they need to be taught explicitely to English-speaking (and reading) children.
- **Phonological Awareness** - This refers to the awareness a reader has of the sound systems in language, including knowledge of syllables, and sentence intonation (a rise in voice when asking a question, for example). Knowledge and experience of rhymes seems especially important in developing this awareness.
- **Decoding** - This includes an understanding of the alphabetic principle, that is, that a letter of the alphabet represents a sound, and that these letters/sounds can be blended to make words. This is trickier in English than in some other languages. English has about 44 sounds (phonemes) but only 26 letters in the alphabet. Thus, the relationship between letters and sounds cannot be one to one.
- **Sight Recognition** - Some words are recognised when reading without the reader needing to decode them, you just know them. Research tells us that, in fact, most adult reading is like this. It is quite rare for us to have to read words we have never seen before, and thus do not know. Children need to build up their repertoires of sight words and the more they can read by sight, the more efficient their reading becomes.

- Once pupils have the skills to recognise words, they can then put these words into language comprehension.

Language Comprehension

- **Background Knowledge** - This refers to the knowledge a reader already has about the information being read which needs to be applied to make sense of this new information. The knowledge about the world which children possess is, it seems, crucial to them reading effectively.
- **Vocabulary** - This refers to the breadth of a reader's vocabulary. Obviously, the more words a reader knows in a text, the more fluent his/her reading of that text is likely to be.
- **Language Structures** - A reader needs at least an implicit understanding of how language is structured, that is, grammar. The debate has been about whether that knowledge needs to be explicit. Most children (and adults) sense when a sentence is not grammatically correct without being able to explain what the problem is.
- **Verbal Reasoning** - Readers need to be able to make inferences and construct meanings from the text, that is, they need to be able to THINK logically about what they read if they are to understand it, and its implications.

To complete this focus on reading and to stress the uniqueness of the vocabulary and complex knowledge that lies within every subject, there is the term 'disciplinary literacy' (Shanahan and Shanahan 2012). This offers subject specialists a lens to look at the differences in the way texts for each subject are written. What is being asked for here is that teachers can support their pupils in developing the skills that will help them to understand the language as a scientist, a historian or a student of religion, for instance.

Disciplinary knowledge is that knowledge obtained by historians, geographers, designers, artists or scholars of literature that is unique to their academic discipline. History is a study of the past and it is through the sources of information, documents and other artefacts that allow scholars to draw conclusions as to a chronology, an informed opinion and a set of facts about the past. A scientist will use analysis from experiments, observations and others' research and the logical sequencing of ideas and events using scientific language. Each subject has a unique vocabulary and approaches to how they arrange text and ideas. Teachers need to understand the barriers to reading that this may create.

Alex Quigley, in his book *Closing the Reading Gap*, suggests we should be mindful of the following 'arduous eight' reasons why pupils might find a text difficult.

1. Background knowledge - the sheer range of necessary knowledge and related ideas in each passage or whole text
2. Range and complexity of vocabulary (including word length)
3. Use of abstract imagery and metaphorical language
4. Sentence length and syntax
5. Narrative or whole-text structures

6 The generic elements of the text, for example, a biographical account in history
7 The scaffolds present, or absent, in a given text, for example, key-word glossary
8 Text length

DISCIPLINARY LITERACY

Mastering the art of reading in the secondary school is to understand that each subject requires a different set of language features. What we want over time is that pupils develop deep and unconscious competence in the skill that allows them to construct sentences; build paragraphs that show they can arrange knowledge into a sequence that flows from a description to an analysis and then to a conclusion, and use grammar, vocabulary and creativity to demonstrate confidence in the manipulation of the English language.

Textbooks have their place in allowing both the teacher and the pupil access to other experts writing for a specific subject. Pupils can see firsthand the disciplinary knowledge that shapes specific subjects. Textbooks can be written to the discipline of the subject and not to the reading age of the pupil so ensuring that pupils are given opportunities to unpick the content, learn the vocabulary and use a variety of strategies that will help them to access the knowledge within, are all important.

ORACY – THE ART OF ACTIVE LISTENING AND SPEAKING WITH CLARITY AND CONFIDENCE

Speaking and listening are just as important as reading and writing in ensuring that all pupils can access knowledge in different subject disciplines. Oracy is not as easy to assess as the written word and much more difficult to organise and keep track of than simply asking pupils to read and digest a piece of text, a chapter or a worksheet.

The Education Endowment Foundation funded research for Greenwood High School to measure the impact of their 'Talk for Literacy' programme (Greenford High School 2014). Through the structured intervention of teaching assistants to support pupils to talk in relation to developing their comprehension skills, the results showed that pupils made three months additional progress as a result of the programme. Planning a real focus on the spoken as well as the written word in classroom pedagogy is a powerful precursor to deepening knowledge and accessing the vocabulary and complex text across subject disciplines.

Structured speech events (Sherrington 2017) are an approach where pupils can express ideas, share their thoughts and engage in debate. The rationale is that communication is an embedded element of our social and political life, of the academic world and in any place of work. It is therefore essential that we focus on ensuring pupils have the same opportunity to practice their skills of speaking and listening as in any other literacy discipline.

Sherrington uses the term 'structured speech event' to cover a range of activities that teachers can deploy where speech is being developed in a planned and structured way. He cites individual or group presentations, speeches or recitals, pupil presentations, structured discussions, role-play and debates as the main means of encouraging the spoken word as part of learning.

There are several important considerations when focusing on the pedagogy that underpins the development of powerful oracy.

- **Confident presence and control** - speaking clearly, confidently using good hand and body gestures, making eye contact and responding to the reactions of an audience
- **Know the content** - organise ideas and shape the content to the audience and purpose of the talk or discussion
- **Talking for exploration** - using debate and sharing ideas to formulate new learning
- **Making presentations** - organising learning to share with others
- **Use of correct grammar and vocabulary –** using language to create the right effect, using rhetoric and intonation to really emphasise the points, ideas and arguments
- **Knowing the audience –** modifying the language, the content and the medium to take account of the needs of all those listening

Confidence in the ability to speak and listen requires pupils to ask incisive questions, to share ideas and explain their own thinking around ideas they may have that differ from their peers or their teacher. They should be able to speculate about certain aspects of their learning and have the opportunity to say what they believe might happen next or what they think could change. They must also, through talking to their peers, working in groups and taking part in discussions and debates, begin to argue their own point, reason a hypothesis or justify their reasons for thinking differently (Quigley and Coleman 2020).

Allowing pupils to think and share ideas or have a point of view builds a mental picture that can make their written work and their understanding of what they are reading far more profound.

One of the most powerful tools when I was teaching was to give different groups of pupils within the class a related topic to work on over five lessons ending with each group making and giving a presentation on their investigation. The approach works best when several elements of the same topic need to be understood. For example, in business studies, this could be a focus on six motivational theorists that pupils need to know.

Here, six groups investigated their own assigned theorist and worked together to create a presentation. It was competitive, challenging and allowed for a real focus on group interaction, shared talk and a lot of discussion in relation to what to put in and what to leave out. The presentations were shared with the whole class, and each group learnt about the motivational theorists from their peers and not from me the teacher.

They listened, learnt well and asked some extremely incisive questions. There is no way that I could have been as interesting teaching each theorist to the whole class over the same period. I was able to follow up with a discussion about the similarities and differences between them and their intrinsic value to the study of leadership and team building. I was also able to counter any misconception and fill in any essential gaps.

Another useful tool to use the spoken word is to use speeches that have stood the test of time. Martin Luther King, Winston Churchill, Barack Obama and John F. Kennedy as well as speeches from Shakespeare's plays for instance. Analysing the language, the rhetoric and what makes their speeches powerful in conveying their message, exploring the need for change or reassuring the listener. Pupils can also focus on body language, the range of registers and their ability to manipulate meaning to persuade others that their point of view is the right one.

The Education Endowment Foundation (Teachers' Tool Kit (2020) state that the average impact of oral language intervention is an additional six months progress over the course of a year which is significant. There is, the research concludes, also an improvement in classroom climate and there are fewer behavioural issues. The evidence is profound and difficult to ignore.

There is a need to ensure that what is happening in the classroom is well planned and structured so that the teacher has carefully crafted a set of questions to support the discussion or debate that will lead to learning. This must be more than noise or chatter. Each pair or group need to know what outcomes they want as part of the conversation and interaction that is taking place. Resnick et al. (2018) have developed a structure to support teachers to consider the importance of accountability in the process of constructive talk in lessons.

Knowledge – ensuring that knowledge is accurate and relevant in the context of the conversation and where it is leading.

Reasoning – pupils should develop the skill of being able to reason so that they can justify their answers, remember important elements and draw their own conclusions.

Community - how pupils interact as a group or in a pair. Can they listen to others points of view, can all members contribute? Is every individual valued and is their contribution seen as relevant and valid in the context of the learning?

Creating the right conditions to allow high-quality interactive learning conversations to take place should start in year 7 and become an essential part of a planned sequence that allows pupils to be active participants in their own learning. Sharing ideas, being able to express a different point of view and listening to others who may have something to say that is different and new can reap benefits for the pupil's capacity to learn deeply. Consider these points when thinking about how to ensure planned conversations and oracy lead to learning. Create opportunities for pupils to listen to discussions, TED talks and debates on the radio and television. Teachers can model effective discussion skills using podcasts where colleagues debate a topic that will become a part of a sequence of lessons:

- Explicitly give pupils an opportunity to focus on what we mean by reasoning. Provide a framework linked to such phrases as, I think this because, I conclude due to the evidence I have found, I agree to a point, but have you thought about this element
- Give pupils lists of the relevant vocabulary they should be using as part of their discussions so that they have prompts to help them move forward with meaning
- Link their talk activities to what they are asked to read and to write so that the talk element provides a rich addition to help with comprehension or is a powerful starting point in thinking about what is going to become a piece of extended writing
- Challenge pupils to be explicit with their language and the conclusions they draw from a debate or a discussion. Ask pupils to explain their reasons, their sources of evidence, the facts to back up their hypothesis

- Use powerful and probing open questions that require a full answer and make the pupil think deeply about being specific and accurate in the shared conversation
- Ensure that the group or paired activity has an aim and a goal so that pupils know what they are aiming to achieve through the discussion. Ensure that there is a feeling of accountability to produce answers, achieve a shared conclusion or agree to differ

Teachers need to work together to develop the skills of positive professional conversations that can help define their own strategies for effective classroom pedagogy linked to their planned sequence of learning, within their own subject area and where there are opportunities for cross curricular discussions. Learning how to listen, give relevant and effective feedback and respect others points of view are essential for teachers as well as pupils (Table 5.1).

Knowing how to ask incisive and open questions is one of the most important and difficult skills to master even for the teacher never mind the pupil. Open questions can only begin with who, what, where, when, how or why. The way they are posed means that the person answering questions cannot answer with a yes or a no, a full answer is the only way.

- How do you know that is right?
- Where does your evidence flow from?
- How might you look at that from a different point of view?
- Who else would say something similar?
- What are the contrasting arguments to that?

Speaking and listening have taken on a new impetus as young people embrace video making, podcasting and other social media outlets. Encouraging pupils to use their skills to be expressive, creative, enquiring and vessels of their own knowledge is an essential pedagogy in a changing world.

Table 5.1 Raising awareness of listening skills for teachers

• What is the optimum noise level in your classroom to ensure that your learners can hear what you and others are saying? • How do you project your voice, vary your tone, use signals and body language to communicate your points? • How well do you know your learners and their ability to listen and concentrate well? • For how long do you talk and expect your learners to listen to you? • How do you instigate time for learners to discuss what they have been listening to with their peers? • How do you make sure that listening is seen as an important skill that learners need to adopt as part of all their learning?	• How do you make learners take responsibility for their own ability to listen actively to what you are saying? • What are your strategies for encouraging note taking or visual representations of what has been said? • How well do you listen to your learners? • How do they know you are listening? • What opportunities are there for learners to compare notes on what they have been listening to? • What can you do to ensure all learners can understand what you are saying and build structure into the content of what you are saying?

WRITING IS THE EVIDENCE THAT CONFIRMS THAT LEARNING HAS TAKEN PLACE

Writing is the culmination of the learning process for many pupils as they progress through their secondary school years. Writing provides the teacher with reassurance that their teaching has made a difference and allowed pupils to build their knowledge through the sharing of ideas, the analysis of the facts and the drawing of conclusions.

Pupils can, of course, demonstrate their understanding and can offer explanations, share ideas through speaking and demonstrate comprehension and deeper knowledge by explaining what they have read, but it is the written word that is the concrete proof for the teacher, the pupil, the parent and, of course, those who judge from an external perspective.

The overarching aim, stated in the key stage 3 programme of study for English, is to promote high standards of language and literacy by equipping pupils with a strong command of the spoken and written word. For writing, the aim is specifically to 'write clearly, accurately and coherently, adapting their language and style in and for a range of contexts, purposes and audiences' (2014).

The written word is not simply the domain of the English curriculum. The range of contexts, purposes and audiences reaches across the curriculum. Where pupils are taught to write with style and clarity right from the first day in year 7, they will become highly competent and ready to answer the questions that will allow them to demonstrate what they have learnt, argue a range of points, provide their own perspective, infer, reflect, justify, evaluate and compare and contrast in all sorts of contexts that will lead to impressive GCSE responses.

Firstly, writing requires pupils to be able to transcribe, spell well, have handwriting that flows and is legible and use keyboard skills to write fluidly. Secondly, they need to develop the skills that will allow them to articulate ideas and manipulate the knowledge they are learning in a variety of ways.

Pupils need to have the ability to see the distinctive characteristics of texts written for different purposes and audiences. Each subject provides the pupil with the challenge of learning how to write to specific disciplines, investigation, analysis and experimentation for science, reflecting on evidence and what it proves in a historical context or impressions, descriptions and preferences when analysing a piece of art or architecture, appreciation of art or a piece of design work.

It is the task of the English department to support pupils to develop the different elements that make up the art of writing well. These are highlighted as a bulleted list in the Research Review series for English (Ofsted 2022).

Knowledge of the writing process and how to teach it.

- Explicit teaching of foundational writing skills, aiming for fluency
- A 'process approach' to writing; beginning, middle and end
- Direct instruction about writing knowledge and targeted practice
- Encouraging pupils' self-regulation, such as pupils monitoring their own performance, setting goals for improvement and assessing their own writing
- Opportunities to write frequently
- Opportunities to work cooperatively on different aspects of writing and stages of the writing process

Some of the above can be applied to learning beyond the English lesson such as opportunities to write frequently and to work cooperatively. Also, a process approach to writing is the setting out of a plan for how pupils draft, revise, edit and publish their writing. Learning how to practise these processes can be taught as part of English language lessons and then applied in any other subject where writing is a part of the pupil's learning.

It is unlikely that many teachers other than those in the English department will have had any training in how to encourage pupils to write with great skill. Creating opportunities for a strategic model of professional development to build the knowledge and confidence for how teachers can support pupils to develop highly effective writing skills is the only way to ensure that pupils can write well in all their subjects and be ready for answering those tricky questions at GCSE and beyond.

The task of writing is complex and becomes increasingly so as pupils move through key stages 3 and 4. Creating a consensus on some of the approaches that will support teachers to have the pedagogy to develop writing skills is important. Here are some tips for creating a dialogue and a shared approach that can be adopted for teachers across the range of subjects that require pupils to write with clarity and in some depth.

- Focus on the vocabulary pupils will need to be familiar with in order that they can access knowledge they are reading or hearing
- Create opportunities to scaffold the development of writing fluently by supporting the development of sentence structure giving pupils sentence starters such as, at first it was thought. . ., a closer look revealed. . .
- Introduce the language of assessment especially the language of mark schemes used in GCSE across all subjects. What is the difference between describe and explain, analyse and evaluate? How do pupils justify an answer? What is a correct formula for compare and contrast?
- Focus on writing in different subjects, creative writing in English, analysis of a text in English literature, the approach needed to write up an experiment, describe a geological formation, show appreciation for a piece of art or of a design or argue a point from evidence in history
- Teach pupils to use a range of planning tools to help them organise and structure their writing. Graphic organisers, fish diagrams and mind maps all provide an opportunity for pupils to talk about the subject they want to write about and organise their thoughts before turning them into the written word
- Explore with pupils how to draft out ideas for a series of paragraphs and reflect on what they want to include before a final piece of work is produced
- Use open questioning to draw out of pupils how they can improve on their writing. Use the sequence towards the higher order questioning in GCSE papers and mark schemes to develop pupils' ability to answer using higher order thinking skills
- Tell your pupils to write, write, write. After all you can't improve on a blank sheet of paper!

Combining reading and writing is the key to effective writing. It is knowledge that pupils need to use to write with authority and depth. Reading also provides a model for their own attempts to write. Writing down facts from reading as notes and annotating key features in a text can all help to define what pupils might write in response. Pupils should summarise what they have read either speaking or writing, both will consolidate their understanding and provide the teacher with the opportunity to check for misconception or misunderstanding.

ENGLISH LITERATURE – A CATALYST FOR SO MUCH MORE

The study of English literature is the domain of the English department and is an essential vein that runs through curriculum study for every pupil as early as their first year in reception and most certainly as they enter their secondary school in year 7. Hopefully, the opportunity to read extensively and absorb the lives and scope of many different people, places, situations, dramas and moments in history will ensure pupils continue to read throughout their lives. Leaving this as a legacy for all pupils is one of the privileges of being a teacher, especially a teacher of English literature.

Literature is also a window to many other subjects and worlds that are to be discovered through the deepening understanding of the words and how they are put together to stimulate our imagination and build pictures that will live within us for ever. As part of this chapter, we cannot ignore the role of the English department and the teachers within it to teach the nuts and bolts of the English language and also to develop a deeper understanding of the power of literature as the embodiment of fluency in writing, deep comprehension and the ability to articulate, debate, share and present as part of learning to speak well and listen actively.

The essence of a strong curriculum is to ensure that all teachers understand the disciplinary knowledge that underpins individual subjects. The question we want teachers to ask in whatever subject they teach is, how do experts in my subject write about the subject? What are the writing conventions and styles that are essential for different contexts and purposes?

It is the role of the English subject leader and their team to decide what pupils will read across their five years of study up to GCSE. They need to create the sequential pathway towards a love of literature and an understanding of how to analyse the plot, know the characters and the parts they play in the telling. The National Curriculum does not specify a sequence to the literature curriculum especially in key stage 3 or 4. However, the subject content requires that pupils will understand increasingly challenging texts, making inferences and refer to evidence in the text, know the audience, for and context of the writing.

They are also expected to be able to recognise a range of poetic conventions, study setting, plot and characterisation, understand how the work of dramatists is communicated effectively through performance and how alternative staging allows for different interpretations of a play.

The choice of texts, plays and poems is at the discretion of the school and those in the English department. There is simply the requirement to study English literature pre-1914 and contemporary, two plays by Shakespeare and quality works from the seminal world of literature.

The use of literature to support pupils understanding of how text is constructed, why an author might choose the prose, the words they use to explain, describe or embellish can really help pupils to begin to see how they can use words and vocabulary to improve their own writing in preparation for their GCSE examinations and beyond. Literature can also help pupils to make sense of their world and the world they inhabit, politics, the environment, history and so on and provide the perfect vehicle for debate and discussion.

It is not the intention in this chapter to look in detail at the English curriculum, that is for English specialists to interpret, but it is essential for all who teach within an English department to be aware of the influence they have on a pupil's ability to use their English language skills to increasingly deepen their understanding of the world they live in and will contribute to in adult life.

THE ROLE OF INFORMATION TECHNOLOGY IN THE DEVELOPMENT OF LITERACY SKILLS

Communication skills remain the essential thread that is the weft of delivering the curriculum. Pen and paper have largely been replaced by electronic devices that provide many different media with which to manage the delivery of the curriculum. However, we do still require our pupils to use a pen and write on paper in examination situations so practicing handwriting skills remains an important principle.

For learning throughout key stages 3 and 4 using spreadsheets, word processing, presenting with PowerPoint, Presi or Canva or using software such a Photoshop and Publisher all provide remarkable tools for expression, analysis and demonstrating deep understanding.

Game technology is proven to be good for the young brain (National Institute of Health 2022). For many parents, the length of screen time their offspring undertake is a worry. Like mobile phones they need to be used with care and respect but have their place. There are many games that help pupils with their vocabulary, spelling and grammar. For pupils with special needs, there is a wealth of technology including text to speech software and touch screen opportunities.

Pupil collaboration can be enhanced using software, such as where they can work together to make their own videos, write for a school newspaper using Publisher, create their own presentation using a range of ever sophisticated software and sharing writing tasks created through group enquiry and collaborative topic work.

The pandemic has seen schools embrace technology in a much positive way with remote learning for pupils who are absent or where there is a blended approach for such elements of learning as homework, flipped learning or revision. The use of podcasts for pupils to hear what has been taught in the class at home is a powerful reinforcement of the learning.

At its simplest, asking pupils to word process their essays can be motivating as they can correct as they go, draft and redraft and work with their peers and their teacher in a formative way that means their final piece of work is the best they can produce. Whether it shows the progress they have made through the process needs careful thought from the teacher but as a tool that gets pupils writing it is valuable.

CONCLUSION

Reading, writing and speaking and listening are the domain of the English department and form the building blocks of the English curriculum in key stages 3 and 4. However, they are also essential skills in the process of learning in all the subjects even those of a practical nature such as art, PE and music.

Those who teach English should be the catalyst for ensuring that there is a whole school vision for ensuring that all pupils are unconsciously competent in the use of these skills and take a lead in professional development that raises awareness of the fundamental part they play in how pupils learn in all subjects and in the pursuance of a connected curriculum. Deep proficiency in reading is where this chapter starts. Year 7 is an important year for all pupils. It is a time when the interpretation of both quantitative and qualitative data will build a picture that will highlight which pupils are not secondary ready and should create the imperative for carefully defined strategies for intervention.

Where pupils are not fluent readers, they will be at an immediate disadvantage and they will find it difficult to catch up. Speaking and listening skills can be so important. Articulating what we are learning and how we are learning can really help to cement the knowledge and create real opportunities for pupils to question, debate, share ideas and build a finished product through group work and collaborative project work. Oracy is a powerful tool in the box of learning and these pedagogical strategies should never be underestimated.

Writing is the evidence that pupils have grasped the concepts, understood the theory, can analyse the plot, know the reasons why. It is a skill that must be taught. Pupils need to be able to learn how to plan, how to put together technically well written sentences, structure paragraphs and pull the threads together with a powerful conclusion.

The use of technology has its place within this chapter as well as in others. Mobile phones, office and learning software can be valuable assets in the classroom as can gaming tools, video and podcasts. Whatever we can use, the old-fashioned pen and paper or the newer technologies we need to find as many opportunities as we can to ensure that every pupil who joins a school in year 7 can read, write and talk with confidence, clarity and purpose. Where this happens, all pupils will succeed in being ready for the next stage in their learning journey.

Ten Top Tips

1. Ensure reading, writing and speaking and listening are explicitly taught in all subjects.
2. Create opportunities for a series of CPD sessions that teachers from across the curriculum can access to improve their own skills.
3. Make sure all subject leaders encourage their teams to refer to the English programmes of study when planning subject specific learning.
4. Look to the key stage 1 and 2 programme of study for English to ensure that there is a profound understanding of the depth of study in literacy that pupils have already been exposed to.
5. Identify pupils who are not secondary ready in year 7 and ensure intervention happens as soon as possible.
6. Prioritise reading as the skill that pupils need for all their learning and create CPD sessions for subject teachers to focus on comprehension, phonics for older pupils, inference, vocabulary, grammar, etc.
7. Find as many opportunities as possible for structures talk so that pupils can present, debate, role play and share ideas.
8. Use famous and memorable speeches to highlight the power of the orator.
9. Build for pupils a pride in their writing and explicitly teach the skills associated with higher levels of response, describe to explain, justify, compare and contrast, analyse to evaluate.
10. Use technology as a learning tool including the mobile phone. Podcasts are a positive way to reinforce learning.

REFERENCES

Beck, I. and McKeown, M.G. (2013) *Bringing Words to Life: Robust Vocabulary Instruction*. New York, Guilford Press.

Blatchford, P., Sharples, J. and Webster, R. (2018) *Making the Best Use of Teaching Assistants*. London, Education Endowment Foundation.

Burns, M.K., Appleton, J. and Stehouwer, M. (2005) Meta-analytical Review of Responsiveness to Intervention Research: Examining Field-based and Research Implemented Models. *Journal of Psychoeducational Assessment*, 23, 381–394.

DfE (2013) *DfE Programmes of Study Key State 1 and 2*. London, DfE.

Education Endowment Foundation (2021) *Teachers Toolkit*, London, EEF.

Greenford High School (2014) *Talk for Literacy*, London, Education Endowment Foundation.

Miskin, R. et al. (2017) *Read, Write Inc.: Fresh Start*. Oxford, Oxford University Press.

National Institute of Health (NIH) (2022, November 22) *News Release*. Bethesda. NIH.

Ofsted (2022) *Research Review for English*. London, Ofsted.

Quigley, A. *Closing the Reading Gap*, (2020) London, Routledge.

Quigley, A. and Coleman, R. (2020) *Improving Literacy in Secondary Schools*. London, Education Endowment Foundation.

Resnick, L., Asterhan, C. and Clarke, S (2018) *Accountable Talk: Instructional Dialogue that Builds the Mind. Educational Practices Series*. The International Academy of Education and the International Bureau of Education. https://www.researchgate.net/publication/324830361

Scarborough, H.S. (2001). Connecting Early Language and Literacy to Later Reading (Dis)abilities: Evidence, Theory, and Practice. In S. Neuman and D. Dickinson (Eds.), *Handbook for Research in Early Literacy* (pp. 97–110). New York, Guilford Press.

Schlink, B. (2011) *The Reader*. London, Orion.

Sherrington, T. (2017) *The Learning Rainforest: Great Teaching in Real Classrooms*, Woodbridge, John Catt.

Steele, A. and Key Stage 3 Phonics (3) (2019) *Workbooks & Teachers Guide*. Independently published.

Shanahan, T. and Shanahan, C. (2012). *What is Disciplinary Literacy and Why Does it Matter?* https://www.shanahanonliteracy.com/upload/publications/50/pdf/Shanahan-What-is-Disciplinary-Literacy.pdf Not sure how to reference this

White Rose Research (2016) *A Systematic Review of Reading Intervention for Secondary School Students*. Leeds, University of Leeds.

6

MATHEMATICS – DEEPENING KNOWLEDGE THROUGH CONCEPTS AND CONTEXT

Contents

MATHEMATICS AS A FOUNDATION FOR LEARNING

Mathematics is everywhere, it is a fundamental element of our lives and creates the building blocks for the world we live in. The study of maths in the secondary school must build on what has been taught before so that pupils can see how their prior knowledge will strengthen their conceptual understanding throughout key stage 3 and ensure they are ready for key stage 4.

Where there is a consensus across the whole school that maths has an important role across the curriculum, the subject becomes more meaningful for the pupil. To create the mathematicians of the future, we must ensure that they see learning maths concepts as essential to their learning in many other contexts. If they are to become adept at reasoning, problem-solving, using evidence accurately and forming their own opinions to argue a point, their depth of knowledge of the maths that will help them is critical.

The Department of Education, along with the National Centre for Excellence in the Teaching of Mathematics (NCETM), published comprehensive guidance to help structure the key stage 3 curriculum so that students develop a deep and connected understanding of mathematics (DfE & NCETM 2021).

They say,

> For maximum impact, all teachers need to work with an agreed curriculum (or scheme of work) which,
>
> - Offers a clear and coherent sequencing of mathematical ideas, concepts, knowledge, and techniques both within each year and across years so that new ideas are built on the firm foundations of existing ones
> - Gives a coherent view of mathematics that highlights important unifying ideas and links between them so that students experience mathematics not as a collection of disparate topics but as a connected whole.
>
> They suggest that the following principles are particularly important for coherent curriculum design,
>
> - Certain images, techniques and concepts are important precursors to later ideas; sequencing these correctly is an important aspect of planning and teaching
> - When introducing new ideas, it is important to make connections with earlier ideas that are already well understood
> - When something has been deeply understood and mastered, it can and should be used in the next steps of learning. (NCETM and DfE 2021: p10)

This document is a very good starting point for establishing the dialogue that will support robust curriculum design that dovetails with key stage 2 learning and is a springboard for key stage 4 and beyond.

SEQUENCING SUBJECT KNOWLEDGE – A CONTINUUM OF LEARNING

Throughout all key stages, the maths teacher must continually assess that pupils can build on their prior learning. Curriculum planning must take account of what pupils have been taught and expected to know and understand by the end of year 6. The programme of study for key stages 1 and 2 (DfE 2014a) should be an essential part of planning the sequence of learning throughout key stage 3. For those planning for key stage 4, the key stage 3 programme of study and other quantitative and qualitative data and information will be essential. This, of course, will dovetail with awarding body criteria and specifications.

Pupils will undoubtedly forget some of their learning from key stage 2. They are primed for SATs tests and there is time after SATs where pupils may learn differently and there is a long summer holiday where they may not learn at all.

Creating the right starting point for pupils in year 7 will provide them with a platform for being able to reason mathematically, understand how their learning is building over time and allow them to become procedurally fluent (2014b). They will develop a bank of essential skills that are important in nearly every other subject and in many elements of life outside school.

In the key stage 3 programme of study for mathematics, the aims are the same as for key stages 1 and 2, to become fluent in the fundamentals, to reason mathematically and to be able to solve problems (DfE 2014c).

The aim of the maths curriculum is to challenge pupils to apply concepts in other contexts that help them to consolidate or master their numeracy skills through challenging problem-solving tasks. Pupils who find it difficult to grasp concepts should have the opportunity to strengthen their understanding through targeted intervention.

It is here that subject leaders and their mathematical teams could work together, if possible, before pupils arrive in year 7, to establish how well they have grasped the concepts and identify which pupils are ready to use them in more challenging contexts and plan the curriculum appropriately for those specific pupils. They must also identify those pupils who have not yet grasped the basics and focus carefully on how to build their knowledge, their confidence and help them to find ways towards ensuring they don't fall behind permanently.

Creating opportunities to identify through positive conversations and highly effective data transfer the level of mathematical understanding of pupils coming into year 7 will reap profound benefits that will translate into more pupils achieving clearly defined end points at the end of key stage 3 and be ready to achieve highly at GCSE.

MASTERY – PLANNING FOR DEEP UNDERSTANDING AND CONCEPTUAL FLUENCY

Mastery is now firmly a part of the educational and curriculum vocabulary. It is often associated with mastery in mathematics but ought to apply across the whole curriculum and beyond. However, it is not new and was first formally proposed by Benjamin Bloom in 1968

(Bloom 1968). The underlying principle is that pupils should have mastery of the subject knowledge in a given context before they can move onto another topic.

There are some issues with mastery and the current model of schooling in our secondary schools. We have a system that focuses on timed slots for learning of different subjects that do not allocate specific time for pupils who need to be challenged or those who need intervention so they can catch up. Therefore, mastery can appear to require time that isn't there to undertake the necessary collaboration with subject teams and teaching assistants and for some, to develop the expertise to deliver either challenge or appropriate intervention.

Dedicated professional development for maths teachers is essential if the concept of mastery is to be an integral part of mathematical study. Teachers and teaching assistants need to work together to focus on the intervention that is most appropriate either for challenge or further teaching and support. Here the following key features of the follow up are essential,

- Teachers and teaching assistants work together to design individualised learning packages for pupils to systematically work towards clearly defined targets for learning and impact.
- When it is identified that pupils need support or are ready for new challenges, intervention is an integral part of what is planned and delivered.
- Time is given so that pupils can achieve the goals that have been set by them, and for them, and they know themselves what success will look like.
- Subject leaders, teachers and teaching assistants all have a clear understanding of what is meant by mastery and what they are working together to achieve.
- Teachers and teaching assistants need time to plan how to create a differentiated classroom where pupils work on different tasks that will lead to similar outcomes.

Mastery is ultimately about the individual pupil and their potential to learn. Whole class instruction and assessment is unlikely to lead to mastery. Creating the right conditions for a mastery approach requires that there is a consensus and a clear understanding of the incremental steps needed to achieve the goals and outcomes set. It is possible through high quality pedagogy, effective coaching strategies and a belief that through the right approaches all pupils can achieve a high standard of maths mastery.

The essence is in looking across the curriculum and ensuring that pupils have grasped the basics. Fluency in maths, for instance, requires that pupils understand negative numbers, fraction work, basic algebra, percentages, solving equations and so forth. These take time to learn and need to be constantly reinforced. They are building blocks for further learning and mastery of that learning. The more practice pupils undertake, the more likely they are to become unconsciously competent in their use of these skills, the learning will move from their short-term, working memory to their long-term memory thus leaving space for more learning and ultimately mastery.

Curriculum planning needs to take specific account of the mastery model in determining the vision for the maths curriculum from year 7 onwards. The NCETM have developed a paper called, 'The Essence of Maths Teaching for Mastery' (NCETM 2015, 2022). Here I have turned the list into a set of questions that should support maths subject leaders to create opportunities for professional conversations and deeply useful CPD linked to the mastery principles (Table 6.1).

Table 6.1 Maths Teaching for Mastery - some questions to promote discussions

• How do we ensure that all our pupils believe that they will become fluent in their learning in maths? • What approaches can we use that will allow all pupils to work together on the same lesson content at the same time sustaining their interest and motivation? • What examples do you have where pupils have grasped the concepts that you have been teaching? • How are we building strong partnerships with Teaching Assistants and the SENCO to support in class intervention? • What evidence do we have that the whole team is working cohesively to identify key points, difficulties and the sequence we want when we teach new mathematical concepts? • How do we know that everyone in the maths team develops procedural fluency and conceptual understanding in tandem? Why is this important? • What strategies and pedagogy in the classroom is evidence that we all create opportunities for practice that reinforces pupils' procedural fluency and develops their conceptual understanding? • How can we use peer to peer interaction as part of developing pupils as masters of mathematics?	• How do we convey the belief to our pupils that if they work hard and are resilient in their perseverance they will succeed as mathematicians? • How can we foster the resilience in pupils so that they will continue to work on areas where they have misunderstood so that they will catch up with their peers? • What intervention strategies can be incorporated into whole class teaching of specific contexts? • How can we share good practice in our approaches to effective questioning, breaking down the content into short tasks and in our ability to explain, model and demonstrate? • How is time planned to ensure that pupils develop deep knowledge of the key ideas that are needed to underpin future learning? • What strategies do we use to ensure that the structure and connections linked to the maths that pupils are learning are emphasised, so that pupils develop deep learning that can be sustained? • What are the approaches to ensuring pupils retain the key building blocks of maths and that they are learnt automaticity to avoid cognitive over-load?

Creating a collaborative approach to the development of a maths curriculum that will create a culture of mastery is predicated on the five big ideas defined in the diagram above according to the NCETM(2017). These are mathematical thinking, representation and structure, variation, fluency and an overarching pursuance of departmental and whole school cohesion (Figure 16.1).

Coherence embraces all the other four ideas linked to how teachers work together to support pupils to master the maths they are taught. Coherence is about progression and the quest for pupils to have a deep connected understanding of maths that they can apply in a range of contexts.

Representation and Structure requires teachers to create opportunities for the pupil to 'see how the maths works' rather than just being able 'to do' the maths. The aim here is that pupils will grasp the deeper concepts and make connections across their learning.

Mathematical Thinking is about conjecture, reasoning and making generalisations. Pupils need to learn and use mathematical language as part of all their mathematical and other learning.

Fluency takes time and requires that pupils have mastered the basics. Pupils should have the capacity to recall accurately key facts and procedures so that they can take on more

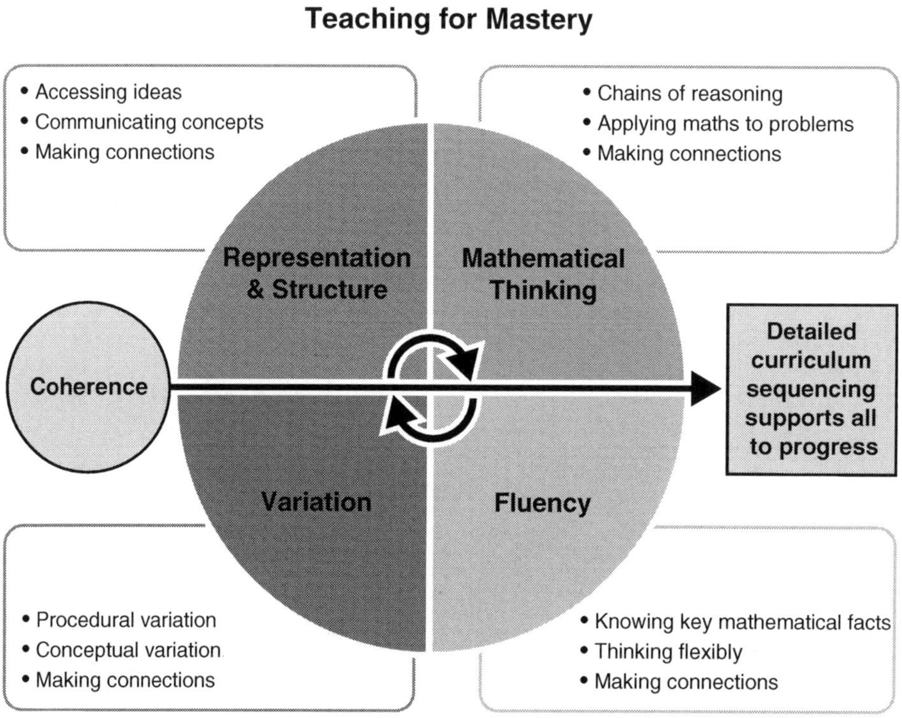

Teaching for Mastery

- Accessing ideas
- Communicating concepts
- Making connections

Representation & Structure

- Chains of reasoning
- Applying maths to problems
- Making connections

Mathematical Thinking

Coherence

Detailed curriculum sequencing supports all to progress

Variation

- Procedural variation
- Conceptual variation
- Making connections

Fluency

- Knowing key mathematical facts
- Thinking flexibly
- Making connections

Figure 6.1 NCETM - The five big ideas in teaching mastery (2017)

demanding concepts and problems to solve. Teachers need to create opportunities for pupils to become fluent through moving them towards more challenging opportunities to recognise relationships and choose their own methods and strategies for solving problems.

Variation requires the teacher to draw pupils' attention towards an understanding that mathematical concepts can be and are sometimes represented in different ways and pupils should have the opportunity to work with such variation.

DEFINING MATHS KNOWLEDGE AS THE FULCRUM FOR FLUENCY, REASONING AND PROBLEM-SOLVING

Subject knowledge in mathematics can be defined as,

- declarative knowledge - the facts and formulae that pupils need to know;
- procedural knowledge - the methods pupils need to use and master in order to deepen their understanding of the principles of mathematics and how mathematics works;

- conditional knowledge - which relates to when one might use certain mathematical concepts in different context to solve problems and find solutions.

It is the role of the subject leader and their team to create the right mix of these three elements. The key facts, concepts, methods and approaches need to be woven together so that the pupil can achieve proficiency.

Fluency comes from practice and the opportunity to apply the skills in a variety of ways and contexts and to understand the patterns and principles that underpin mathematics. Reasoning asks that pupils follow a line of enquiry, where they can see patterns and relationships and make general references and assumptions. To reason is to be able to participate in an informed argument or debate, justify the hypothesis or show a belief that something is right, using mathematical language and results. It is the combination of procedural and conditional knowledge to demonstrate an understanding of mathematical principles, facts and methods that form the declarative foundations of the subject.

Problem-solving, like reasoning, is not just the domain of maths but a distinct element of the maths curriculum and therefore needs careful consideration by all those planning their sequential and knowledge-rich maths curriculum. Problem-solving creates an opportunity for pupils to demonstrate autonomy and their own approach to finding solutions. To be adept, problem solvers pupils need to have a sound grasp of the basics.

Pupils need to be taught through the linking of declarative and procedural knowledge to make connections between facts and method. Where the teacher is confident that the pupil has the core knowledge, more complex concepts become much more achievable. With the basics in their long-term memory, pupils can take on more potential learning.

Ofsted are looking for evidence of the following features,

- Pupils understand and remember the mathematical knowledge, concepts and procedures.
- Planning sequences knowledge, concepts and procedures to build mathematical knowledge and skills.
- New material is divided into manageable steps lesson by lesson.
- There are opportunities for pupils to use mathematical reasoning and problem-solving to make connections with their learning elsewhere.
- There are opportunities for pupils to revisit previously learnt knowledge, concepts and procedures over time.
- Gaps in mathematical knowledge are identified and strategies built into planning to support pupils to fill them.
- Assessment considers when pupils have gained intended understanding and unconscious competence in knowledge, concepts and procedures.
- Teaching models new procedures and uses resources and approaches that enable pupils to understand the maths they are learning.
- Pupils' mathematical knowledge is developed and used, where appropriate, across the curriculum (Ofsted 2024).

CREATING THE RIGHT BALANCE BETWEEN NEW LEARNING, PRIOR LEARNING AND PRACTISING FOR RECALL AND DEPTH

Curriculum planners must ensure that pupils are deepening their learning over time and can reflect on their prior learning and how conceptual knowledge, facts and methods they have used in the past can dovetail into new learning.

It should be clear that the core content is firmly embedded as part of prior learning and that pupils and teachers have the time to consolidate their learning and understand its value for what they will learn next. Therefore, pupils should not be rushed through the content but given time to consolidate their learning through, retrieval, recall and rehearsal and the opportunity to share this with their peers and teachers.

The foundations must be there. Being presented with information is not sufficient in the development of a powerful curriculum for maths. It is the organising structure that is at its heart. The term 'Intellectual architecture' (Myatt 2018) is relevant here. The architect constructs the drawing and imagines the final concrete image of a building or a structure. Creating the right opportunities to focus on what it is that we want pupils to know and be able to do at critical end points allows the teacher, and the pupil, to work together towards that end, building on the foundations from previous stages.

We need patterns and connections that pupils can link together to make sense of their learning. For instance, pupils learn about the concept of measurement in their quest to find the angle size of a triangle or the diameter or circumference of a circle. They need the basic skills that help them identify the scale, imperial or metric, the ability to estimate the degree of an angle. How they then apply this to a problem in relation to more complex trigonometry such as 'apply angle facts, triangle, congruence, similarity and properties of quadrilaterals to derive results about angles and side, including Pythagoras' Theorem and use known results to obtain simple proofs.' DfE Key stage 3 Programme of Study for Maths (2014) is determined by their growing knowledge and how they recall it and use it.

In order to create the balance between new learning and prior learning, there needs to be:

- opportunities for pupils to make links with prior knowledge so that it is part of their newly acquired knowledge;
- an orchestrated plan to ensure curriculum sequencing and progression and is not arrived at by chance or happy accident;
- aligned so that new learning directly relates to classroom discussions about prior learning;
- given the time needed to ensure that those pupils who are at risk of falling behind can catch up and are not excluded from the main learning in the classroom.

By the end of key stage 3, pupils need to have procedural fluency and a bank of key skills in things like negative numbers, fraction work, basic algebra, percentages and solving equations (Tomsett and Myatt 2021). It is here that pupils should be given the opportunity to see how these basic skills can be applied in a variety of contexts, where pupils can gain conceptual understanding and begin to think and work like mathematicians.

Taking a whole class to the next stage when some pupils are unable to grasp a basic principle that underpins that next stage will be problematic. Teachers, their departmental leads and, where appropriate, teaching assistants need to work together to identify those pupils who are flying, those pupils who are coasting and those who have still to grasp the basics.

DIFFERENTIATION – EVERY PUPIL A HIGH ACHIEVER

Metaphors abound when it comes to trying to describe planning the curriculum for maximum impact and creating a learning experience that inspires all pupils. The image I have conjured is the tapestry, the weaving together of the threads that lead to learning. Earlier in this chapter, I talked about Mary Myatt's illusion to intellectual architecture. For this section, I am struck by Tom Sherrington's imagery linked to the rainforest. To create the right conditions for excellence (Sherrington 2017), he focuses on the roots of a tree that will thrive in the rainforest if the conditions are right.

His metaphor focuses on the need to have the foundations that will create the right pathways that build a curriculum structure linked to the knowledge and skills that pupils will need and how the teacher will nurture pupils to achieve their potential. I have used this metaphor here as it links closely to the concept of mastery as the route to success and focuses on the need to aim for the highest outcomes for all pupils. In order to do this, there is an imperative to plan the learning so that the content of the lesson is aimed at those pupils who are the highest achievers. In this way, all pupils are given access to the most stretching content. Less able pupils are often lifted by the challenge and the atmosphere when the lesson is stimulating and aspirational.

This does not mean that all pupils will achieve the same end results. Defining a pupil's ability is often arrived at by looking at data which may not reflect their true ability or potential. Creating a classroom of aspiration and challenge will allow some pupils the chance to show that they can outperform what data and preconceived notions suggest. Essential scaffolding for some pupils and a clear understanding of the different outcomes that pupils might achieve helps to ensure that pupils achieve through this model.

In order to create a vision for excellence that defines stretch and challenge, subject leaders build a consensus that the core subjects are taught in mixed ability classes. Where pupils are grouped according to their ability, higher achievers can be complacent, they often achieve but are not challenged. Lower ability pupils never see what is out there in terms of challenge and will continue to bump along the bottom of the achievement graph as their more competent colleagues sail away into the distance of self-belief and attainment and hopefully achievement. This approach requires a consensus that,

- Subject leaders and teachers develop an attitude that all pupils can master the highest challenge in the maths they are expected to achieve by certain age-related benchmarks.
- Teachers work together and have the training to support them in the development of positive pedagogical strategies that will encourage pupils to rise to the challenge.

Teachers understand the underpinning principles of a growth mindset (Dweck 2007). They adhere to the absolute statement, 'You can't do it *yet*'.

- Lessons should be vibrant and varied in content and be collaboratively planned to support pupils to be masters of their own learning. Pupils should, where possible, work together in group. Specific and dynamic problem-solving activities should be set including incisive questions that require deeper enquiry, higher level thinking and some data analysis.

TEACHING TO THE TEST: MATHS IN KEY STAGE 4

The maths programme of study structures how subject leaders and their teams need to build on what has been taught in key stage 3. The essential additional knowledge and skills to be learnt are highlighted in bold text in the key stage 4 programme of study (DfE 2014). A key stage 4 curriculum for maths needs to ensure that it builds on what has been taught and learnt in key stage 3. Planning time at the end of key stage 3 should provide those planning for key stage 4 with the collaborative opportunity to build a sequenced strategy for learning that will prepare pupils for sitting the GCSE examination at the end of year 11.

The verbs and phrases that populate the key stage 4 programme of study indicate what teachers should be focusing on in their quest to challenge their pupils to be able to work mathematically. Creating the right collaborative dialogue that focuses on how to teach and facilitate the learning that allows pupils to,

- **apply** systematics listing strategies;
- **estimate** powers and roots;
- **calculate** exactly with fractions;
- **change** recurring decimals into their corresponding fractions;
- **simplify** and manipulate;
- **argue** mathematically;
- **interpret** simple expressions as functions;
- **interpret** the reverse process as the 'inverse function' or interpret the succession of two functions;
- **calculate** or estimate gradients;
- **solve** linear and quadratic inequalities in one variable;
- **deduce** expressions to calculate quadratic sequences;
- **know and apply** in a variety of contexts;
- **calculate** and interpret in a number of contexts;
- **construct** and interpret diagrams for grouped discrete data and continuous data;
- **construct** and interpret equations;
- **describe** the changes and invariance;

- **apply** and prove;
- **apply** the concepts.

The more opportunities pupils encounter these verbs, know what they mean in terms of outcome and have many opportunities to practice using them, the more likely they are to be ready to answer questions in an examination situation.

The dangers of simply 'teaching to the test' are problematic. Past papers will not necessarily represent what pupils will see on the day. The goal is for pupils to have mastered the concepts, understood the principles and through practise, recall, positive formative assessment and the sequenced introduction of new knowledge, attain the unconscious competence to know how to answer an exam question.

The best actor adjusts their performance when the unexpected happens, the best driver remains alert in the face of a challenge from outside their car and the best teacher abandons the plan when what was intended isn't working. It is this resilience and ability to think quickly in the face of the unlikely or unrehearsed question that the pupil needs to have developed. It is the role of the teacher to give pupils an abundance of opportunities to be that actor, that driver or that teacher. Rote learning won't give pupils what they need when it comes to the question that has a vocabulary and an approach that doesn't absolutely match what has gone before.

The cry I hear all the time is that 'we must cover the content' and that can sometimes mean that the foundations that should be in place are left to chance. However, much content one teaches it is of no use at all if the pupil simply forgets, didn't have a clue or has misunderstood or misinterpreted. The best constructed maths curriculum is a sequence of learning that builds a strong foundation in key stage 3 and creates the qualitative and quantitative data that will help those planning for key stage 4 to make sure that pupils are well prepared for GCSE.

A scan of the mark schemes for maths GCSE papers also requires the teacher to impress on their pupils, from as early as possible, that answers require more than just something that is correct, they must show the workings and processes that led them there. Accuracy is key and English skills for spelling, grammar and punctuation also have a place in the planning.

A further look through GCSE maths question papers across the awarding bodies will show there are many questions that draw references from other areas of the curriculum. In one paper, there is a question that relates to pay and a graph linked to earnings. The opportunity to relate the maths here to earlier work on personal finance could be helpful. There is a question that uses the shape of a garden as an example of a shape where pupils must calculate the area and potential erection of a fence. Look for similar opportunities for pupils to relate their learning about geometry in maths and its relevance in design technology. A speed/time graph has applications in PE and in science. There are several references to terms like relative frequency, averages, ratios and percentages in terms of sales and marketing all that have relevance in business studies.

Creating the right foundations for maths is about the window of opportunity the subject offers teachers to give pupils as wide a perspective as possible in order that they are ready for summative examinations. The data the exam provides are a snapshot in time and it gives the examiner and many other stakeholders a view, not of what happened on the day of the exam but for the six or seven years that led up to it, from upper key stage 2 through to year 11.

PROFESSIONAL DEVELOPMENT: CREATING A CULTURE OF DIALOGUE AND SHARED LEARNING

Being a mathematician is no guarantee of being a successful maths teacher. Many teachers have only about nine months to consolidate their pedagogical expertise and then they are let loose in the classroom. In fairness, the new Early Career Framework does require two years to see a novice teacher learn their craft through a systematic programme of learning, the support of a mentor and regular review and appraisal. Ofsted's research series review of mathematics acknowledges that teacher training in terms of pedagogical, and subject specific knowledge can be variable (Ofsted 2021) and that some teachers of mathematics will need careful development.

It is recommended for novice mathematics teachers that these approaches may be useful:

- Regular opportunities to observe and be mentored by experienced and successful teachers of mathematics
- Provision of sequenced schemes of learning, matching textbooks and teacher's notes to aid explanations and help the novice teacher to bring the subject to life
- Systematic plans to build these models of instruction and rehearsal over time so that future generations of teachers can benefit
- Collaborative planning with more experienced and successful teachers of maths (Ofsted 2021)

I would argue that the above list is not just for novice teachers but for all teachers working in a secondary school. I like Chris McGrane's booklets that he talks about to Tom Sherrington in *Huh: Curriculum Conversations between Subject and Senior Leaders*. He says, 'For every teacher in my department the booklets spell out a number of things, beginning by spelling out the specific topic. The tasks and the booklets bring the curriculum to life. They embody what we value and what we see as being the essential building blocks of mathematics. The booklets are a catalyst for pedagogical change. If we are moving towards using an approach which is quite novel, the tasks and examples in the booklet can support the teacher' (Myatt and Tomsett 2021: pp195–196).

Any kind of shared approach to best practice is to be welcomed. Maths is the domain of the maths department, but all pupil-facing staff should be aware of what is being taught, the methods used and the sequencing of the learning.

Creating the cohesion and sequenced content that is relevant to the local context of the school and the goals and aspirations in the creation of a powerful curriculum plan all lead to deeper learning opportunities and positive outcomes for all pupils.

MATHS AND NUMERACY – CONCEPTS INTO CONTEXT ACROSS THE CURRICULUM

The Ofsted review from 2015, *Key Stage 3: The Wasted* years? highlights the problem with many elements of key stage 3 curriculum planning discussed in chapter 4. Here, specific reference is made to the lack of priority given to numeracy.

> Developing pupils' literacy skills is seen as a high priority in many schools. This same level of priority is not evident for numeracy. The headteachers we spoke to were able to explain how they were improving literacy in Key Stage 3 but only a quarter could do the same for numeracy. This is reflected in inspection evidence, for example from monitoring inspections, where HMI's reported improvements in literacy nearly three times more than they did numeracy. (Ofsted 2015)

The Ofsted Inspection Handbook devotes a whole paragraph in its Quality of Education section in Part 2 of the publication (Paragraph 263). The one bulleted statement relevant here is,

> The school's curriculum identifies opportunities when mathematical reasoning and solving problems will allow pupils to make useful connections between identified mathematical ideas or to anticipate practical problems they are likely to encounter in adult life. Pupils have sufficient understanding of, and unconscious competence in prerequisite mathematical knowledge, concepts and procedures that are necessary to succeed in the specific task set. (Ofsted 2024)

We have previously discussed mastery within mathematics. However, if mastery of each and every mathematical procedure and concept is the ultimate goal for the maths department, then it will be far more likely to be realised if there is true synergy with the rest of the curriculum.

The quest for mastery and the desire to ensure that pupils become 'unconsciously competent' in their ability to apply mathematical concepts is an aim that will support pupils when they sit their maths GCSE and will also help them when they encounter a maths problem in other examinations such as science, design technology and geography.

The term 'unconscious competence' was first used in a 1960 textbook called *The Management of Training Programmes* (DePhillips et al. 1960). It is useful for teachers of any subject and provides us with a framework for creating a pathway to mastery.

If we use the analogy of learning to drive, before we get into the car, we are unconsciously incompetent, we have no idea we can't do it. Once we are behind the steering wheel for the first time, we know we can't do it and we are temporarily consciously incompetent. Over time, with a great deal of practise in different conditions, we begin to cautiously work it out and become consciously competent in our approach. We pass a test and probably for a while, we are still only just consciously competent. We soon become unconsciously competent and drive without thinking at all about the learning we did and the practise that led us to where we are now.

Unconscious competence in maths is all about creating opportunities for learning new methods, procedures and concepts and then weaving in opportunities to practice, recall and use different scenarios to cement the learning through application and problem-solving within the maths curriculum and across the wider curriculum.

THE ROLE OF THE NUMERACY COORDINATOR

Appointing a numeracy coordinator is a positive first step in ensuring that numeracy is a thread that runs through all learning and not just in maths lessons. A numeracy coordinator can work closely with heads of departments and raise the profile of maths and its prevalence in many subjects. The numeracy coordinator does not necessarily have to be a mathematician, but in most cases, they are part of the maths team and can help to create the learning communities that can foster a numeracy pathway that reaches beyond just maths lessons.

The table below provides the numeracy coordinator with some indicators they can use to determine their role as part of creating the dialogue and the connections between subjects where maths features as an essential element of knowledge acquisition and its analysis and evaluation.

The role of numeracy coordinator is an important one. Their influence can have a significant impact on GCSE results and the general development of pupils' attitudes to, and enjoyment of, maths. Creating a higher profile for maths as a subject that transcends maths lessons has the potential to raise the confidence of both teacher and pupils as they deepen their mathematical knowledge and learn how to use that knowledge as part of learning elsewhere.

The numeracy coordinator should have a role in creating a school culture that celebrates how maths shapes our world, building for pupils and teachers a sense of wonder as to the patterns and beauty of mathematical knowledge and its significance to practically everything we do. Every pupil and teacher embracing maths as part of their learning will reap untold benefits and ultimately improve the summative data that is so important for GCSE and beyond.

The Numeracy Coordinator should have the opportunity to be a part of the conversations that determine the curriculum intent, the vision and rationale for what the school wants in terms of curriculum implementation. It is their role to ensure that maths is seen as integral to all learning. They also need to be a part of the planning for implementation for subjects where maths has a deep relevance, such as science, geography, art, design and computer science. They must also show other departments where maths can enhance learning, such as in history with statistical evidence or languages focusing on currency, distance and vocabulary (Table 6.2).

Table 6.2 The strategic role of the Numeracy Coordinator

Strategic vision	
• Create a strategic vision for numeracy • Keep up to date with pedagogy, resources, assessment strategies, record keeping • Encourage a high profile for maths and numeracy around the school	• Work closely with the senior leadership team to devise a numeracy policy linked to the National Curriculum • Have a clearly defined action plan and strategy that is reviewed and updated regularly
Monitoring and evaluation	
• Monitor the implementation of the numeracy strategy • Evaluate the effectiveness of strategies that are implemented • Create an internal standardisation process to monitor a consistent approach to the teaching of Maths and numeracy • Keep records of meetings connected with the development of a numeracy strategy • Provide regular updates to all stakeholders about numeracy	• Create mechanisms for supporting staff to analyse and use data for progression and assessment • Monitor how different teams are using data to measure learning, achievement and progression • Liaise with the SENCO regarding those pupils who need support • Create a cross-curricular team who meet every half term to assess progress and plan next steps • Monitor and evaluate how well ECTs and recently qualified teachers are embracing policy
Resource management	
• Coordinate the development of cross curricular resources • Work closely with the ICT Coordinator to identify and find relevant e-learning tools and software • Arrange for maths subject specialists and other subject experts to work together to share resources and ideas	• Work with subject specialists to encourage the sharing of resources and ideas to enrich numeracy teaching in different contexts • Build a bank of materials and resources that can support every teacher and teaching assistant to develop their own numeracy skills
Professional development	
• Identify and facilitate the professional development of all staff • Regularly attend training delivered by exam boards and other organisations • Invite financial institutions such as banks to talk to teachers and to pupils	• Create a suite of training opportunities that staff can dip into as part of their own upskilling of maths and basic numeracy skills • Encourage each department, team and whole staff meetings to regularly agenda time for a discussion about maths and numeracy • Have a designated area where teachers and others can meet to share ideas about maths and numeracy

CREATING THE CULTURE OF DIALOGUE ABOUT MATHS AND NUMERACY ACROSS THE CURRICULUM

There is a place for maths or numeracy in every subject. The danger is that we overemphasise maths skills over the skills that are essential for the learning in subjects other than maths. The key is to create a deep understanding that maths provides the substance, the depth and the opportunity to analyse a situation, justify an answer or present evidence in a more informed and analytical way. Graphs give us shape to represent all sorts of data in many subject areas. Scale is an essential skill in map reading in geography, in designing a product in design technology, in art in the representation of the human form. Calculation provides the opportunity to measure time in history; ratio is an essential element of the preparation of successful short crust pastry. Algebra is frequently a part of chemistry and physics.

In our current system of secondary education, it is difficult to build a curriculum map that would allow the teaching of the relevant maths topic at the same time as, say, teaching coordinates and grid referencing in geography, working out the amount of wood needed to create a picture frame or measuring the angles to create the apex of a bird table roof in design technology. However, there are some simple techniques that can support a more informed curriculum map that defines the numeracy and maths skills and ensures that those that teach maths are able to refer to where the methods, procedures and concepts being taught in maths apply in other contexts.

Firstly, where subject leaders and their teams are planning the content of a series of lessons linked to a topic or sequence of learning, if they have access to the maths programme of study, they can find the mathematics that apply and use the right terminology to add as a reference in their scheme of work and make pupils aware that they are using the same method, technique or procedure as in their maths learning.

Secondly, create opportunities for maths teachers and other subject teachers to plan together so that foundation subject teachers can share their approaches to teaching the maths content in their subject and build through professional dialogue a greater synergy and understanding of where maths plays a part in another subject.

Thirdly, plan some opportunities for lesson observation where teachers from subjects other than maths are invited to observe maths lessons. This is a profound way to support a shared understanding of terminology, methods and pedagogical approaches for subject specialists across the curriculum.

A useful resource that can be used to create opportunities for a shared dialogue about maths across the curriculum is a set of questions that support non-specialists to work together to look at some of the principles they need to consider. This resource is replicated as a table here. Put the questions onto cards or into a proforma that teachers can use as a prompt to aid a positive dialogue about numeracy and their subject.

It is also useful to think about how these specific skills are taught in maths lessons. Maths teaching may use different vocabulary, methods and outcomes. In maths, the aim is to teach the concept. In other subjects, the concept is being used to strengthen understanding of a set of data in science, the construction of a model in design technology, a study of symmetry or perception in art or the reasons for density of populations in certain cities in geography (Table 6.3).

To complete this section focusing on the plethora of maths that is prevalent in other subjects, I draw on some work that we undertook for teachers to use with their pupils to think about how maths is essential for their everyday lives, their academic achievement and their future in terms of work and economic security. This has proved invaluable in setting the scene for why, alongside English, maths is so important and forms part of the core learning.

Table 6.3 Questions linked to how maths is integral to learning across the curriculum

Calculations	**Estimating and checking problems**
• How do you identify where learners use calculation? • What mathematical methods and terminology do you/the learners use? • How do you work with maths teachers to ascertain how they teach similar strategies to those you teach?	• Where are estimating skills used as part of the learning? • How do you teach pupils to assess whether they have made a reasonable judgement? • How do you encourage pupils to make a guess or take a risk? • How do you assess the skills of estimating and checking? • How are these skills taught in maths lessons?
Reasoning and problem-solving	**Measuring**
• How do you identify opportunities where pupils can work independently to solve problems? • How do you assess how well pupils are able to reason and problem solve? • What opportunities do you have to talk about different ways you encourage pupils to reason and problem solve?	• Where is measuring an integral part of learning in your subject? • How do you know that each member of your department uses the same methodology and terminology? • What standards are in place to ensure accurate assessment of measuring is embraced by all? • How do you create a synergy between the way measurement is taught in all subjects?
Algebra	**Data handling**
• To what extent do you use algebra as part of learning or to support problem-solving? • How do you know that learners have the underpinning skills for new learning, or do you teach them prior to putting them into context? • How are these skills assessed in relation to learning?	• To what extent do pupils use data to find their own solutions, to analyse a situation or provide an explanation to a question or a problem? • How well do pupils manipulate data to put it into new formats and use it as part of a presentation or conclusion? • What opportunities are there for pupils to use data as part of their ability to analyse, justify and evaluate knowledge they are processing?
Use of graphs, charts and tables	**Geometry**
• What would you say is a definitive understanding of the difference between a graph, a chart and a diagram? • How do you ensure that pupils have the relevant skills to complete and interpret graphs, charts and diagrams accurately? • What strategies do you use to ensure that pupils know when to use graphs, charts and diagrams in different circumstances? • How do you know that there is a uniform approach to the use of graphs charts and diagrams across the department?	• How do you ensure pupils know the conventional terms for shapes and angles where they apply? • How do you ensure pupils use the criteria and appropriate language and technologies for the congruence and properties of triangle and other shapes? • What occasion might the understanding of the properties of parallel lines and alternative corresponding angles apply? • Identify where Pythagoras Theorem apples in the context of learning in subjects other than maths?

Ask pupils to think about the importance of numeracy in the ability to answer the following questions:

- How would you get to school in time? How would you know when to leave home?
- How would you know to be on time for a bus, a train or a plane?

- How would you be able to read a timetable, a schedule or the clock?
- How would you be able to read the number on the front of a bus?
- How would you know how to manage your money?
- How would you work out when there was a percentage discount on something you wanted to buy?
- How would you know the position of your favourite football team, goal difference calculations or the price of a ticket and whether you can afford it?

For both the maths department and other departments across the curriculum, it is important that we all focus on the maths that is everywhere across the curriculum.

A revealing professional development activity is to bring together subject leaders from across the curriculum to share exam papers, textbooks and pupils' work and focus on the amount of maths and numeracy that is clearly evident. Science, geography, design and PE all have questions that rely on the pupil understanding the maths concept that they need in order to answer the question. Also, for every subject, pupils need to focus on the marks awarded and think about how much time to allocate to the answer.

CONCLUSION

Maths is everywhere and the patterns, shapes and essential calculations, however, simple or complicated, shape our world. It remains a subject that some pupils, and some teachers, understand and can do without too much difficulty. This is probably because they were taught the fundamentals well and were given opportunities for continuous recall, reflection and rehearsal as well as building new knowledge and skills over time. However, some pupils and some teachers have not had the structure laid down successfully and, for whatever reason, find maths difficult to make sense of especially where new complexities are not built on strong foundations. For pupils, their secondary school experience should be a time to consolidate learning and continue to build the fluency, reasoning skills and become adept problem solvers. Careful professional development can build confidence for new and experienced teachers in their own ability to teach maths concepts.

Alongside English, maths is an essential part of the core curriculum. Maths subject leaders and their teams must work together to focus on the sequencing of maths concepts over time and create opportunities for pupils to recall, refresh and reflect on their developing skills as mathematicians. It is also key to deep learning in many other subjects and it is important to foster awareness of the impact maths has on how pupils learn in other subjects.

Ten Top Tips

1 Curriculum intent relating to the maths curriculum must include positive conversations and highly effective data transfer from year 6 to year 7

2. Ensure that there is a consensus across the school that celebrates maths learning and conveys the message that all pupils can and will achieve well in their mathematical endeavours
3. Focus on the concept of problem-solving as an essential element of maths curriculum planning as well as elsewhere across the curriculum where it is pertinent
4. All curriculum planning for maths should involve a clear understanding of prior learning and an explicit focus on the clearly defined end points expected at given points along the learning journey
5. Planning should also take account of how lessons and a series of lessons take account of the need for pupils to recall, review and reflect on how they are developing as mathematicians
6. Those planning the key stage 4 curriculum for maths should have allocated time to work with others to ensure that key stage 3 learning is dovetailed into a sequenced programme for years 10 and 11
7. Create as many opportunities as possible for pupils to use the verbs in relation to outcomes they are aiming for throughout key stages 3 and 4
8. Create cross-curricular opportunities for subject teams from across the curriculum to share teaching methods and maths concepts that exist in subjects other than maths
9. Give teachers and teaching assistants time to work together to build consensus on how to use differentiated learning activities within a lesson or series of lessons so that intervention is inclusive
10. Appoint or review the role of a Numeracy Co-ordinator, they have a very important part to play in raising the profile of maths and numeracy and will enhance the learning, the professional dialogue and the synergy of maths as an integral part of the whole curriculum

REFERENCES

Bloom, B. S. (1968). *Learning for Mastery. Instruction and Curriculum.* Regional Education Laboratory for the Carolinas and Virginia, University of North Carolina (UNC) Topical Papers and Reprints, Number 1. Durham, UNC.

Department of Education (DfE) and National Centre for the Excellence in Teaching Mathematics (NCETM) (2021) *Mathematics Guidance: Key Stage 3.* London, DfE & NCETM.

DePhillips, F.A., Berliner, W.M. and Cribben, J.J. (1960) *The Management of Training Programs.* Homewood, IL, Richard D. Iwrin Inc.

DfE (2014a) *Programmes of Study for Mathematics Key Stage 1 & 2.* London, DfE.

DfE (2014b) *Programmes of Study for Mathematics Key Stage 3.* London, DfE.

DfE (2014c) *Programmes of Study for Key Stage 4 Mathematics.* London, DfE.

DfE (2021) *The Early Career Framework.* London, DfE.

DfE and NCETM Key Stage 3 Guidance London. DfE. Bristol, NCETM.

Dweck, C. (2007) *Mindset: The New Psychology of Success.* New York, Ballantine Books.

McCourt, M. (2019) *Teaching for Mastery*. Woodbridge, John Catt.

Myatt, M. (2018) *From Gallimaufry to Cohesion*, pp. 82–85. Woodbridge, John Catt.

Myatt, M. and Tomsett, J (2021) *Huh: Curriculum Conversations between Subject and Senior Leaders*, pp. 195–196. Woodbridge, John Catt.

National Centre for the Excellence in Teaching Mathematics (NCETM) (2022) *The Essence of Mathematical Teaching for Mastery, Paper*. London, NCETM. https://www.ncetm.org.uk/teaching-for-mastery/mastery-explained/the-essence-of-mathematics-teaching-for-mastery/

National Centre for the Excellence in Teaching of Mathematics (NCETM) (2017) *Five Big Ideas in Teaching for Mastery*. London, NCETM. https://www.ncetm.org.uk/teaching-for-mastery/mastery-explained/five-big-ideas-in-teaching-for-mastery/

National Centre for the Excellence in Teaching of Mathematics (NCETM) (2015) *The Essence of Maths Teaching for Mastery*. Bristol, NCETM.

Ofsted (2024) *Handbook for School Inspection*. London, Ofsted.

Ofsted (2021) *Research Review: Mathematics Education*. London, Ofsted.

Ofsted (2015) *Key Stage 3: The Wasted Years?* London, Ofsted.

Sherrington, T. (2017) *The Learning Rainforest*. Woodbridge, John Catt.

7

SCIENCE – CONTENT, KNOWLEDGE AND VALUES THAT COULD CHANGE THE WORLD

Contents

- The science curriculum in key stage 3
- The science curriculum in key stage 4
- Capitalising on science learning in the primary phase
- Working scientifically
- The literacy of science
- The sequencing of knowledge from year 6 to year 11 and beyond
- The weaving together of maths and science purposeful practical science
- Pedagogy for deep sequential science learning

THE SCIENCE CURRICULUM IN KEY STAGE 3

Science is a part of the core curriculum at key stages 3 and 4. In key stage 3, pupils are expected to study all three of the science disciplines, biology, chemistry and physics. The content of each is systematically documented in the National Curriculum programmes of study for science (DfE 2014).

The National Curriculum for science aims to ensure that all pupils:

- develop **scientific knowledge and conceptual understanding;**
- develop understanding of the **nature, processes and methods of science;**
- are equipped with the scientific knowledge required to understand the **uses and implications** of science.

Science subject leaders need to have the expertise themselves to be able to support pupils with,

- extended specialist vocabulary;
- applying mathematical knowledge to their understanding of science;
- using mathematical knowledge to collect, present and analyse data;
- understanding the importance of the social and economic implications of science;
- using different contexts to maximise pupils' engagement and motivation.

The programme of study expects that pupils develop a deeper understanding of the three subjects. Planning should also ensure that pupils will be able to see connections between biology, chemistry and physics. It states that pupils should become aware of 'some of the big ideas' underpinning scientific knowledge, such as,

- links between structure and function of living organisms;
- the particulate model as the key to understanding the properties and interactions of matter in all its forms;
- the resources and means of transfer of energy as key determinants of all these reactions.

In 2010, Wynne Harlen edited a publication called *Principles and Big Ideas of Science Education* which drew together ideas from international science education experts exploring how to transform the teaching of science from a series of disconnected facts into content and learning experiences that would be interesting and engaging for pupils to study. The subsequent report gathers together the big ideas and, 'considers the progression from small ideas about specific events, phenomena and objects to more abstract and widely applicable ideas and significant aspects of pedagogy that are required to support progression' (Harlen 2010).

Harlen and colleagues suggest these 14 'big ideas' which are divided into 'Ideas of science' and 'Ideas about science'. A subsequent paper published by Harlen et al. in 2015 focuses on the teaching sequence for these big ideas. There is a useful grid that suggests how the sequence the teaching of the big ideas from year 1 to post 16 (Table 7.1).

A key stage 3 curriculum must create a sequenced plan that defines how pupils will learn and become excited by their growing and deepening understanding of science as a discipline. The intent should outline that the curriculum will develop pupils' ability to think objectively

Table 7.1 Big Ideas of and about science

A precis of Harlen's big ideas	
Defining the broad picture of ideas of science	**Ideas about science**
• Materials in the universe and how they are made • Objects and how they move • Energy in the universe • The composition of the earth and its atmosphere • The solar system and its place in the universe • Organisms, what they require, what they require, how they survive and their diversity • Genetic information and how it is passed down	• Cause and effect • Scientific explanations, theories and models • Knowledge and technology • The ethical economic, social and political implications of science **A possible CPD opportunity** Ask your science teams to share pedagogy and learning strategies they use in relation to their sequencing from small ideas to the teaching of their own thoughts on the big ideas. Find Harlen's version of the big ideas and discuss the potential of these big ideas to help with planning at key stage 3 to ensure that pupils are engaged and excited by the science curriculum they will be taught across the three disciplines.

Source: Adapted from Harlen (2010).

and learn how to work scientifically. Sequenced learning should create an awareness of the role of science in the pursuance of the new as well as the already ascertained and understand that science knowledge changes and grows to take account of new evidence and hypotheses. There should be reference to the need for pupils to know the importance of peer review among the science community in furthering scientific ideas and research.

The science curriculum at the beginning of key stage 3 should make clear that pupils are encouraged to work autonomously, to decide themselves what is appropriate in relation to the type of scientific enquiry undertaken. They should be given a voice to pose their own questions and find the answers through their collection and analysis of data. There should be an explicit understanding that, by the end of key stage 3, pupils should have the ability to evaluate their results and identify further questions arising from them (DfE 2014).

All those involved in the development of the key stage 3 curriculum for individual science subjects should work together to identify the subject vocabulary that pupils bring with them from key stage 2. Adding further vocabulary will create deeper meaning to aid their growing understanding of the different science disciplines.

The curriculum demands that there are opportunities for pupils to work together, in pairs, in groups and with their teacher to talk and articulate their growing scientific understanding. Where pupils debate, share ideas and present findings, they are honing their use of scientific vocabulary, demonstrating their growing knowledge of scientific concepts and principles and can consolidate their understanding. The spoken word also gives the teacher a window into misconception and misunderstanding.

The purpose of study, aims and scientific knowledge and concepts at the beginning of the programme of study offer a clear view that content should be interwoven so that pupils learn core knowledge and can see the relationships between different elements within each discipline and the interconnections that exist. For example, in biology, pupils are expected to calculate the energy requirements in a healthy diet and in physics, they must compare energy values of different foods.

'Working scientifically' gives the curriculum its rigour. Teachers must have the skills to create pedagogy that fosters deep enquiry and analysis that leads to profound scientific understanding. Key stage 3 curriculum planning should weave the disciplinary knowledge and the skills outlined in the 'working scientifically' section of the programme of study, into a plan as to how the different concepts and substantive knowledge will be taught as an integral part of pupils' developing understanding.

THE SCIENCE CURRICULUM IN KEY STAGE 4

Science is a compulsory subject at key stage 4. Pupils can follow two different pathways towards GCSE science. There is the combined science outcome which is worth two GCSEs, or pupils can opt to take triple science and study the three separate disciplines.

For pupils who have special educational needs or disabilities (SEND), there are qualification outcomes at Entry Level, below grade 1 GCSE. There is also vocational applied science.

Key stage 3 study is the foundation for what is planned for key stage 4. However, the introduction to the key stage 4 National Curriculum document approaches this in a slightly different way. Here the focus is on the essential methods, processes and uses of science. Teachers should have the pedagogical skills to support their pupils to 'help them to appreciate the achievements of science in showing how the complex and diverse phenomena of the natural world can be described in terms of key ideas relating to the sciences which are inter-linked, and which are of universal application' (Key Stage 4 Programme of Study for Science, DfE, 2014).

The key ideas from the programme of study are:

- the use of conceptual models and theories to make sense of the observed diversity of natural phenomena;
- the assumption that every effect has one or more cause;
- that change is driven by interactions between different objects and systems;
- that many such interactions occur over a distance and over time;
- that science progresses through a cycle of hypothesis, practical experimentation, observation, theory development and review;
- that quantitative analysis is a central element both of many theories and scientific methods of enquiry.

In 2015, Harlen and colleagues revisited their 2010 work on 'big ideas' in science. Their focus was on the application of these big ideas in the development of pupils' deepening understanding of science. They took each big idea and exemplified a strategy for teaching it at each educational stage. These provide those planning key stage 4 strategy with an overview, a progression model from age 5 to 17 and provide those with the task of planning the key stage 4 curriculum with possible answers to these questions:

- What should pupils know and be able to do by the end of key stage 3?
- How is the key stage 4 curriculum designed to build on prior learning and create the pupil who is able, through their growing science knowledge, to make sense of the world?
- How can the key stage 4 planned curriculum ensure that all pupils are motivated to want to continue to take their learning of science beyond GCSE?
- What are the skills and capabilities pupils have learnt in order to prepare them for study towards GCSE and beyond?
- To what extent have pupils developed an appreciation of science as intrinsic to learning in other subjects such as mathematics?

Harlen et al. (2015)

Key stage 4 is dominated by the need to ensure that pupils have the right knowledge and the skills to achieve highly when they sit their GCSE examinations. The danger is that the curriculum content is linked to a series of disconnected facts that may come up as exam questions and provide the pupil with little opportunity to deepen their understanding of science in its wider world context.

> An ambitious curriculum … needs to identify the most important concepts for pupils to learn, It must also teach pupils how these concepts are related so that, over time, the logical structure of each science discipline is made explicit. For example, pupils studying biology should learn how the theory of evolution provides a central structure to organise and connect many other concepts such as variation, adaptation, and natural selection. (Ofsted, 2023)

The programme of study explains that a key aim for key stage 4 science is to support pupils to have access to knowledge that enables them to be curious about the natural world. There should be clearly defined opportunities for pupils to undertake scientific enquiry that will give them access to nature, and processes and methods of science in the pursuit of deeper understanding of the world they inhabit.

A further aim is to create the right opportunities for pupils to learn through observation, practical activities and modelling, as well as developing skills in problem-solving and relevant maths skills in order that they can be analytical and motivated to find out more. A fourth aim is to develop the right content and activities that will allow pupils to question and analyse claims based on scientific research and practical discovery. They should be able to demonstrate their ability to explain methodology, the evidence base and the conclusions drawn. They should learn and be able to analyse and evaluate qualitative and quantitative data.

There is a tacit acceptance within the programme of study that maths skills are essential to science. All staff planning the key stage 3 and 4 curriculum should be clear where maths will enhance learning and use the maths programmes of study as a starting point for planning how maths concepts will apply in the context of science. This becomes increasingly important in key stage 4 as the maths content in GCSE examination papers plays a significant part in assessing pupils' scientific knowledge and understanding.

There is also a clear statement that key stage 4 teaching should reflect how scientific ideas have developed over time, looking at the historical content and modern developments that have built on them. Science is an ever-changing subject and pupils need to know how it can be a powerful driver of change and create the solutions to some of the pressing issues and problems that they will inherit as adults.

WORKING SCIENTIFICALLY

The importance of the 'working scientifically' section of the programmes of study from key stage 1 to key stage 4 cannot be underestimated. Working scientifically provides the basis for how all three science subjects are taught in order that pupils can develop the skills they need to be able to perform as scientists. The main points associated with the programmes of study in key stages 2 and 3 are set out in Chapter 3 where a focus on what pupils know and can do in terms of their science learning should be seen as essential to the planning of a science curriculum in year 7 and throughout key stage 3 in readiness for key stage 4 and beyond.

Key stage 3 should be seen as the time when pupils develop their scientific knowledge. Subject leaders and teachers should identify the pedagogy that will enhance pupils' ability to develop scientific attitudes, to experiment and investigate so that they are the ones asking questions, making predictions and using appropriate techniques. Pupils should be learning to be analytical and to evaluate, interpret, present reasoned explanations and evaluate data.

In key stage 4, pupils should be developing as scientific thinkers, use experimental skills and strategies, apply the cycle of collecting, presenting and analysing data and develop and use increasingly complex scientific vocabulary, units, symbols and nomenclature. The subject leader must look to create pedagogy that supports pupils' independence in the pursuit of scientific enquiry, investigation, use of mathematics, presentation, objectivity and accuracy.

Pupils must be exposed to the disciplinary knowledge that is an essential part of working scientifically. Learning substantive knowledge passively through a didactic approach is unlikely to allow the learning to deepen or create the conditions for pupils to become unconsciously competent in how they apply their growing skills in working scientifically. Below is Table 7.2 with an abridged version of the working scientifically section of the key stage 4 programme of study. Notice the verbs which clearly denote it is for the pupil to know how, to develop, plan, consider and so forth.

It is through the opportunity for pupils to recognise and understand key ideas in all three science disciplines that they can develop as scientists. In each of the specific subjects, the programme of study is set out as a list of disconnected concepts. It is through expert pedagogy and opportunities for a shared approach to planning how knowledge can be taught in creative

Table 7.2 The development of scientific thinking abridged from the key stage 4 programme of study (DfE 2014)

The development of scientific thinking	Experimental skills and strategies
• Know how. . .. • Explain concepts and methods • Understand limitations • Consider. . . • Evaluate evidence • Argue a point . . .. • Understand. . ..	• Develop and test hypothesis and explore phenomena • Plan experiments • Make observations • Select appropriate techniques, apparatus, materials and methods • Demonstrate understanding and accuracy • Know how to use sampling techniques • Suggest potential improvement
Analysis and evaluation	**Vocabulary, units, symbols and nomenclature**
• Translate data from one form to another • Use mathematical and statistical analysis • Make estimations of uncertainty • Identify patterns and trends • Present reasoned explanations • Evaluate data objectively • Identify error • Communicate the scientific rationale	• Deepen scientific vocabulary and nomenclature • Understand how scientific quantities are determined • Use SI and IUPAC where appropriate • Use prefixes and powers of ten. . . • Change units from one into another

and innovative ways that will lead to pupils being able to think and work scientifically and hopefully want to continue to study science beyond GCSE.

THE LITERACY AND VOCABULARY OF SCIENCE

Science is an everyday part of our lives, we see it in everything we do, our journey to school, cooking a meal, watching the ice melt in winter or the sun high or low in the sky depending on the season and the time, the tides and their rhythm and the beauty of a rainbow after rain. The more we can convey the importance of science to our pupils and build a sense of awe and wonder about the natural world and the part we play in the development of scientific knowledge and understanding, the more likely pupils will be able to relate their learning to life in and out of school.

The knowledge that pupils are expected to absorb is increasingly complex. It requires context to make sure it is understood. Creating a curriculum plan that ensures pupils are interested and motivated to learn requires a focus on relating it to their lives. One school case-study cited in the IMPACT magazine (Flynne, Summer 2019) looks at this in relation to relevance to pupils from disadvantaged backgrounds.

Their project was called the 3 Cs, Choice, Control and Change science curriculum, 'Beyond the Classroom Door'. It is an enquiry-based curriculum that uses questioning at its heart. Their example is, 'How can we use scientific evidence to help us make healthy food and activity choices?' They were looking to create a science curriculum in school that went beyond the classroom and ensured the teaching should be 'towards agency, creating for pupils the context for why they are learning' (Mallya et al. 2012, p265).

Making science relevant in this way allows for some pupils to access the science within the context of their own lives. The C3 curriculum may not be relevant or available, but the idea of choice, control and challenge has possibilities, such as:

- What would you do if your mobile phone was lost over a whole weekend?
- How does your journey to school impact on the air quality of your neighbourhood?
- What is the main ingredient in bread and how is it made?
- Examine the different materials that were used to build the place where you live, the doors, the roof, the walls, the floors, the furniture the fixtures, explain why these might have been chosen as the most suitable.
- How is your home heated? How much does it cost over a year? What alternatives are there?
- What contribution are you making to reduce your 'carbon footprint'?
- What causes a rainbow to appear in the sky?
- How do the changing seasons make you feel?

Creating the right conditions for pupils to make connections with their science lessons and the real world provides them with a greater sense of the purpose of learning science. Where pupils see science as a key element of their daily existence, the more they will engage (Millar and Osborne 1998).

All vocabulary needs to be carefully thought about in relation to a sequential science curriculum. Pupils will not learn if they cannot connect words they are exposed to. Where teachers work together to look at lesson content, focus on the language and the potential for misunderstanding, lack of comprehension or unfamiliarity there are opportunities to explicitly teach key words and find ways to make sure they are visible throughout the learning phase or process.

In the process of working scientifically, pupils may be exposed to words such as hypothesis, prediction, data, quantitative and qualitative, experiment or variable. These are words pupils might have encountered in other subjects or outside school. Creating opportunities to share their meaning and define their context within a science topic helps with comprehension. Words associated with specific science subjects such as chromosome, chloroplast, photosynthesis in biology, compound, electron, isotope, atom and electron in chemistry and convection, centripetal, gravity and kinetic in physics all need to be taught, reinforced and recalled over time to ensure that they are learnt, remembered and used in relevant contexts.

The examples I use above are a small proportion of many words that are relevant across the three disciplines and can apply in a variety of contexts elsewhere in the curriculum. Creating a word bank and having space within every science classroom for a wall of words and meanings can be useful. Having weekly multiple-choice quizzes can help pupils to learn terminology and give the teacher some means of knowing where misconceptions are occurring.

Many words in science have more than one syllable and contain root words which can aid deeper understanding and provide opportunities for connections to other words with the same root. For example:

- The root word 'form' means shape and forms part of words such as uni**form**, **form**ality and in**form**ation.
- The root word 'act' means to do and forms part of words such as re**act, act**ion and **act**ivity.
- The root word 'aqua' means water and forms parts of words such as **aqua**marine, **aqua**tic, **aqua**rium and **aqua**duct

Many words that occur in science teaching occur in other subjects. Atmosphere could be created by lines in a play; it could explain the weather in a geography lesson. Energy is a vital concept in science, it is also necessary for sports activity, to bake a cake or use a power tool. Cell is a term with a very definite meaning in science, it can refer to where a victim of Henry VIII's punishments was kept in the Tower of London or a name to describe a kind of telephone or battery. If it is just heard and not written down, it may be perceived as being the word 'sell', to persuade someone to buy.

Pupils may also encounter scientific terminology in textbooks, journals and research papers. The more opportunities pupils have to read widely, interpret what they have read and demonstrate that they understand and can analyse and evaluate the knowledge they gain, the more likely they are to learn, remember and apply. Shared reading can support pupils to articulate their ideas, develop deeper comprehension skills and offer the teacher an awareness of any misunderstandings and misconceptions.

Writing scientifically is a whole science in itself. A comprehensive suite of training opportunities for teachers to use are available on the STEM website, www.stem.org.uk. Teaching pupils how to write scientifically should be an essential part of learning any science topic. The more opportunities pupils have to learn how to write as a scientist, the more adept they will become at creating informative, factually accurate and evaluative pieces of extended writing.

There are conventions that relate to all extended writing and science teachers should seek the expertise of English subject specialists to share pedagogical ideas on how to write for the specific contexts, audiences and purposes that science demands. Encourage pupils to find their own style and to know how important it is to ask the right questions in relation to planning their own writing:

- What are the questions I need answers to?
- What is the best way to capture what I observe?
- What can I surmise from my observations and experiments?
- How can I say with clarity what I have found out?
- What is the evidence to back up what I think is the answer?
- Where else can I look to find out more?
- What have I learnt and how can I convey it in my writing?

The science teacher can model good writing by taking pupils through stepped approaches such as point, evidence, explain, or plan, do and review. The teacher can share planning tools such as fish diagrams, mind maps or graphic organisers.

Pupils also need to become adept at producing written work that is discursive, where opinion is backed by evidence, and learn how to use persuasive arguments aimed at changing the point of view of the intended audience. Scientific writing is an art form in itself, teachers need to know how to teach it and pupils need to be aware of the conventions. A great way to build confidence for teachers is to share and moderate their pupils' written work, to define where it has the capacity to be simply a piece of descriptive writing; or shows potential in how it demonstrates higher level thinking through analysis, evaluation and, potentially, original or creative thinking.

SEQUENCING KNOWLEDGE FROM YEAR 6 TO YEAR 11, AND BEYOND

Science, as with other subjects, is, to some extent, made up of both substantive and disciplinary knowledge and through weaving these two elements together a high quality and meaningful curriculum can emerge. Those responsible for developing the science curriculum need to see it as a continuum that builds on prior learning from the primary phase, especially years 5 and 6, and map out a clear pathway that deepens pupils understanding and creates for them a desire to learn more about the possibilities of science as part of their future.

Substantive knowledge in science encompasses the key concepts that pupils need to build over time such as energy, atmosphere and force. Disciplinary knowledge is the way that scientists arrive at their conclusions through working scientifically and being able to act as scientists in the pursuit of accurate analysis, the ability to draw conclusions or investigate new ideas. Over time pupils need to learn how to use disciplinary knowledge to help them make sense of the substantive factual knowledge that is listed in the National Curriculum programmes of study. In Ofsted's recent report *Finding the Optimum: the science subject report* (2023), they offer four content areas that pupils learn more about as they move from year to year, these are the knowledge of:

1 methods that scientists use to answer questions;
2 apparatus and techniques, including measurement;
3 data analysis;
4 how science uses evidence to develop explanations.

Ofsted's findings suggest that substantive knowledge is often the focus of curriculum planning. Opportunities for pupils to develop their disciplinary knowledge are not evident in many settings. There is a need to pay attention to the 'working scientifically' section and plan the curriculum to dovetail the substantive and the disciplinary together. Create a set of cards out of the phrases in Table 7.3 below that ask teachers to think about how they can build science learning through the desire to develop the skills and attributes that will help pupils to begin to think like scientists.

The science curriculum needs to be planned with end points in mind so that pupils develop deeper knowledge and understanding of science over time. We want a pupil to move from being a novice with vague notions of the relevant concepts and move towards a deeper understanding of the underlying principles.

Each element of the science curriculum needs to be analysed in terms of how best to break down the components into manageable and accessible pieces of content that bind together to create deep learning. We want pupils to be able to see how science over time has changed perceptions and can mirror pupils' own misconception and misinterpretation. Teachers need

Table 7.3 Activity that focuses on the dialogue of working scientifically

• Understand the need for objectivity • Use and analyse research results and peer review • Test predictions through scientific enquiry • Use a range of methods for different investigations • Apply sampling techniques • Use tables and graphs to present data and observations • Evaluate data showing awareness of potential error • Use and derive simple equations • Pay attention to health and safety	• Show concern for accuracy and precision • Ask questions based on observation of real-world situations and problems • Identify, independently, dependent and control variables • Evaluate the reliability of methods and suggest improvements • Use and apply relevant mathematical concepts • Use data and information to identify patterns • Identify questions that might arise from evaluating results • Carry out appropriate calculations • Use and apply simple statistical techniques	• Know that scientific methods develop because of new evidence • Ask questions based on prior knowledge • Make and record observations and measurements • Use appropriate techniques, apparatus and materials • Present observations and data using appropriate methods • Use data and observations to draw accurate conclusions • Understand and us SI units and IUPAC • Undertake basic data analysis • Make predictions using scientific knowledge

to allow pupils to see why they have not yet understood and create opportunities for them to strengthen their understanding without deflating their potential (Ofsted 2021: p13).

How different ideas are introduced is also important. Starting with what pupils already know and building from there in a sequential process allows the jigsaw pieces to come together to make sense of many potential meaningless bits of unconnected content. What we don't want is to teach the content as a series of disconnected facts. Jasper Green, in his book *Powerful Ideas of Science*, describes the difference between meaningful learning and rote learning in relation to learning about electricity (Green 2021: p75). He describes meaningful knowledge as the careful integration of new knowledge structures that lead to the forming of a chain of understanding.

THE WEAVING TOGETHER OF MATHS AND SCIENCE PURPOSEFUL PRACTICAL SCIENCE

Maths and science have close links. It makes sense to build the science curriculum with opportunities to work with the maths department. Curriculum planning should create synergy between the teaching of certain topics in science and how these are taught as concepts in maths. It remains an issue that this collaboration is not evident in many schools (Ofsted 2023). Where there are opportunities for collaboration and a sharing of ideas, methods and language, the results are profound.

Almost every scientific explanation or experiment is likely to require some kind of mathematical skill, such as using negative numbers, calculating, estimating and recording, creating and interpreting graphs, ratio, applying formulae and solving equations.

A powerful CPD opportunity is for those who teach science and maths to look at their own planned sequence of learning from year 7 to year 11 and share some of their approaches to the pedagogy that they use to teach the method, the concept and the application. It can be very interesting to watch as different approaches, different language and different methods emerge and it does not take very long for there to be a dawning realisation that if there are so many diverse ways to teach the same concept that it is understandable that pupils may be confused.

There is great potential to re-order the teaching of certain maths concepts to align with teaching them in science so that pupils can see the connections to the context for which it fits in the real world. I worked with a school that developed a powerful partnership arrangement between the maths and science departments. They planned together using their respective programmes of study to ensure that schemes of work dovetailed the maths with the science, were careful to use the same language, terminology and methods and came together to team teach when learning had synergy and would be enhanced through joint project work.

What is also striking, when maths teachers start to delve into the science curriculum, is that some maths concepts are used in science *before* they are ever taught in the maths. There is an obvious issue here for pupils who are struggling with their maths learning to be suddenly confronted with maths that is out of their comfort zone. Acknowledging this is important and teachers from both maths and science need to focus on how to address this in their planning and teaching (Boohan 2016).

Applying maths concepts in as many science lessons as possible builds pupils' confidence. In science, pupils are expected to understand the importance of accuracy in measurement, this is also true in maths. They will use and apply graph work in both contexts and need to understand how to create equations and interpret formula.

There are three types of mathematical knowledge that were highlighted by Dowker (2009). Factual knowledge, which is the basic skills of number facts; procedural knowledge which is how to carry out mathematical operations and thirdly, conceptual knowledge where pupils know how to use mathematics in a variety of different situations. Knowing this is important for the scientist who has the task of creating the right pedagogy that will lead to pupils knowing how their competence in maths translates into their learning in science.

Where pupils find the maths difficult, they will undoubtedly find the science nearly impossible to access especially where they have not mastered their procedural and conceptual mathematical knowledge. From as early as possible in the planning of a sequential curriculum for science, the science teaching team should work together to identify potential barriers and share ideas as to how they can work with maths teachers to minimise the risk of misunderstanding, misconception or creating pupil beliefs that they 'can't do' maths or science.

Where there is a synergy between maths and science departments and faculties, professional development can support professional dialogue that will strengthen pedagogy and learning. All of the main elements of mathematical teaching have their place in science so, work together to share ideas about how to plan learning through:

- Identifying where calculation is an integral part of learning?
- Knowing the processes that will support the skill of estimating?
- Identifying how we teach pupils to reason and be effective problem solvers?

- Instilling the importance of accuracy when measuring?
- Applying the concept of algebra essential in a scientific context?
- Supporting pupils to use and interpret data accurately and incisively?
- Choosing to use a graph, a chart or a diagram as an aid to learning?
- Knowing how geometry applies in a scientific context and how can we share ideas as to how to teach it?

PURPOSEFUL PRACTICAL SCIENCE

Practical work is essential and creates many opportunities for pupils to demonstrate their disciplinary knowledge and show that they can work scientifically. Through practical work, pupils are exposed to different methods of science enquiry, to the textures, smells and phenomena of changes to matter, to substances and to living things.

According to Ofsted (2023), research suggests that practical work is not always effective. Their own research suggests that practical activity is not always carefully planned or linked to a deeper learning panorama where it has a clear purpose in relation to a wider sequence of lessons. The Education Endowment Foundation cite practical work as one of their recommendations in their review of secondary science. EEF (2022). Section 5 of their guidance report is headed 'Practical Work: Use practical work purposefully as part of a learning sequence'. They cite the following recommendations,

- Know the purpose of practical activity
- Sequence practical activity with other learning
- Use practical work to develop scientific reasoning
- Use a variety of approaches to practical science

The Holman (2017) has also produced a deeply comprehensive guide where they have ten recommendations for ensuring practical science is an essential element of highly effective science learning. Their focus is on how a good science education leads to many opportunities for pupils' future careers and opportunities for further study post-16. Practical science has the potential to create the awe and wonder we want from science learning. Here are the ten headings that define their benchmarks for good practice in teaching practical science.

1 Planned practical science
2 Purposeful practical science
3 Expert teachers
4 Frequent and varied practical science
5 Laboratory facilities and equipment
6 Technical support
7 Real experiments, virtual enhancements
8 Investigative projects
9 A balanced approach to risk

Assessment fit for purpose - The key stage 3 National Curriculum programme of study makes it clear that schools and their science teams should create opportunities for pupils to make their own decisions about scientific enquiry,

> Pupils should decide on the appropriate type of scientific enquiry to undertake to answer their own questions and develop a deeper understanding of factors to be considered when collecting, recording and processing data. They should evaluate their results and identify further questions arising from them. (Ofsted 2023)

The key stage 4 curriculum also emphasises at the beginning of the 'Working scientifically' section of the programme of study that pupils 'develop understanding and first-hand experience of developing their scientific thinking, their experimental skills, their ability to analyse and evaluate and their use of vocabulary, units, symbols and nomenclature'.

UNDERSTANDING HOW THE MIND WORKS FOR MEMORY AND LEARNING

It is important for those who plan and teach science to understand how the memory works and how easily pupils can become overloaded with knowledge and will not remember what they have been taught. All teachers, especially those involved in the teaching of science because of the high content requirement, need to have a good understanding of cognitive load theory. This is one of the recommendations of the Education Endowment Foundation's research paper 'Improving Secondary Science' (2022).

Pupils need to have time to absorb knowledge in small amounts and revisit the knowledge they have learnt so that it is retained in their long-term memory. Pupils also need to feel connected to their learning and be stimulated to want to learn more. Therefore, the opportunity for the teacher to find different ways to revisit certain concepts and apply them in different contexts can really support how pupils absorb and retain knowledge over time.

Planning and teaching science knowledge has to be carefully chunked and sequenced so that pupils have a chance to absorb the knowledge, use it, have opportunities to recall and revisit it and continually use science vocabulary in as many places as possible. Complex tasks need to be broken down into constituent segments in order to sequence them. This must be the job of the expert teacher who understands how the sequence fits together and can decide how to build knowledge so that pupils develop their understanding over time and do not overload the working memory (Lovell 2020: p49).

Teachers need to pay attention to cognitive load and its implications for ensuring pupils can understand the knowledge taught and allow it to deepen over time. The teacher needs to follow these steps:

- For new learning, pupils need the relevant background knowledge.
- Think about how information is presented. Pupils find it difficult when their attention is split between two or more pieces of information about the same principles.
- Create opportunities to take pupils through each sequence of a new task or topic and review their understanding.
- Give pupils the opportunity to share their understanding with their peers and as presentations to the whole class so that they articulate their growing knowledge.

To maintain the knowledge that we want pupils to retain, there must be opportunities for them to review their learning. This is part of being ready to take on new learning and reinforces the learning they have already processed in their long-term memory. Think about the sequence, review, retrieve and reflect as an essential part of the planning process for how you can ensure that all pupils are moving in the right direction towards deep learning of a growing body of scientific knowledge that they remember and can recall.

PEDAGOGY FOR DEEP SEQUENTIAL SCIENCE LEARNING

Teaching must ignite a passion for learning more, going deeper and allowing the pupils to discover a love for science as an essential part of their lives.

The science teacher must foster their pupils' attainment and engagement as the two are synonymous with achievement. Knowing the facts is not enough, certainly in the quest for the top grades. It is through highly competent science pedagogy that pupils will have the skills and disciplinary knowledge to demonstrate that they are working scientifically, through enquiry, effective group work, practical experimentation and observation, analysis and evaluation and use of evidence that they know will help them to absorb the substantive knowledge and demonstrate their skills as scientists.

Science leaders and their teams should have a shared commitment to a pupil-centred approach to pedagogy and create a strategy that will help pupils to be masters of their own learning. Encouraging pupils to think for themselves, find solutions to problems posed by the teacher and by their own investigations, is uplifting and motivating.

Self-regulated learning is the second of seven Education Endowment Foundation recommendations contained in their review of secondary science (EEF 2022). They cite a distinct link between self-regulation and attainment in science. To foster the right conditions in the classroom, the teacher needs to create a strong foundation for pupils to learn well. The teacher needs to ensure that pupils have the skills, such as the ability to measure accurately, read and understand, sift and select relevant information and use evidence to back up their hypotheses. Pupils also need to have a range of metacognitive skills that develop as they progress. These might include the ability to take notes and listen actively to others, to a video or to their teacher. They need to learn to process information from a variety of different sources, create pictures in their minds through graphs, diagrams or charts and use questioning to further their own understanding.

It takes teachers out of their comfort zone to be told to allow pupils to do their own learning. Teachers who have mastered this often initially feel as if they are not doing their job, that they should be at the front doing the talking and their pupils should be passive listeners in order that they can be the beneficiaries of their expertise and understanding. Some pupils learn in this way, but it is likely that the majority don't.

Creating opportunities for pupils to plan their own learning starts with the teacher. They will set the scene with the learning objective or goal. The teacher must then ascertain what pupils already know about the topic they are going to be investigating.

- What have they learnt previously?
- How well can they remember the vocabulary they have gathered along the way?
- What strategies helped them absorb the knowledge they have retained?

Then, the teacher can introduce the next phase in the learning process.

- What are we looking to find out?
- What is the problem we want to solve?
- What are the steps along the way?
- What is the evidence we are looking for?

Expert learners will relish this approach and embrace the challenge of working independently, novice learners may struggle with the process. Identifying the novice learner and creating smaller learning elements and opportunities to learn in different ways can help them build the confidence that comes from developing expertise of a particular process or task.

A lot can be achieved when pupils work in mixed ability groups. Novices, coasters and experts all working together learn from each other; the experts consolidate their learning by sharing it with others less expert in the group and those who tend to just coast are challenged to be more proactive with their learning. Lower ability learners are exposed to the highest learning encounters and rise to the challenge. (Taylor et al. 2018).

There is a great deal of pedagogical skill in this approach. The teacher is the facilitator of the learning, which is particularly important in science, where we want to foster the enquiring mind. Spinning the plates to ensure all pupils are working as a group, and not just in a group, carefully working with pupils who are struggling to grasp the concept and challenging those who have to go that few steps further is hard work, but learning and remembering is more likely here than through didactic teaching from the front.

Formative assessment, using highly effective questioning techniques and building confidence through positive feedback, creates an atmosphere of learning where all pupils feel they have been part of the process. Pupils need to also assess themselves in terms of their own success criteria, asking questions such as: What went well? What worked that I didn't think I could do? What would I do differently next time? What are five things I have learnt from this?

Asking the right questions is a critical learning curve and allows pupils to become more motivated to find the answers. Here are some that might support and encourage independent learning in science:

- What are the questions I need answers to?
- What methods might be most appropriate here?
- What is the best way to capture what I observe?
- What can I surmise for my observations or experiments?
- How can I best describe what I have found out?
- What is the evidence to back up what I think is the answer?
- Where else can I look to find out more or to be reassured that I am on the right track?
- What have I learnt?
- How can I use this knowledge in other situations?
- How will I remember what I have learnt?

Here the teacher's role might be to model some of these answers to the whole class, or to groups as they complete an assigned task, and then he or she asks pupils for their own answers. There can be brilliant opportunities for shared dialogue where pupils can answer questions and share their thoughts with the whole class or group. The teacher is there to set the boundaries, look for misconceptions and allow everyone to contribute. The learning that takes place from structured discussion is profound, uplifting and creates a real feeling of pupils' being masters of their own learning.

CONCLUSION

Science is a core subject in the National Curriculum and its content defines the world we live in. Invention, experimentation and research shape all our lives. The content is vast and spans three separate disciplines. The role of the subject leader is to inspire their teams to create a sequential, knowledge-rich curriculum that embraces essential substantive *and* disciplinary knowledge that will allow all pupils to work scientifically and develop a range of useful skills. They must also work with their senior team to create a vision for science that is relevant and well-taught.

Many elements need to be planned into the development of a science curriculum and time should be given for teams to work together to define their plans for weaving together the different threads that lead to deep learning. The learning needs to be sequenced; pupils need to be able to learn new concepts but have the opportunity to revisit prior learning. They need to feel confident and motivated to find out for themselves, experiment, hypothesise and predict without fear of being judged.

Ten Top Tips

1. Create time to plan a sequential curriculum where teams can build on prior learning and where incremental steps to deep learning are set out carefully over time.
2. There needs to be an understanding that only teaching substantive knowledge will not necessarily mean pupils remember their learning.
3. Focus on 'working scientifically' and ensure opportunities exist for pupils to develop their own skills and knowledge of the science disciplines.
4. Make sure all pupils have enough opportunities to take part in high-quality practical work that has clear purpose in relation to the curriculum
5. Create opportunities for cross-curricular collaboration to ensure that the science curriculum dovetails with other subjects, especially maths.
6. Build a team approach to misconception and misunderstanding. Know the common threads and how best to support pupils to become secure in their learning before they move onto a new topic.
7. Create CPD opportunities to share good and best practice in science pedagogy and learning.

(Continued)

(Continued)

8 Ensure that teachers have planned carefully how they can support pupils to connect new learning to prior learning.
9 Create opportunities for pupils to present their learning in different ways to help to create the right conditions for pupils to remember and use this in different contexts.
10 Find ways to relate science learning to pupils' own experiences of life outside school and use the vocabulary of science to create an understanding of how science is in everything we do.

REFERENCES

Boohan, R. (2016) *The Language of Mathematics in Science*. London, Association of Science Educators (ASE).

Department of Education (2014) *Programmes of Study for Science Key Stage 2, 3 and 4*. London, DfE.

Dowker, A. (2009) *What Works for Children with Mathematical Difficulties?*. Oxford, University of Oxford. Research report RR554 Paragraph 4.3 page.

Education Endowment Foundation (EEF) (2022) *Improving Secondary Science -Seven Recommendations for Improving Science in Secondary Schools*. London, EEF.

Flynne, S. (Summer 2019) *Science Literacy – Science in Education for Everyday Life. Issue 6*. London, IMPACT.

Green, J (2021). *Powerful Ideas in Science and How to Teach Them*. Abingdon, Routledge.

Harlen, W. (2010) *Principles and Big Ideas of Science Education*. London, Association of Science Educators.

Harlen, W., Bell, D., Devés, R., Dyasi, H., Fernández De La Garza, G., Léna, P., Millar, R., Reiss, M., Rowell, P. and Yu, W. (2015) *Big Ideas of Science Education*. Association for Science Education. https://www.ase.org.uk/download/file/fid/6740

Holman, J. (2017) *Good Practice Science*. London, The Gatsby Foundation.

Lovell, O. (2020) *Cognitive Load Theory in Action*. Woodbridge, John Catt.

Mallya, A. Mensah, F.M. Contento, I.R., et al (2012) Extending Science beyond the Classroom Door. Learning from Students' Experiences with the Choice, Control and Change (C3) Curriculum. *Journal of Research in Science Teaching* 49: pp244–269.

Millar, R. and Osborne, J. (1998) *Beyond 2000: Science Education for the Future*. London, Kings college, School of Education.

Ofsted (2023) *Finding the Optimum - The Science Subject Report*. London, Ofsted.

Ofsted (2021) *Research Review Series: Science*. London, Ofsted.

STEM website. www.stem.org.uk

Taylor, B., Hodgen, B., Tereschenko, A. and Archer, L. (2018) *Dos and Don'ts of Attainment Groupings*. London, UCL. Institute of Education.

8

THE HUMANITIES – SINGULAR AND INTERTWINING DISCIPLINES THAT MAKE SENSE OF OUR PLACE IN THE WORLD

Contents

HUMANITIES: A SUITE OF SINGULAR AND INTERTWINING DISCIPLINES

The subjects that make up the humanities curriculum are usually considered to be history, geography and religion. Business studies is sometimes included as a part of a humanities faculty as are the social sciences of economics, classics, law, philosophy, politics, psychology and sociology. Citizenship often finds its way into this classification. The National Curriculum sets down the content for the three main humanities subjects separately. However, there are many exciting opportunities to design content that combines themes and concepts from across the humanities discipline and sets the scene for pupils to have a deep, broad and knowledge-rich curriculum.

The depth and breadth within the humanities offers such potential to inspire pupils to want to find out more, to feel a sense of wonder at the achievements and events of the past, the forces that have shaped our physical world and allowed us to develop as economically viable communities. There are many common themes and transferrable concepts that can aid understanding and provide opportunities for deeper knowledge across subjects and give pupils time to consider humanity and its huge capacity for diversity, exploration, conflict, ambition, beliefs and cultural ingenuity.

It is to humanities that we look to explore ethics, the human condition and our place within the local context of our experiences and the wider context of our ability and our imagination. The inter-relationship between the subjects provides the potential for curriculum planners to create knowledge-rich content that places individual subjects within a wider perspective where history, culture, religious belief and the natural environment all inter-relate to shape events and explain change over time.

There is also a huge opportunity to create a tapestry that binds together pupils' local context with their place in the wider and more remote, international community of nations, beliefs, landscapes and cultures (Myatt 2018: p170).

FOSTERING CHALLENGE, CURIOSITY AND CREATIVE THINKING

The previous three chapters looked in detail at the core learning of English, maths and science. Humanities is one of the key areas that allows pupils to use many of the skills learnt in core subjects. It provides them with further opportunities to deepen their literacy and numeracy skills, their metacognitive skills and their understanding of how science can help to make sense of the world.

Pupils must have the opportunity to gather evidence themselves, find justification for their hypothesis and their supposition. They will need to analyse a situation, synthesise information and build their knowledge to demonstrate their progression to higher level thinking that is essential for success at GCSE. Where pupils are able to think critically about what they learn, what they discover for themselves and what they interpret from evidence, the more they are able to draw informed conclusions.

Teachers must have the pedagogical skills to coach pupils to reflect on their methods, or their sources of information, and create for them alternatives or make suggestions that acknowledge different interpretations, partial or inconclusive evidence or other factors that change the outcome. Many elements of the humanities curriculum provide great challenge and opportunities for debate and give pupils an insight into the need to look for different perspectives that will alter their own thinking (Brooks 2018).

The humanities curriculum focuses on what happens over time to the physical world and the people who inhabit it. Creating a curriculum must looks at the humanities not only as single subjects but also as a unique perspective for pupils of their place in the world.

- What has influenced them?
- What are the opportunities awaiting them as adults?
- What are the critical decisions being made now that will affect them the most?
- How can they have a say in the shape of things to come?

The same questions will have different answers from pupils from different backgrounds, ethnicities or experiences. Learning that the decisions made by individuals may impact both favourably and unfavourably on others is a keen lesson that will help pupils to become discerning and objective. The humanities curriculum can help pupils to understand that change happens because of physical and human powers that are unpredictable and difficult to control, and this will impact their own lives. Pupils need to be aware that different perspectives, narratives and interpretations will affect their own thinking, views and beliefs and can allow them to find their own answers to complex questions that remain as yet unresolved (Conventon 2022).

HARMONY BETWEEN THE NATURAL WORLD AND HUMAN SOCIETY

The positioning of certain elements within the humanities curriculum can ensure that learning builds from a local context, where pupils can relate the landscapes and environments that are familiar, to wider contexts that are unfamiliar and difficult to imagine. This can give pupils a sense of their place in the world and a sense of belonging. There is a case for the weaving together of some of the concepts within the wider humanities curriculum especially in key stage 3. This enables pupils to experience natural phenomena and how over time communities, settlements and places have evolved to take advantage of the topography, natural resources and environment.

The combination of a geography of place and topography linked to a history of people, ingenuity and progress can help pupils to make connections between the past and the present and the influence of the natural world on the people that inhabit it (WAG/HWB 2021).

The opportunity to define concepts linked to these interactions is reflective and will help pupils to make connections and profoundly understand their meaning in relation to how humanity interacts with the natural world. Concepts such as change, significance, place, settlement, cause and effect and continuity apply in a range of contexts that will support deeper understanding and retention of knowledge over time.

Pupils can explore the consequences of choices that societies and communities local to them have made in the past that impact on their local environment and quality of life. They have the opportunity to see their place in society and can consider the choices and consequences that they and others around them can make that will influence their future potential. There is a story in every community, often hidden but very much there in the minds of those who have lived through change. Local archives, books, photographs and accounts visual and written can all offer insight into the landscape and the environment. Real opportunities for investigation and exploration into the shaping of their world, as they inhabit it, can be meaningful and motivating for even the most disinterested.

SEQUENCING OF KNOWLEDGE TO FOSTER PROGRESSION AND DEEP LEARNING

The key stage 3 curriculum is the starting point for planning a sequential learning pathway for the secondary humanities curriculum. There is also the imperative to build on what has been taught and learnt in the primary school. The key stage 3 humanities curriculum can be delivered as a stand-alone model where the humanities subjects are taught discreetly or woven together using themes and concepts from across the suite of subjects. Whatever the chosen approach, the goal here is to create a pathway that builds on prior learning and creates a sequential structure that embraces what pupils need to know by the end of key stage 3 whilst acquiring understanding and higher-level thinking skills needed for success at GCSE and beyond.

Within the history National Curriculum programme of study (DfE 2014a), it states that the purpose of study is to inspire curiosity and fascination about the past, the world and its people. There is a clear indication in the history curriculum that pupils should be able to ask perceptive questions, think critically, weigh evidence, sift arguments and develop perspective and judgement (Ofsted 2021a). In the geography curriculum, the disciplinary skills are defined as being able to collect, analyse and communicate, interpret a range of sources and communicate geographical information (DfE 2014b; Ofsted 2021b).

The sequence of learning should ensure that pupils are deepening and broadening their knowledge over time and are increasingly exposed to a range of concepts that are related to particular areas of study but that also transcend the different disciplines. Where pupils can make connections within the individual subjects and can see links to other humanities subjects and the wider curriculum, especially in English, maths and science, their understanding is reinforced and their knowledge strengthened and retained. Different viewpoints can be explored through one lens in one subject or can be viewed from several different perspectives (Spielman 2018).

What is required is a growing sophistication in the use and application of the disciplinary knowledge or skills that pupils need to develop to access the substantive knowledge of each subject. They need to develop accuracy and fluency in how they use their growing understanding to tell their story and understand patterns in natural phenomena and human development.

Pupils should be able to share ideas and write about change and the consequence of change and understand and make sense of the similarities and differences between places, eras and ideas. What the humanities curriculum should achieve is to shape the pupil who knows their place in the world, who can see how time has impacted on their place in society and give them the skills and confidence to be reflective and responsible citizens who have the potential to make a difference (Myatt and Tomsett 2021).

A DEEP DIVE INTO THE COMPULSORY HUMANITIES CURRICULUM

Humanities subject leaders need to shape the vision for a meaningful and innovative curriculum that ensures pupils have a deep understanding of the compulsory key stage 3 disciplines that pupils choose to study at GCSE. Alongside geography and history, these could include business, economics, sociology or psychology. This requires knowing what the planned curriculum will achieve for pupils by the end of year 11, in preparation for further study, life and work.

For humanities in all its different guises, there is something else to focus on as well. It is about pupils understanding about ethics, values, the human experience, considering different perspectives and understanding the global challenges that are an integral part of their future.

Humanities subject leaders must translate the vision into a coherent curriculum that embraces each individual discipline and can, through careful collaboration and co-construction, be woven together to create deep meaning for the pupil. The essential ingredients are:

- Breadth and depth of knowledge acquisition so that pupils are able to use the knowledge they are gaining to be coherent in their pursuit of meaning
- A balance between learning the content and developing the disciplines that allow pupils to become independent and confident citizens
- An understanding of the purpose of each of the disciplines and how they interrelate
- An understanding that the core skills of literacy, numeracy and the wider metacognitive skills are an integral part of the learning

Planning how the curriculum is to be taught should be thought through carefully in relation to what pedagogies and classroom management strategies are relevant to teaching humanities in a meaningful way. These questions are useful as discussion points for those within the humanities faculties.

- How do we plan the need to focus on the local context and then broaden out to wider and more abstract concepts?
- What do we teach and when, to ensure that the widest possible potential for deepening the learning is achieved?

- How do we create coherence so that all pupils can find meaning and are deepening their knowledge over time?
- What are the strategies we can use to ensure all learners have the same access to a rigorous and knowledge rich discrete and cross-curricular experience?
- How do we ensure that pupil voice is heard so that they share ideas, opinions and solutions through reasoned debate, discussion and constructive argument that embraces different beliefs, cultures, religions, politics and opinions?
- How do we select the right content that is most relevant for our own cohort without narrowing the potential for deeper learning?

Below is a table that sets out what outcomes teachers should be striving to ensure happen so that pupils are the masters of their own journey to deeper understanding (Table 8.1).

The history curriculum is set out as distinct periods and events that have shaped Britain and our influence in history over time. There are many non-statutory examples where the history team can decide specific content linked to their interests and expertise.

The concepts that are explored within the non-statutory examples provide further opportunities for professional dialogue about the depth and breadth of content and how to teach it. Here are a few that lift off the page; the importance of religion, the emergence of parliament, society, economy and culture, revolt, social and economic impact, conflict, the interregnum, restoration, succession, enlightenment, slavery, franchise, politics, social reform, suffrage, depression, welfare, time, social history, revolution. It is the vocabulary as well as the context that needs to be explored to ensure that pupils can access knowledge and encourage them to continue to learn history beyond GCSE. (Quigley 2018: p97).

Table 8.1 Key learning outcomes in history and geography (DfE history and geography programmes of study for key stage 3 (DfE 2014c))

For history pupils should:	**For geography pupils should:**
• Extend their chronologically secure knowledge • Have a well-informed context for wider learning • Identify significant events • Make connections • Draw contrasts • Analyse trends within periods and over time • Use historical terms and concepts • Pursue historically valid enquiries • Create accounts supported by evidence that is relevant and structured • Understand the importance of historical sources • Discern why contrasting arguments and interpretations of the past have been constructed	• Consolidate and extend their knowledge of major countries, physical and human features • Understand how geographical processes interact to create distinctive human and physical landscapes that change over time • Become aware of increasingly complex geographical systems • Develop greater competence in using geographical knowledge, approaches and concepts • Develop their skills in analysing and interpreting different data sources • Enrich their locational knowledge and spatial and environmental understanding

The geography curriculum at key stage 3 sets the subject content out as four distinct elements.

- Locational knowledge
- Place knowledge
- Human and physical geography
- Geographical skills and fieldwork

Key concepts that are explicit within the explanation of the generic subject content include: spatial awareness, environmental regions, key physical and human characteristics, geographical similarities and differences, geological timescales, plate tectonics, weathering, weather, climate, glaciation, hydrology, coasts, population, urbanisation, international development, economic activity, primary, secondary, tertiary and quaternary sectors, natural resources, natural systems, ordnance survey, grid referencing, scale, topography, thematic mapping, aerial, satellite, GIS.

The vocabulary here can be complex and difficult to access for the novice geographer. So, ensuring that pupils can access meaning as well as context is an important consideration in planning the key stage 3 curriculum (Quigley 2018).

DEFINING RELIGIOUS EDUCATION AS AN INTEGRAL PART OF HUMANITIES

Ofsted's research review for religious education (2021c) suggests that pupils have the opportunity to see religion and non-religion in society. It would be difficult to teach any kind of religious studies without some reference to place, historical context or events and natural phenomena that have shaped thinking and ideas about religious belief or otherwise. Religious education should dovetail with curriculum planning for other humanities subjects to explore events, places and conflicts that are significant for the subject.

There is no statutory programme of study for religious education. There is a plethora of literature and much of what is published recommends some form of prescribed and detailed curriculum content. Schools have the opportunity to set their own local framework to take account of our complex multi-religious and secular society.

There are many possibilities for ensuring that religious education has a place in the wider humanities family and provides pupils with an opportunity to see religion in its widest context linked to human endeavour, frailty and invention as well as ambition, community and national identity.

There are many examples of how religion links to history and geography and to ignore the significance of religion in the unfolding of certain key historical events or to the importance of physical geography, places of deep meaning and issues of displacement and conflict would be a travesty. For example:

- The nativity and its power to evoke story is set in a place where conflict is still a reality
- Henry VIII and his fight with the Pope that led to the English Reformation

- The power of the dynasty in China or Russia and the subsequent control of religious belief
- The Northern Ireland story linked to place and identity and the conflict between Catholic and Protestant communities
- The bitter struggle between the Greeks and the Turks and the collapsing Ottoman Empire and the Gallipoli campaign

The curriculum for religious education focuses on the substantive knowledge of religions, their traditions and locations within local communities and origins across the wider world. There are opportunities for structured debate and conversations about beliefs, non-belief and possibilities in relation to helping pupils to be tolerant of difference, to see similarities between their own ideals and those from other religions or communities. The Ofsted research review (2021c) asks that schools ensure their curriculum planning for religious education is given the same credibility as any other subject.

In July 2023, the Religious Education Council for England Wales published a document outlining their proposal for a National Entitlement Statement that they would like to see adopted in schools. They want the religious education curriculum to explore the nature of religion and world views and their importance for us all. They say, 'this means enabling all pupils to become knowledgeable, open-minded, critical participants in public discourse, who make academically informed judgements about important matters of religion or belief which shape the global landscape' (Religious Education Council 2023: p9).

Asking pupils in lower key stage 3 the question 'What is religion?' provides an opportunity to look at the religion of pupils in the school, where these originate and how perhaps parents or other family members came to Britain and why. Creating opportunities for a deep discussion about the concept of religion to different members of the class will be relevant for contexts linked to other humanities subjects, concepts and facts. Asking pupils to consider how religions change over time might provide the opportunity to explore significant concepts developed through the ages, understanding theories of atonement, the Qur'an in Islamic traditions or it can be linked to geography to look at the significance of place where people feel they belong or have to flee from persecution. The development of significant concepts is also explored through these considerations, the concept of power, values, tradition, icons, for instance.

In key stage 4 where religious education is an examinable subject as well as a requirement of the wider curriculum offer, there is the potential to focus on how religion impacts on our lives, the sanctity of life, for instance, within the Catholic religious community, the wearing of the hijab by Muslim women in some countries or the observance of certain religious festivals (Religious Education Council 2021). The opportunity for reflection, debate, understanding and developing a view of context in relation to the depth of observance has huge potential to help pupils to develop higher-level thinking skills for use in a much wider set of parameters.

The teaching of religious education is compulsory. However, there is little consensus on what should be taught and how. Whether it is taught discreetly, or as part of Spiritual, Moral,

Social and Cultural education (SMSC), these questions can be an integral part of the planning process and in preparation for high quality implementation:

- What is the school policy for religious education?
- What content knowledge do we want pupils to have by the time they leave us?
- How do we ensure CPD builds expertise in subject knowledge?
- How do we make sure we know, and make use of, research on what religious education should look like in the secondary school?

Religious education creates an opportunity for humanities curriculum planners to embrace disciplinary knowledge that is relevant across other subjects, such as:

- Concepts within religious education that transcend the subject and provide a backdrop for learning in history, the social sciences and in SMSC
- Religious education lessons provide opportunities for pupils to develop positive attitudes and values and to relate their learning to their own experience
- Through their growing knowledge of different religions and their traditions pupils can become more informed about the world around them, their peers and their environment
- Pupils can articulate their own beliefs and learn not all people hold religious views
- The fact that there are several integrated world views linked to a variety of religions provides pupils with an opportunity to look at the origins, similarities and differences and powerful traditions
- Religion provides a rich tapestry of tradition and can create some wonderful lessons in preparing food, replicating festivals and traditions, looking at music of different religions and traditional buildings such as temples, sacred places, churches and monuments

BUILDING ON PRIOR LEARNING FROM THE PRIMARY PHASES

What has been taught in upper key stage 2 should be an essential part of the planning for subject-specific history, geography religious education teaching. The key stage 2 national curriculum defines the sequential content and expects there to be an overview of the different elements as well as a depth to study that will help pupils to understand the long arc of development and the complexity of aspects of the content.

Key stage 2 geography is equally detailed and sequenced towards deeper knowledge and understanding by the end of year 6. In the same way, there is detailed content and structure that defines what should be taught and the themes, skills and processes and linked closely to the key themes within the key stage 2 programme of study (DfE 2014c).

The history and geography programmes of study stand alone in terms of their content, but there are some wonderful examples of how to create joined up learning opportunities across the transition bridge.

- A joint fieldwork project linking why the landscape shaped history, perhaps the proximity of a hill for a battle or raw materials for the industrial revolution, or maybe a study of a river, its powerful journey from youth to old age and the history unfolding along its course.
- The Roman invasion of Britain in terms of where the Romans came from, where and why they settled here and how they changed the landscape
- Changing patterns of land use linked to historical contexts that define place and settlements and human behaviour and characteristics
- Erosion, eruption and tremor, the geography and the consequences on human history and economic survival
- The complexities of war and the essential nature of identity, place and beliefs

SKILLS THAT ENHANCE LEARNING ACROSS THE HUMANITIES

The humanities curriculum has an abundance of opportunities to enhance pupils' core and wider learning skills. Here, literacy skills play an important part in pupils' ability to absorb knowledge across humanities subjects.

There are many opportunities to enhance learning through literacy in all of the compulsory humanities subjects, developing speaking and listening skills through debate and discussion linked to specific areas of dispute or where different theories exist. The use of role-play can really bring a period in history alive or a re-enactment of why a group of people chose a particular place to settle.

There is an abundance of opportunity for using different styles of writing to support pupils to think about the audience and purposes to which they are writing, or where they are exposed to the writing of others, such as letter writing, explanations that have changed over time, writing linked to scripture texts, accounts of historical events and descriptions of landscapes in different guides and diaries. These are rich opportunities for pupils to read unfamiliar and difficult texts that require a great deal of thought and concentration (Hockman and Wexler 2017).

Maths and numeracy are integral to much of the learning in geography and in history and religious education as well. In geography, there are many examples of maths skills, such as data handling, scale and proportion, percentages, graphs and charts and population statistics. Creating opportunities for pupils to analyse data and statistics can also help to strengthen their writing skills and their ability to demonstrate the higher-level thinking skills needed for GCSE and beyond.

There is also a wealth of opportunity to develop pupils' wider thinking and metacognitive skills, such as developing creative ways to present accounts of periods in history, expressing opinions with evidence, finding sources of information to back up arguments about events in the past or examining the theories around different geological and geographical structures. There are opportunities for pupils to work together in groups to share their investigations, develop their presentations and accounts and work together towards a play, a short story or a podcast about their learning.

THE HUMANITIES CURRICULUM AT KEY STAGE 4

Not all pupils will study geography, history or religious education in key stage 4. It is likely they will choose only one, as that is often the way option choices work. All schools should continue with some kind of religious education study into key stage 4. It is worth considering how departmental heads and their teams can ensure the content and the creativity employed in delivering humanities subjects in key stage 3 empowers pupils to continue to study them in key stage 4.

The National Curriculum for these subjects at key stage 4 does not contain a definitive set of parameters for what should be studied, or a clear structure for how each subject should be taught as with the key stage 3 specifications. The content for geography and history at key stage 4 is explained in two DfE documents that set out the knowledge, understanding and skills that the government want to see in all specifications produced by awarding bodies. The task of the awarding body is to design their specification so that it ensures progression from key stage 3 and prepares pupils for possible A level study.

Subject aims and learning outcomes for geography state that pupils should understand more about the world. This makes a tacit assumption that pupils have a bank of knowledge and associated disciplinary skills as they embark on GCSE study to build on what they already know and can do. The GCSE course is designed to deepen understanding of:

- geographical processes;
- the impact of change;
- the impact of complex people-environment interactions;
- the dynamic links and inter-relationships between places and environments at different scales.

Planning the subject content and how it should be taught should also develop pupils' competence in using a wide range of geographical investigative skills and approaches.

There is also a progression statement that emphasises the need to build on what has been taught and learnt during key stage 3. The focus is on:

- broadening and deepening understanding of locational contexts;
- a greater emphasis on process studies that lead to an understanding of change;
- a greater stress on the multivariate nature of human-physical interactions;
- developing pupils' ability to form generalisations, abstractions and theoretical perspectives;
- pupils planning and undertaking independent enquiry linked to geographical questions;
- enhancing pupil's competence in a range of intellectual arguments and debates to synthesise and evaluate content and material.

(DfE 2014b)

For history, the GCSE subject content document is set out in a similar way. The subject aims and learning outcomes for study at key stage 4 should deepen pupils' understanding to:

- think critically;
- weigh evidence;
- sift arguments;
- make informed decisions;
- develop perspective and judgement.

There is further amplification of the scope of study for history which includes the study of mediaeval, early modern and modern history. Pupils should have the opportunity to study on three timescales, a depth study, a period study and a thematic study. There should also be an opportunity to study British history, European history and wider world settings.

Historical knowledge, understanding and method should be carefully planned for implementation so that pupils demonstrate:

- Knowledge and understanding of the key features and characteristics of the periods studied
- An understanding of first-order historical concepts such as constitution, nation, revolution, society
- That they can reach substantial conclusions through finding, sifting and selecting knowledge and understanding and create relevant written narratives
- An understanding of the key features and characteristics of the periods they are studying in relation to second order historical concepts such as continuity, change, cause, consequences, significance and similarity and difference within situations
- An understanding of the connections, contrasts and trends between different periods and events, local/regional, national/international, cultural/economic/social/political/religious/military
- An understanding of the importance of source material appropriate to the period
- Their understanding of how knowledge is used to make historical claims and being discerning in their own interpretation

(DfE 2014a)

For religious education, all of the awarding bodies offer qualifications at key stage 4 and 5. These have options to study Christianity and its influence, as well as other religions. They also focus on ethics and beliefs, such as in marriage and family and how individuals live and die. There are also themes linked to crime and punishment and living in conflict.

PEDAGOGY AND LEARNING THROUGHOUT THE HUMANITIES CURRICULUM

Each subject within the humanities is unique and the knowledge pupils need to have as they progress from year 7 to year 11 should be progressive, sequenced and lead to a readiness for decisions about GCSE options.

Here we are looking at the curriculum and how generic curriculum thinking can support positive cross-curricular professional development and consistent and high-quality pedagogy. Key principles to consider here are:

- It is essential that across the humanities subjects, there is a symbiosis between the teaching of disciplinary and substantive knowledge.
- Teachers should work together with their subject leader and others within their team to determine the content to be taught and to focus on the pupils and the local context to prioritise what is the most important content pupils need to learn.
- Pupils need to develop a range of skills in analysis, use of argument, debate and enquiry and the providence of evidence to hone their disciplinary knowledge.
- The substantive concepts need to be clearly defined at the beginning of the topic or sequence of lessons.
- Pupils should be exposed to as many challenging and relevant texts to reinforce their learning and allow them to deepen their knowledge over time.
- Teachers should know the misconceptions that are common in each topic or series of lessons. Teachers should share ideas as to how these will be identified and addressed.
- Pupils must have the time and space to apply what they been taught and conversely where they are asked to apply their skills and knowledge they are secure enough to be able to do just that.
- Teachers should be aware of the problems caused when pupils are expected to cover content quickly, frequently shallow learning of content will lead to pupils who are unable to retain the content for any length of time.
- Teachers should ensure that planning takes account of prior knowledge and is structured towards carefully defined end points.
- Assessment should check both that pupils have secure substantive knowledge but can also apply that knowledge effectively in associated context.

OTHER SUBJECTS UNDER THE HUMANITIES UMBRELLA

There are several other subjects that fall under the jurisdiction of humanities such as the social sciences and business studies. It is usually in key stages 4 and 5 that these subjects become optional. The curriculum is quite crowded in key stage 3 so it is unusual for schools to opt for them as part of a key stage 3 offer. However, the opportunity to introduce variety into new subjects for pupils to study from year 9 or 10 is often a new start and an opportunity to try something new and different. Within this suite of subjects, the same humanities approach should be adopted if the goal of depth and breadth of knowledge is to be realised.

The social studies of psychology and sociology require deep understanding of people and their values. There are opportunities for pupils to learn through understanding society and the people who have shaped it, learning about systems of government, democracy and the influence of direct and indirect action. There are opportunities to explore concepts such as equality, freedom, gender identity inequality, to name a few. The emphasis may be different, but there are connections between these subjects and the other humanities subjects we have looked at in more depth.

Pupils who opt to study business will explore the economic realities of business in its many different shapes and sizes. They will look at the elements of supply and demand, how a company promotes and goes to market, ways that businesses stay afloat and make critical decisions about their costs, growth and profitability. Once again it is to the disciplinary learning of key elements such as enquiry, questioning, data handling and debate that shape pupils' ability to achieve well as they approach their GCSE examinations.

THE POSSIBILITIES FOR HUMANITIES BEYOND THE CLASSROOM

Here one immediately considers the possibility of fieldwork in the geography context. It is a compulsory part of the National Curriculum for geographers and there is a very clear steer as to what pupils should learn and be able to do as part of undertaking fieldwork. These are:

- Build on their knowledge of globes, maps and atlases and apply and develop this knowledge routinely in the classroom and in the field
- Interpret Ordnance Survey maps in the classroom and in the field, including using grid references and scale, topographical and other thematic mapping, and aerial and satellite photographs
- Use Geographical Information Systems (GIS) to view, analyse and interpret places and data
- Use fieldwork in contrasting locations to collect, analyse and draw conclusions from geographical data using multiple sources of increasingly complex information

(DfE Programme of study for Geography key stage 3, 2014b)

This is explicit within geography as a means of gaining disciplinary knowledge that will strengthen pupils' understanding of their local context and also in using some geographical navigation tools necessary to be a geographer. There are also opportunities to build this kind of fieldwork into a wider humanities context and ensure that pupils studying history and religious education, as well as social sciences and business studies, have the opportunity to study these subjects in more depth, in the real world outside the classroom.

I live in the small market town of Bridgnorth in Shropshire where I could and would love to plan a humanities fieldwork experience because of my own local knowledge. What I can do each and every teacher can also do within the confines of their locality.

Here goes for a trip into what is rich learning territory.

- The birth of the industrial revolution in Ironbridge with its museums, a deep gorge, the meandering middle age River Severn and the history of bone china, coal mining and pipe and tile manufacture

- Benthal near to Much Wenlock with a truly magnificent manor awash with the history of the English Civil War and how the topography helped in the demise of the King and his troops as well as the destruction of the village of Benthal
- Wroxeter where there is a Roman fortification and a real opportunity to look at the geography of why this site was chosen as well as the historical context.
- Then there is Much Wenlock with its priory and mediaeval town. Nearby the Wenlock Edge, a truly magnificent limestone escarpment and interesting geology and the imposing Wrekin, not an actual volcano but consisting of lava and ash. Also, the home of the first Olympic games and a mascot for the games in 2012

This approach brings substantive knowledge to life, in terms of the vocabulary and real events. It creates images and experiences that will translate into deeper and more meaningful understanding of more than just a local study. In geography, it brings the opportunity to see firsthand a meandering river in middle age, the topography of a unique and iconic 'volcanic' hill, the shape of the undulating land as represented on a map and the settlements that are nearby and are there because of the river and the rich soils of rural Shropshire.

The opportunities to develop the disciplinary knowledge associated with fieldwork is also profound not just for geography but also for history and religion. In my local example, this could encompass debates about the Catholic faith and republicanism, discussions about the reason for the siting of Wroxeter and the importance of the beginnings of the industrial revolution in Ironbridge.

CONCLUSION

The humanities is unique in the way that it provides a rich cornucopia of knowledge that is familiar and accessible to pupils and to teachers who are involved in planning a learning experience. The main subjects of history, geography and religious education, all compulsory in key stage 3, provide an interconnected body of study that can help pupils to make sense of their own place in the world. The focus in this chapter has been to look at humanities as a whole, rather than at each subject individually. Through professional dialogue and a shared understanding, subject leaders and teachers can work together to strengthen the potential for pupils across all three disciplines to become equipped with the disciplinary knowledge and the core and wider skills that will help them to achieve at GCSE and beyond.

If schools can establish a consensus and develop innovative planning for challenge and depth of study in each of the disciplines at key stage 3, this will lay the foundations for pupils to want to continue to study one or more humanities subjects at key stage 4. There is huge potential to use disciplinary knowledge, concepts and skills from the humanities to enhance the depth of learning in the core subjects of maths, English and science and ensure pupils are becoming unconsciously competent in a range of higher-level thinking skills so important in the quest for success in examinations, life and work.

Ten Top Tips

1. Create opportunities for cross-curricular teams to work together to define the common themes and transferrable concepts.
2. Planning should inevitably start with a focus on the potential of the local context, the topography, history and the nature of the cohort of the pupils in the school.
3. Make explicit the importance of the core skills of maths and English in how pupils access knowledge and demonstrate their depth of understanding.
4. Create opportunities for pupils to investigate, problem solve, ask questions, share ideas and argue a point.
5. Foster partnerships with primary schools in order to ensure you are building on prior learning and can support pupils to reinforce and reflect on their learning.
6. Ensure all those who teach within the humanities suite understand the aims and purpose of study in the relevant National Curriculum programmes of study.
7. Explore the descriptions of learning as set in the Welsh curriculum document as part of an opportunity for a professional dialogue about what we mean by learning.
8. Gather together the rich vocabulary contained as part of each of the humanities subjects and ensure all pupils can access the language and understand the meaning of words and concepts as well as a focus on where they exist across the curriculum in other contexts.
9. Make sure that subject leaders and their teams of teachers understand the vision and ambition for humanities so that there is agreement that we plan for what we want pupils to know and be able to do at certain carefully defined end points along the learning journey.
10. Carefully focus on the mark schemes for all three main humanities examination subjects and consider how you can develop pupils higher level thinking skills from as early as year 7.

REFERENCES

Brooks, C. (2018) *Debates in Geography Education*. Abingdon: Routledge.

Conventon, A. (2022) *Redrawing the Cross-Curricular Map: An Interdisciplinary Approach to Curriculum Design in Humanities*. London, IMPACT magazine, Issue 14, Spring, Chartered College of Teaching.

DfE (2014a) *Key Stage 3 History Programme of Study*. London, DfE.

DfE (2014b) *Key Stage 3 Geography Programme of Study*. London, DfE.

DfE (2014c) *Key Stage 2 Programmes of Study for History and Ggeography*. London, DfE.

Hockman, J. and Wexler, N. (2017) *The Writing Revolution*. San Francisco, CA, Jossey-Bass.

Myatt, M. (2018) *From Gallimaufry to Cohesion*. Woodbridge, John Catt.

Myatt, M. and Tomsett, J. (2021) *Huh Curriculum Conversations between Subject and Senior Leaders*. Woodbridge, John Catt.

Ofsted (2021a) *Research Review for History*. London, Ofsted.
Ofsted (2021b) *Research Review for Geography*. London, Ofsted.
Ofsted (2021c) *Research Review for Religious Education*. London, Ofsted.
Quigley, A. (2018) *Closing the Vocabulary Gap*. Abingdon, Routledge.
Religious Education Council of England and Wales (2023) *National Content Standard for Religious Education*. Nottingham, Religious Education Council.
Sherrington, T. (2018) *The Learning Rainforest -Great Teaching in Real Classrooms*. Woodbridge, John Catt.
Spielman, A. (2018) *Commentary on the New Education Inspection Framework*. London, Ofsted.
WAG/HWB Curriculum for Wales overview (2021). Cardiff: Welsh, Assembly Government.

9

CREATIVITY AND EXPRESSIVE ARTS

Contents

- The creative subjects: an opportunity for expression
- Defining the school vision creativity and the expressive arts
- Collaboration and partnership across the transition bridge from key stage 2 to 3
- Building expression in key stage 3 art and design
- The pathways into music appreciation and skills for future study
- Design technology a unique conduit for invention, design and technical skill
- Overlapping concepts in the creative subjects
- Increasing breadth and depth of learning – pedagogy and progression
- The arts at key stage 4 – building a future of creativity

THE CREATIVE SUBJECTS: AN OPPORTUNITY FOR EXPRESSION

Artistic expression takes on many forms and is difficult to pin down as an integral part of the static National Curriculum. There are many different genres that exist within art and each one can capture the imagination or spark the desire to want to learn more. Painting, drawing, ceramics, sculpture, graphic design and print all have their place. Within each genre are diverse elements that require nurturing talent to create a gateway for future development. In painting, for instance, there are different media, pastels, oils, water colour and ink. Often it is the expertise and talent within the respective creative studies departments that will determine what pupils are exposed to in terms of what they learn and can understand.

Music is much more than the National Curriculum could ever capture and is part of the fabric of all our lives. There is a tradition that goes back before writing, before the birth of civilisation that builds music into storytelling, emotional expression and the backdrop for many of the experiences that shape the human condition. However, as a secondary curriculum subject, it is perilously close to extinction.

Film, photography and digital media also have a seat at the expressive arts table and provide a powerful medium for many pupils to combine interests in technology and what it can achieve as part of artistic expression. Here the curriculum might embrace games design, print media, production, hosting live events, creating podcasts, videos and filming live presentations. There are opportunities for pupils to learn about light and sound, how to edit, how to use a camera or an audio machine.

Design technology is included in this section, but it could just as easily have found its way into the science chapter. There is much maths in design technology too. However, it is fundamentally about creativity, new ideas and a deep understanding of structure, form and style. It examines what society demands in terms of the evolving of ideas that will shape the future and take the best from the past.

Drama is not compulsory in key stage 3 and is not offered at GCSE in all secondary schools. However, it deserves its place in this chapter. Drama can bring together all the other subjects that fall under this umbrella and provide opportunities for pupils to express themselves and to use their skills in music, creativity and design. There are also opportunities to link drama to English both for creative writing and literature. Creating opportunities to bring characters alive, design sets and costumes and tell stories create real-life connections that help to make sense of the written word.

DEFINING THE SCHOOL VISION FOR CREATIVITY AND THE EXPRESSIVE ARTS

Art covers such a wide spectrum of potential learning that it is essential for each school to consider which aspects of the subject to include and which to omit. Much will depend on the expertise within the teaching team. Each area of study has its own distinct identity, skills and knowledge that require time to fully explore. Time is often at a premium and sometimes the creative elements of learning are marginalised in consideration of other foundation subjects.

In relation to curriculum intent, it is important to recognise that developing skills and knowledge in these subjects provides pupils with potential future opportunities in a variety of creative jobs. The creative industries make a significant contribution to the UK economy of £115.9 billion (Ofsted 2023).

Studying art, music and other creative disciplines provides pupils with an appreciation of how art can bridge the gap in cultural and social differences across countries, eras and beliefs. Where pupils can learn about the history of art, the evolution of music styles and expressions and how design has shaped our world, the more they can relate the creative world to other elements of their learning and their life.

Creativity allows pupils to express themselves in a variety of different ways. Exposure to different genres in both music and art, different approaches and styles to design technique and expression can help pupils to articulate their own artistic preferences. They can see how important it is that individuals can express their creativity. This gives them freedom to be themselves and can be beneficial socially, emotionally and physically. Being at liberty to be expressive nourishes the spirit, enhances well-being, fosters self-esteem and builds resilience (HWB 2019).

The inclusion of a wide-ranging creative curriculum, especially during key stage 3 when pupils can use their creativity in a wide variety of contexts, can strengthen the vision for deep learning. The potential to see the creative arts as overlapping with core and foundation subjects make it a vital addition to a deep and rich curriculum. For example, history can explore how art and music have evolved over time. The inspiration of landscape, both rural and urban, in art offers a clear link to geography. The development of different types of architecture, its relationship with society, the juxtaposition between wealth and poverty, urban and rural design and the preservation or destruction of iconic buildings all play their part in pupils' deeper understanding of the society that they live in, places where other people see things differently and a look at some of the monumental mistakes and successes in the design world.

Finally, the creative arts offer the opportunity for pupils to explore how art, music or design makes them feel, how it impacts on their world and that of others. Opportunities to explore, debate, experiment and practise a range of skills provide them with a better cultural identity and they are more confident in their ability to be themselves.

COLLABORATION AND PARTNERSHIP ACROSS THE TRANSITION BRIDGE FROM KEY STAGE 2 TO 3

We have a whole chapter devoted to transition and rightly so. However, it is widely acknowledged that many primary school teachers are not specialists and are unable to provide the depth and breadth of subject knowledge that subject experts in the secondary phase would expect in the creative arena.

The answer for many key stage 3 curriculum planners is to start again, accepting that pupils have little knowledge or skill in the creative subjects. In the book *Huh* (Myatt and Tomsett 2021), which is a suite of curriculum conversations between subject and senior leaders, this lack of focus on what has gone before year 7 is borne out in the art and music chapters.

In the chapter about the art curriculum, there is little reference to what pupils should have experienced through the study of art in key stage 2. In the music chapter, there is a tacit understanding that the ability of pupils as they arrive in year 7 is varied mainly because of parental influence which makes it difficult to find the right starting point. This is not a criticism of the book or its concept. It is informative and instructive in its approach and the opportunity to read about practical conversations with experts and their senior leaders is so useful.

Design technology follows the same path. The curriculum at key stage 3 is firmly described as a starting point. There is no significant reference to how the design curriculum in key stage 3 might be enriched through the opportunity to share with primary school partners and pupils the learning they have had in year 6 and before.

When comparing the key stage 3 programmes of study for art, music and design technology with those from key stages 1 and 2, it is revealing to see what pupils should have been exposed to in primary school. The 2019 Ofsted framework focuses on curriculum depth and breadth at every key stage. So, for those teaching in the secondary school, there should be an understanding that pupils will have been exposed to wide ranging opportunities in art, music and the different elements of design technology.

A review of the key stage 2 programme of study for art and design provides year 7 art and design teachers with potential questions to ask of their primary partners.

- How can we have access to the sketch books that pupils have used as part of their artwork?
- What different kinds of art, craft and design have pupils used during their learning in art?
- How do you assess pupils' control and their use of materials?
- What examples do you have of how pupils review and revisit ideas?
- What are the different techniques that pupils have used and been introduced to in key stage 2?
- How do you plan art topics to ensure pupils are developing their techniques over time?
- Which great artists, architects and designers have pupils learnt about in key stage 2?

A review of the key stage 2 programme of study for music provides year 7 music teachers with potential questions to ask of their primary partners.

- How do you assess that pupils are becoming more confident in their ability to sing and play musically?
- How is the music curriculum sequenced across key stage 2 to ensure there is increasing accuracy, fluency, control and expression?
- What are the inter-related dimensions of music that pupils are introduced to during key stage 2?
- How well do individual pupils improvise and compose their own music for different purposes?
- What are the mechanisms for ensuring pupils listen and understand and can recall sounds so that they are enhancing their aural memory?

- To what level of understanding of staff and other musical notations have pupils reached?
- What kinds of live and recorded music have pupils been introduced to, from what traditions and from which composers and musicians?
- Which aspects of the history of music have pupils been exposed to and have learnt about?

A review of the key stage 2 programme of study for design technology provides year 7 design technology teachers with potential questions to ask of their primary partners.

- What kind of research do pupils undertake as they work towards developing their design criteria that will inform their designs of useful and fit for purpose products?
- How can secondary subject leaders and their teams share the design ideas and relevant sketches and diagrams produced by pupils in year 5 and 6?
- What tools and equipment are available in years 5 and 6 for pupils to use when performing practical tasks as part of their design work?
- What materials and components can pupils in their primary school work use when making different products?
- What kind of existing products do pupils investigate and analyse?
- How can secondary design teams work closely with primary design teachers to understand how pupils evaluate their own design ideas and products against their own design criteria?
- What key events and individuals do pupils have the opportunity to learn about and to what depth?
- What complex structures do pupils come into contact with when asked about the need to strengthen, stiffen or reinforce?
- How do you assess how well pupils can understand and use mechanical and electrical systems as part of production?
- What experience of computing in relation to programme, monitor and control of products do pupils have?

It is likely that primary schools have worked very hard in recent years to create a curriculum that embraces the arts and creative studies. It is a travesty for pupils if this is ignored. The visual, sensory and auditory nature of the work produced can easily be saved digitally so that each pupil has a portfolio of what they have designed, produced, investigated and evaluated. Where pupils can show their growing competences across a variety of media they grow in confidence, feel that what they have learnt is meaningful and are more motivated to want to learn and become masters of their own creativity.

BUILDING EXPRESSION IN KEY STAGE 3 ART AND DESIGN

Key stage 3 is a time when pupils can develop their skills and learn about art in its many different forms. Pupils can study, painting, sculpture, drawing and print making and photography, performance and digital media. There is also typography, graphics, textiles and ceramics which come under the umbrella of design and craft but are embraced within the art community.

There is a balance to be drawn for the subject leader and curriculum designer in relation to the practical skills that pupils need to develop and the academic disciplines that are related such as the history of art, aesthetics and art criticism. There is an imperative to be selective with the many different forms of art that might define a curriculum for key stage 3 (Ofsted 2023).

For some pupils, key stage 3 is the last time they will have the creative opportunities that art provides. To give pupils sufficient time to be creative and deepen their practical skills, they need more than the traditional hour lesson to plan, review, reflect and evaluate their own and others' work.

In key stage 3, the art curriculum should create the progression opportunities that will allow pupils to grow as artists, increasing their confidence and show that they are developing a range of skills in a variety of contexts and media. The team that plans sequential learning pathways here should have answers to these questions.

- What content do we want to include as part of a key stage 3 curriculum?
- How do we create a sequential pathway to ensure that pupils are deepening their learning cumulatively?
- What should be the ratio of practical learning and theoretical knowledge we want our pupils to have by the end of key stage 3?
- How do we ensure that our curriculum choices provide sufficient breadth and depth of learning so that pupils have a substantial opportunity to become confident and competent and find their own style in the areas of study we choose to teach?

The art curriculum does not specify how pupils will use the knowledge and skills they learn as part of a sequential plan, but it does set the boundaries for what pupils need to know. Pupils need to learn basic practical skills and knowledge that are an essential part of learning about art such as, mixing colours, line drawing, colour washing or sketching. What they then do with that knowledge can vary (Lonsdale 2018).

The Ofsted research review (2023) refers to this as divergent and convergent end points in the curriculum. There is an imperative to teach about art which is convergent and more prescribed. However, pupils also need the opportunity for free expression and time to work with techniques they have learnt about.

The National Curriculum sets out the knowledge that constitutes the convergent end points. There should be opportunities for pupils to use this knowledge to try out their own ideas and experiment with their growing understanding of new techniques. Art and design subject leaders need to be clear as to the end points they want their teachers to plan towards. These questions are a good starting point in determining how the vision for the art curriculum will translate into a sequential plan for deep learning.

- What knowledge do we want our pupils to acquire by the end of key stage 3?
- How do we build in time and space for pupils to practice their growing skills?
- What evidence can we draw on to show that there is a sequence to the learning and pupils are growing in understanding and depth of knowledge over time?

- How can we build the content so that pupils can re-encounter subject components in different contexts?
- How do we balance the need to teach the practical with ensuring pupils have a diverse range of experiences of different art media and artists?

Within the range of potential learning opportunities on offer, curriculum planners need to think carefully about the knowledge they want pupils to gain along the way. The substantive knowledge we have encountered in other subject areas gives way to a more theoretical and practical approach within art. Disciplinary knowledge remains an essential component of creativity where pupils can see how art has the power to create expression, mood and atmosphere. Knowledge in relation to arts education is contentious in terms of trying to quantify what should be taught in relation to creativity (Hyman 2017).

(Ofsted 2023) suggest that pupils will gain practical knowledge as they learn about materials and the different media. Pupils should encounter as many different 'areas of making' as possible (The National Society for Education in Art and Design 2019). These include, drawing, painting and sculpture, which are mentioned in the National Curriculum and others such as ceramics, textiles and photography which may form an element of the curriculum for many schools.

Defining the vision for the art curriculum requires a collective view on what should be covered in depth. The aim is to ensure pupils are not looking superficially at too wide a range of 'areas of making'. Pupils need time to work with varied materials, associated technical vocabulary and the use of different tools and techniques.

Alongside opportunities to work with tools, techniques and different media, pupils need to learn the theory of art. Decisions need to be made as to which artists, designers and sculptors pupils will learn about. Learning about art in this way, in key stage 3, gives pupils a foundation in how to look for meaning in works of art, how to interpret what the artist is trying to convey and provides an anchor as to the connections and changes in art over time (Myatt 2018).

Curriculum planners need to carefully consider the balance between theory and practice. The following questions are useful to support planning linked to the vision for a cohesive art curriculum that will allow for the practical learning and in sufficient time and depth of content for pupils to see how their own artistic development is mirrored in the work of others.

- How does the planned curriculum for teaching the theoretical knowledge dovetail into the practical skills pupils are developing over time?
- How can we work together to define the pedagogy that ensures pupils develop the ability to articulate meaning in the works they study?
- How can we encourage pupils to be interpretive and positively critical in their assessment of the art they learn about?
- How can we ensure that over the time pupils study the theory of art in key stage 3 they are able to contextualise art, craft and design traditions?

- What is the evidence that there is diversity in the choices made about the artists and artistic traditions studied as part of learning theory in any depth?
- How do we work together to build a rich tapestry of threads of theoretical knowledge that will inspire and engage pupils to deepen their appreciation and create for them a desire to continue to study art and practice their chosen media in key stage 4 and beyond?

Disciplinary knowledge in this context is about the value of a piece of artwork and the different feelings art can evoke. Disciplinary knowledge transcends different areas of making and focuses on purposes of art (Ofsted 2023). It is useful to build into planning, from as early as possible, opportunities for pupils to consider answers to such questions as:

- How does a piece of art make you feel?
- How can we judge what makes a piece of artwork valuable or worthwhile?
- How have certain design structures made a difference to a community?
- How has art reflected a particular culture, religious beliefs and the human condition?
- How has art depicted conflict?
- How do we judge the aesthetic value of a piece of art?
- What is it in certain works of art that changes our mood or sets the scene?

Theoretical and disciplinary knowledge are intertwined and the development of practical knowledge will allow the learner to make their own judgements about their growing competences. Where pupils are encouraged to talk together and with their teachers about their interpretations and feelings about art and design they are exposed to, and have created themselves, they can share their thoughts on the nature of art, the value individuals place on pieces of artwork, the style of different artists and the purpose for which the artwork has been created (Ofsted 2023).

THE PATHWAYS INTO MUSIC APPRECIATION AND SKILLS FOR FUTURE STUDY

Music is a compulsory subject up until the end of key stage 3, but the quality of music education is variable and finding the expertise is sometimes difficult. The ability of pupils is also an issue, some are exposed to music because their parents pay for lessons, there is a musical tradition in the family or they are interested in contemporary music because of the influence of an older sibling, perhaps.

Pupils need to develop technically so that they can play an instrument, sing or use music technology. They must learn how musical components combine to construct musical sound and they must be able to express their appreciation and understanding of the quality of sound in music. The role of curriculum planning is to intertwine these three elements, technical, constructive and expressive into opportunities to perform, compose and listen to music (Table 9.1).

Learning about music is progressive and requires teachers and their subject leaders to build sequential pathways that help pupils to become better at their musical endeavour of choice.

Table 9.1 Interweaving the technical, the constructive and the expressive within the music curriculum

Technical competence	Constructive	Expressive
Controlling sound	Knowing the dimensions or elements of music	Depends on highly developed technical expertise
Developing fine motor skills	Applying knowledge of different components	Requires extensive listening opportunities
Ability to listen actively	Knowing the boundaries and ranges of chosen concepts	Using the components of composition
Creating composition	Learning sequences	Understanding the wider culture from which the music derives
Improvising	Consolidating	Understanding musical theory
Sequencing knowledge	Creating music	Knowing the power of emotion in music
Practicing	Composing	Allowing autonomy in expression
Music vocabulary	Harmony	
Reading and decoding musical notation		
Developing automaticity		

Pupils can't retain the knowledge required to learn the piano, for instance, by studying it for one term only, they must practice and build their skills and knowledge over an extended period. The development of musical ability is about creating the conditions for the learning to become second nature and move into the long-term memory. The constraints of the secondary curriculum with its many priorities won't provide sufficient time for all pupils to become proficient in the playing of a musical instrument (Lovell 2020).

Music education must fight for its place at the curriculum table. With competing priorities, creating the right amount of lesson time to develop pupils' competence as well as teaching a range of enriching musical experiences is difficult to achieve. It is important that curriculum planners:

- consider the quality of the content of the music curriculum that will ensure music is seen as an essential part of a broad and balanced curriculum offer;
- ensure there is time for pupils to develop their procedural knowledge if they choose to learn to play a musical instrument or learn to sing or compose;
- ensure teachers are aware of the constraints of music on a pupil's working memory and should ensure there is sufficient time for pupils to consolidate and deepen their learning over time;
- know that practice is an essential element of a music curriculum and should be built into the plan for music;
- create opportunities to ensure music education is extended by including it as a part of cultural literacy.

Music must retain its place as an asset to the secondary curriculum. There is such potential to enhance the learning for all pupils through cultural literacy and many opportunities to hear music, see how music is an essential element of film and other forms of theatrical performance and how it is celebrated across all cultures. Music has profound links with all religions, there are links to cultural festivals and celebrations. There are opportunities for collaboration with the history department where music plays a leading role in the cultural understanding of certain historical events and can be the backdrop to a period of time with all its heritage, characters and events (Lovell 2020; Ofsted 2021).

DESIGN TECHNOLOGY A UNIQUE CONDUIT FOR INVENTION, DESIGN AND TECHNICAL SKILL

Technology is evolving and the subject leader must create a meaningful curriculum that will equip pupils with a deeper understanding of design and its impact on all our lives.

Ofsted in their research into curriculum design ask:

- What do teachers think is their objective in teaching their subject? (intent)
- How likely is it that the teaching methods used will deliver the teacher's objectives for the subject? (implementation)
- What is the potential impact of the course of study on the pupil? (impact)

Design technology, as with other practical subjects, requires pupils to focus on procedural knowledge and the potential to design and make a product, cook a meal or design an outfit. There is also the need to consider the conceptual knowledge that underpins purpose. Pupils need to have exposure to knowledge of materials, the processes involved in manufacturing, areas of functionality, design processes and understand how to be constructively critical and judge the impact a product is likely to have.

Barlex et al. (2017) talk about the big ideas in design technology as essential elements of a broad and balanced curriculum. These ideas describe design technology's fundamental nature and the conceptual knowledge that underpins the subject.

- Through design technology, people develop technologies and products to intervene in the natural and made worlds.
- Design technology uses knowledge, skill and understanding from itself and a wide range of other sources, especially but not exclusively science and maths.
- There are always many possible and varied solutions to technological and product development challenges, some of which will meet these challenges better than others.
- The worth of technologies and products developed by people is a matter of judgement.
- Technologies and products always have unintended consequences beyond intended benefit which cannot be fully predicted by those who develop them.

(Barlex et al. 2017)

The secondary design technology curriculum should be planned to use increasingly sophisticated resources. The development of the skills and abilities will be nurtured if the equipment and environment allows for the design and production of useful products. There are several elements to the design technology potential in a school such as product design, textiles, electronics, engineering, graphics and food technology. Developing the potential of pupils through teaching should allow them to be creative and use their imagination across all these areas.

Design technology has a place within the context of creativity and expressive arts but could just as easily have a place in other faculty groups. The STEM agenda includes science, technology, engineering and mathematics. The overlap here is obvious. A focus on design linked to projects that have a scientific basis or are linked to existing or emerging technologies is a vehicle for pupils to develop skills as problem solvers and critical thinkers.

There is now STEAM, the A standing for art. STEM exists to promote innovation and analytical thinking in science and the other subjects within the STEM family. Adding in the arts, it is argued, provides opportunities for pupils to be analytical and creative. Adding the arts to the STEM family makes curriculum sense if we are looking to create a holistic offer that creates for pupils the opportunity to develop as designers, thinkers and problem solvers. Embracing the arts gives pupils the freedom to capture the possibilities and cascade the potential of technological and scientific progress.

OVERLAPPING CONCEPTS IN THE CREATIVE SUBJECTS

Each of the creative subjects stands alone as a curriculum area. Where pupils find their niche or realise their talent for a particular area of study, then it is essential that it is nurtured. There must be a balance between creating such opportunities across the creative subjects.

Equally, such subjects are dependent on each other and provide many opportunities for collaboration in topic or themed activity. Pupils can work together to share ideas, learn from each other and work out how to create roles for a team or group. Pupils learn to be resilient, accept that sometimes things go wrong and need to be rethought, redrawn or discarded altogether.

Pupils might work to put on a play, a concert, design a garden, build a piece of furniture, organise a careers fair, make Christmas cards and toys to sell for charity, make clothes for a fashion show, make a film or a video, design a new board game and so on. All these activities require a combination of skills and knowledge from across the different arts subjects. Through this kind of process, pupils will develop an understanding of how to plan, how to draft and redraft. They will act as designer and as critic and have opportunities to share, solve problems, learn about time constraints and work together in the pursuit of a collective goal.

They will have to be sure of their audience and whether what they are planning or making is fit for purpose and appropriate in a given context. They will learn how to work safely and be aware of the safety of others. They will also learn about the constraints on them in relation to resources, materials, time, the contribution of others and finding alternatives when what they need isn't available. All the skills and knowledge they will gain here are needed for work and life.

It is important that any integrated programme of learning defines its purpose and is in line with the school's vision and curriculum intent. Ofsted talked about theme-based learning in a presentation focusing on their development work for the then new inspection framework

(Harford, 2017). There are many examples of different approaches such as cross curricular learning, integrated topics and imaginative learning projects. However, it is important to have a clear understanding of how the grouping of subjects will enhance the learning for all pupils. These questions may help where individuals from different subjects work together to plan a theme-based approach.

- What are the key skills, knowledge and learning that will define the end points for the topic?
- How will teachers work out who does what as part of the teaching and support process?
- How do we keep subject specific learning distinct as part of the process?
- What subject matter can we combine in supporting pupils to make connections and deepen their understanding?
- How do we ensure that pupils know which elements of different subjects their learning contributes to?
- How do we assess the learning in relation to outcomes we want to see as a result of pupils working together to achieve through a theme-based approach?
- How do we assess the learning from the individual subjects that been a part on the process?

INCREASING BREADTH AND DEPTH OF LEARNING – PEDAGOGY AND PROGRESSION

The aim for any practical subject is to ensure that pupils make progress through the incremental development of a range of skills linked to creative endeavour. Pupils need the opportunity to build confidence in their ability, to experience different media, interpret different ideas and forms and choose their own media with which to create. They should feel safe in the knowledge that they can create and experiment without fear of ridicule or disapproval. Pupils need encouragement to evaluate their own work as well of that of others and understand the process as well as the product that emerges from it.

Many of the techniques and skills pupils will learn are medium-specific but many transcend individual subjects. Providing pupils with the space and the time to link new learning to what they already know helps pupils towards greater sophistication and deeper conceptual understanding. They need to be creating, refining and interpreting and they need to think critically about theirs and others' work and understand the social and cultural contexts within which it sits.

For pupils to make progress, planning must be sequenced and carefully structured to ensure opportunities to incrementally develop practical skills and knowledge. We need to define the pedagogical skills required to allow pupils to:

- explore different approaches and techniques and use different materials;
- work with different techniques, materials and processes to know more about how they impact on the work of other artists and on their growing ability to make use of them;
- celebrate the power of creative endeavour and understand social and cultural differences;

- communicate their own feelings about how art, music, design or other media make them feel and affect their mood;
- give pupils the opportunity to find their own voice in order to give their own critical interpretation of the arts;
- give and receive constructive feedback about their work and that of others, suggesting areas for improvement or change;
- make connections with their own work and that of others and understand the context within which the work has been constructed or created;
- share their emotions in relation to how artists and designers have depicted the mood of the time, the emotions of a situation or the context to which they are attempting to convey.

In order to give pupils the time and opportunity to combine their skills and knowledge to express their emotions, feel free to be as creative as they can be and use their imagination to be innovative and different, we must allow pupils to:

- understand that their creative endeavours should reflect their audiences and the purpose to which they want the work to lead to;
- grow in their ability to use a range of different techniques and slowly become more competent and technically attuned;
- develop a sound knowledge of design and learn how to be critical, reflective and ready to make changes;
- become increasingly confident to share and exhibit for a familiar and an unfamiliar audience;
- be able to absorb constructive criticism and use positive feedback to improve and continue to grow;
- know how to use the tools and techniques used in their work safely and with dexterity and always understand the proximity and needs of others.

Creativity is a powerful word in the lexicon of learning. It is a gift that needs to be nurtured. For the teacher, it encompasses how to develop pedagogy that can allow creative minds to flourish. For pupils, it is giving them the confidence to try, the dexterity to make a start, the knowledge of technique and the opportunity to learn the practical skills they need to develop over time. The vision for the highest quality outcomes must come from a deep desire to offer pupils the opportunity to express their creativity and to feel confident to develop their artistic or design flair.

THE ARTS AT KEY STAGE 4 – BUILDING A FUTURE FOR CREATIVITY

The changes to the curriculum in 2014, with the introduction of the English Baccalaureate, have had a significant impact on the number of pupils taking up subjects in the arts in key stage 4. The EBacc is the composite qualification outcome that pupils will achieve on completion of their GCSEs at key stage 4. The EBacc consists of English, maths, science, a language and one of the humanities subjects. This cluster of subjects is meant to represent academic rigour. Pupils must also choose from three other subjects that may or may not include something from the arts suite.

A petition created by a drama teacher from Essex and called 'Include expressive arts subjects in the EBacc' with over 102,000 signatures triggered a debate in parliament in 2016. The ensuing debate focused on how important the arts are to our economy and how skills shortages were a feature of many creative businesses. There were over 200 arts organisations took part in the debate all who showed solidarity in the opinion that current education policy, and specifically the EBacc, risks damaging Britain's rich history of creativity and cultural achievement.

The lack of emphasis on the creative subjects as part of the EBacc does not preclude pupils taking these subjects at key stage 4. In fact, the White Paper published by the Department for Culture, Media and Sport says, 'All state funded schools must provide a broad and balanced curriculum that promotes the spiritual, moral, cultural, mental and physical development of pupils. Experiencing and understanding culture is integral to education. Knowledge of great works of art, great music, great literature and great plays and of their creators is an important part of every child's education' (DCMS White Paper 2016).

Ofsted want to see a broad and balanced curriculum offer which would not be possible without the inclusion of some element of culture and creativity. Therefore, in creating the school vision, the curriculum intent should, and must, include the creative subjects as part of option choices for GCSE. The skills and knowledge that pupils gain through the study of any of the arts provides them with wide-reaching skills linked to many other subjects that are highly relevant for higher education or work (Ofsted 2024).

Designing the curriculum for the arts must start with a look at creativity and its potential in developing the whole person. A rich and deep curriculum offer should contain opportunities for pupils to develop creatively over the whole of their time in secondary school. There should be equitable opportunities to include all disciplines. There should be clear pathways towards greater complexity, the development of deep knowledge and skills and pupils should, by the time they start a programme towards GCSE, be able to work independently and collaboratively. They should have the opportunity to experience seeing artistic and design media in other contexts, learn to appreciate and be critical and share their own growing talent.

CONCLUSION

Creativity is at the heart of our nation. Our creative industries are some of the best in the world and we continue to be leaders in design, art, theatre and music. It is to our schools that we must firstly look to ignite the passion that will make our pupils lifelong lovers of a wide range of cultural endeavours. It is also essential that we nurture the talent of those pupils who have a gift for painting, the talent to play a musical instrument, or the flair to design and make innovative products.

We must create the vision to ensure we plan and deliver the most ambitious curriculum we can with the resources we have. We must also build the self-esteem of pupils so that they know their worth, are rich with cultural literacy and want to take their creative flair further than the end of key stage 3.

Ten Top Tips

1. Make it an essential element of departmental policy to share with primary school partners what pupils have learnt and produced in key stage 2 especially in years 5 and 6.
2. Create opportunities for a review of the strengths and expertise within departments and across the suite of arts subjects.
3. Focus on thinking carefully about the whole school vision and how creativity has an impact on pupils' skills and attributes across all their learning.
4. Share with colleagues across the curriculum where the expressive arts dovetail with other subjects and areas of the curriculum.
5. Give pupils time to share their own ideas about how music, art, design, film or other media make them feel.
6. Be clear about the balance to be drawn between the practical skills pupils will develop and the theoretical knowledge they need to have.
7. Create time for practice, reflection and critical appreciation and remember that learning new techniques can create cognitive overload.
8. Ensure pupils are given opportunities to enhance their cultural literacy with visits to galleries, theatre trips and other opportunities to experience culture at first hand.
9. Have deep discussions with departmental colleagues and those in other practical subjects about what pupils should know and be able to do at significant end points.
10. Create deliberate strategies to encourage pupils to want to continue their creative and artistic endeavours into key stage 4 and the study of relevant GCSEs.

REFERENCES

Barlex, D. Givens, N. and Steeg, T. (2017) *The Curriculum: A D & T Perspective on the Ofsted Curriculum Survey (2017) D & T by D & T.*

DfE (2014) *Programmes of Study for Art & Design Key Stage 2 and 3.* London, DfE.

DfE (2014a) *Programmes of Study for Music Key Stage 2 and 3.* London, DfE.

DfE (2014b) *Programmes of Study for Design & Technology Key Stage 2 and 3.* London, DfE.

Department of Culture, Media and Sports (2016) *The Culture White Paper.* London, DCMS.

Harford, S. (2017) *Curriculum: Intent, Implementation and Impact.* Development work for the new inspection framework. London, Ofsted.

Hyman, P. (2017) *Anatomy of Learning*. Londoon, Royal Society of Arts Journal Issue 3.
HWB (2019) *Welsh Curriculum for the Expressive Arts (2019)*. Cardiff, Welsh Assembly Government.
Lonsdale, M. (2018) *Knowledge: A Dirty Word in Arts Education*. London, Royal Society of Arts.
Lovell, O. (2020) *Cognitive Load in Action*. Woodbridge, John Catt Educational.
Myatt, M. (2018) *The Curriculum Gallimaufry to Coherence*. Woodbridge, John Catt Educational.
Myatt, M. and Tomsett, J. (2021) *Huh Curriculum Conversations between Subject and Senior Leaders*. Woodbridge, John Catt Educational.
Ofsted (2021) *Research Review into Music*. London, Ofsted.
Ofsted (2023) *Research Review into Art and Design Education*: London, Ofsted.
Ofsted (2024) *Ofsted Handbook for Schools* London, Ofsted.
STEM Learning website. Available online: http://www.STEM.org.uk
STEM to STEAM *The 'Arts' and Its Importance in STEM Education Irwindale USA*. Available online: https://steamacademies.org/understanding-stem-and-steam-education/
The National Society for Education in Art and Design (2019) *Parallel Curriculum*, London.

10

PHYSICAL, EMOTIONAL, SOCIAL AND CULTURAL LEARNING FOR WELL-BEING AND MENTAL HEALTH

Contents

CREATING CURRICULUM PATHWAYS FOR PHYSICAL, EMOTIONAL, SOCIAL AND CULTURAL LEARNING

To learn, pupils must be physically, mentally, emotionally and socially secure. Where this is not the case, pupils' life chances are diminished. It is through positive curriculum planning that we ensure that pupils are ready to learn, feel safe within the school environment and have as many opportunities as possible to develop strength and competence in physical activity.

In the Ofsted handbook (2024), social, moral, spiritual and cultural (SMSC); personal, social, health and economic education (PSHE) and relationships and sex education (RSE) are discussed separately as part of the section on Evaluating Personal Development. However, they are not and should never be seen as separate to the main body of the curriculum. There are many opportunities to weave these essential elements through other subjects and extra-curricular activities.

Physical education (PE), on the other hand, is a compulsory subject and requires time to be given to the teaching of it in both key stages 3 and 4. We know that physical activity enhances well-being, is health giving and provides pupils with opportunities to develop fine motor skills, learn rules, strategies, tactics and skills such as team working, resilience and evaluation.

The curriculum vision and planning should embrace the physical and the quest to develop healthy, confident culturally and socially aware learners who can succeed in school and beyond. It is essential that pupils develop the self-esteem to become competitive, empathetic, able to fail before they succeed, take risks with their learning and embrace different roles and responsibilities as part of their growing understanding of their place in society.

PHYSICAL EDUCATION AND THE SECONDARY CURRICULUM

Pupils should arrive in their secondary school having developed a broad range of skills in primary school. Teachers of PE in year 7 should consider how pupils have already learnt how to communicate, collaborate and compete through physical activity. They should be able to reflect on their own ability in the sports they have learnt and evaluate and recognise their own success.

The National Curriculum for PE aims to ensure that pupils:

- develop competence to excel in a broad range of physical activities;
- are physically active for sustained periods of time;
- engage in competitive sports and activities;
- lead healthy, active lives (DfE 2014a).

Many pupils will exceed timetabled PE time because they have an aptitude or love for a particular sport. Some parents will have the time, will and motivation to support extra-curricular activities and schools will have teams in sports they favour. There will be inter-school competitions and matches. For other pupils, they will be happy with the bare minimum and if possible, try to avoid that.

The vision for PE should encompass not just a range of sports and other activities but also how pupils understand the value of physical activity in ensuring they will lead healthy lives. It should be possible to show the links between physical health and what we eat, how exercise affects our sleeping patterns and the functions of our brains and memory.

Curriculum planners need to look at how curriculum design decisions can impact on pupils' physical and emotional development. It is acknowledged in the research review series for PE (Ofsted 2023) that the subject draws on a range of disciplines including physiology, psychology and sociology.

Beyond physical activity, PE is about pupils' self-esteem, their identity, if they support a local football, rugby or cricket club for instance. It is about pupils' admiration and ambitions as they dream of emulating sporting heroes. It has the potential to teach pupils about fairness, equal opportunities, sportsmanship, etiquette and empathy.

One of the most powerful messages for me was seeing the video that won London the Olympic games in 2012. It asked the question, what can sport do for the world and focused on the children who could be the successful sportspeople of the future? Sport is unique in its potential to inspire and foster the dreams and hopes of our young.

PE IN KEY STAGE 3 – LAYING DOWN THE FOUNDATIONS

Key stage 3 is a time of consolidation in the development of expertise and techniques across a range of sports and physical activity. Pupils should have the opportunity to try out new skills, experience sports and activities they haven't tried before and deepen their understanding of the rules and techniques of the sports and games they experience.

For some, they will go on to take a formal qualification in key stage 4 either a GCSE or a vocational course. Key stage 3 should be carefully planned to nurture the potential of all pupils and give them the chance to show their competence in a given sport or physical activity such as dance or gymnastics.

Key stage 3 curriculum planners should focus on these questions linked to the National Curriculum subject content for PE (DfE 2014a).

- What expertise do we have within the PE department to create a broad and rich curriculum offer that will embrace all pupils?
- How can we make the best use of the facilities we have in school and in the wider community?
- What is our preferred approach, a thematic approach where the focus is on teamwork for example or where pupils try several different sports over time?
- How can we create a sequenced curriculum for various aspects of PE that develops pupils' techniques and sees their performance improve over time?

- What is available locally that will allow us to plan outdoor and adventurous activities which present intellectual and physical challenges?
- How do we nurture talent and promote positive attitudes to supporting pupils who have potential?
- How do we build pupils' self-esteem, resilience and the ability to reflect on their performance and how it can be improved through our own professional development as coaches?

A themed approach is explained in a case study from Stratford upon Avon School in Myatt and Tomsett (2021). They follow a traditional model of teaching one sport and then move to another sport. The themes as they work through activities such as athletics, cricket, football and handball are:

expectations and standards;
fundamentals and movements;
desire to improve;
teamwork;
commitment and fitness.

These work on more than one level for me. Pupils who are good at one of the sports develop these important life skills. Those who may not excel in terms of skill can still show their understanding of the need for high expectations and the qualities of effective team working. The emphasis on fitness and healthy living may help many to be more self-aware and determined to change their lifestyle.

Healthy participation in sports and other physical activity is a national curriculum aim. Key stage 3 is a turbulent time for many young learners, their bodies are changing, their identity and place within their friendship groups and their self-belief can mean they are finding their time in school troubling. PE can either be a salvation or a trial. There are many challenges both for those who are instinctively active and talented and those who are not.

Pupils disinclined towards PE can be enticed through raising their awareness of the power of physical activity to enhance health and well-being, such as weight loss or toning the body. For those who want to study PE towards a qualification outcome, it is important that they are given the opportunity to become competent and confident in the techniques they are learning and can apply them across different sports and physical activity.

Pupils need sufficient opportunity to develop their own techniques and be able to explain what it is that makes certain moves, tactics or actions successful. In preparation for the deeply theoretical content of the GCSE, pupils should be introduced to the physiology of exercise, effective team participation, the setting of SMART targets, the use of data, how to prevent injury and the importance of perseverance and fitness.

PE AND KEY STAGE 4

PE in key stage 4 is statutory for all. Pupils should be encouraged to see the inclusion of PE as a way of ensuring that they remain healthy, able to concentrate and to learn. They should be encouraged to make informed choices about what kind of physical activity is most appropriate and how it can support them in their quest to be healthy and to learn well.

Those planning this programme should consider the following questions:

- What opportunities are there for pupils to take part in team and individual games?
- How are pupils building on their learning from key stage 3 in terms of using and developing tactics and strategies to overcome opponents?
- How is the curriculum planned to allow for a choice of other activities such as gymnastics, athletics and dance?
- What is planned to encourage pupils to take part in outdoor and adventurous activities which ensure pupils are exposed to intellectual and physical challenges?
- What is planned to encourage pupils to develop team building skills to strengthen their ability to problem solve, trust others and work co-operatively?
- What feedback techniques are effective at creating opportunities for pupils to evaluate their own performance and what they need to do to continue to develop their competences?
- What links are there with outside sports clubs and the wider community that encourage pupils to take part in competitive sport and activities?

(DfE 2014a)

The potential to develop transferable skills and capabilities that transcend the PE curriculum abound. For instance, opportunities to combine a geography field trip with climbing a mountain, canoeing along a fast-flowing river or an orienteering trek with map and compass could be part of a planned PE strategy that embraces the wider curriculum.

In key stage 4, pupils could be introduced to other activities they may pursue in later life such as Pilates, yoga or spin. The concentration should be on the pupil and their interests and needs. Emphasise that the approach is towards their own self-improvement, personal fulfilment and enrichment.

The content of the PE GCSE is the same across exam boards. Each will have certain elements that are explored in different ways. For those who are taking a GCSE in physical education, the stakes are high. Much of the content is theoretical, has links to anatomy, physiology and psychology and has a written examination and the requirement to demonstrate physical performance in different activities. The potential to combine this optional subject with biology or psychology may support pupils to reinforce their learning. For those pupils who have career aspirations in the world of sport, the qualification structure looks amazing.

There is potential in creating a scheme of work that builds the declarative with the procedural so that the learning is practical and the theory flows for the pupil out of the physical activity that has sustained their interest in wanting to study the subject at this level.

Declarative knowledge is factual knowledge which in PE focuses on movement, rules and tactics in team games, the strategies a team or an individual might engage with and how they ensure they are fit and ready to undertake a given physical activity. Alongside this, pupils need procedural knowledge to focus on why they have succeeded or failed within a particular sport or activity.

For GCSE, pupils will also need to have a depth of theoretical knowledge in order that they begin to develop a deeper understanding of the human body and mind (DfE 2014b). There are four main areas that are the same across all specifications:

- Physical factors affecting performance
- Socio-cultural influences
- Practical performance
- Analysis and evaluation of performance (DfE 2014b)

The GCSE should equip pupils with the ability to demonstrate and apply relevant knowledge and understanding of what affects performance in a wide range of sports. Pupils will deepen their vocabulary and use it to demonstrate their growing competence in sports science. They should gain the ability to analyse performance data and draw conclusions that are supported by evidence. They should also be able to use a wide range of techniques and strategies to demonstrate skill and controlled performance (OCR 2023).

FOOD TECHNOLOGY AND HEALTHY EATING – COOKING AND NUTRITION

The curriculum for food technology should promote the importance of healthy eating and the well-being agenda. Food is a part of the design technology programme of study under the heading, cooking and nutrition. The first emphasis within the specification is to 'understand and apply the principles of nutrition and health' (DfE 2014c). It is, therefore, a much wider remit than learning how to cook several dishes and becoming competent in a range of cooking techniques, although this is important.

Space is needed for pupils to develop their skills in cooking food for themselves as it is an essential element of the National Curriculum in key stage 3. The design technology programme of study explicitly demands that pupils:

- cook a repertoire of predominantly savoury dishes so that they are able to feed themselves and others a healthy and varied diet;
- become competent in a range of cooking techniques;
- understand the source, seasonality and characteristics of a broad range of ingredients (DfE 2013).

There are opportunities to dovetail the experience of cooking with a wider focus on healthy eating. For example, consider a rich scheme of work that allows pupils to develop their skills in the kitchen and broaden their understanding of food in a wide variety of other subjects and contexts.

In terms of cooking and nutrition, the scheme of work should encompass a sequence of learning that allows pupils to develop a deeper understanding the importance of food to their lives. The plan should ensure that ingredients, and recipes studied come from the major food groups alongside the guidelines for a healthy diet.

Table 10.1 The potential for integrating food across the curriculum

English	**Maths**	**Science**
Descriptions of food in literature Descriptions of how to cook a recipe Discussions about techniques and use of ingredients Food in poetry	Budgeting for a meal Costs of ingredients Measuring ingredients Ratio within shorting of pastry Calorific value	Food safety Growing healthy crops Heat transference Conduction and convection How radiation works The reaction of ingredients as a result of cooking and blending methods Chemical properties of food Shelf life of food
Geography	**History**	**Religious education**
Where do different foods originate? Trade routes and the implications of food miles Organic and conventional farming Sustainability Food from different countries Environmental issues related to food	Food through the ages Food as part of culture and status The history of tea, coffee, spices, etc... Rationing in the first and second world wars Slavery and food production Changes in how we shop over time	Traditions from different religions Festivals, ceremonies and rituals Food in the bible, the Queran or other sacred works
Music	**Art and Design**	**Languages**
Music to create moods and atmosphere in restaurants Choice of music to go with food at festivals, traditional events and rituals **Drama** Food in plays and dramas Role-play of food demonstrations and cookery programmes The influence of food in film now and in the past	Photography for cookery books The history of food in art Artistic design in food preparation Food colouring in paint and dyes Food packaging Marketing over time Advertising on the television and film	Vocabulary of food Understanding the culture of food from its country of origin Ordering food in another language **Physical Education** Metabolism and different foods Food and nutrition Different foods needed to boost energy Food and healthy eating

The current concern in many English schools is the prevalence of poor diet and unhealthy eating patterns. The school can play its part by stressing the importance of maintaining a balanced diet and the kinds of foods that will provide them with the nutrition to enhance their well-being, control their weight and ensure they maintain a healthy lifestyle.

From age 11, pupils go through a series of changes to their bodies and to their understanding of the relationships they forge, the identity they want to convey and the image they want to project. Social media has a lot to answer for in shaping the ideas, values and beliefs that pupils might want to aspire to. It is important that the curriculum supports pupils to make informed choices to help them to be healthy in body and mind and can forge good habits in their choices of what they eat, how they exercise and how they maintain a healthy lifestyle Public Health England (2015).

Linking food to the wider curriculum exposes pupils to the importance of a healthy diet and the influence food plays in all aspects of society and culture. This can extend from local food businesses, chefs and restaurants to the wider influence of food in religion, cultural traditions and festivals.

There are many examples of where food spills out of the design and technology context and is an integral part of learning in other curriculum areas. Above at the end of the section on food is a Table 10.1 of ideas.

PERSONAL DEVELOPMENT WITHIN AND BEYOND THE CURRICULUM

PE and food technology are part of the National Curriculum. They are included here because they are an integral part of the personal development of pupils as part of their progress towards healthy adulthood. The rest of the chapter looks at the other aspects of personal development that schools must plan for in a rich and deep curriculum.

In the Ofsted handbook (2024), 'evaluating personal development' is one of four main categories they want schools to focus on. There is an acknowledgement that it is unlikely that the impact of the provision for personal development will be assessable during pupils' time in school. It is also acknowledged that schools are crucial in preparing pupils for their adult lives, teaching them how to engage with society and providing them with opportunities to do so.

Creating evidence that there is a clear thread throughout the curriculum in all subjects that contributes to pupils' personal development is essential. Use the questions below to consider your school's approach. Share with colleagues, what is working well and what could be improved.

- How do we ensure that all pupils have access to extra-curricular activities outside school?
- What evidence can we draw that we emphasise the stated British values of democracy, individual liberty, the rule of law and mutual respect and tolerance?
- What actions do we take to promote equality of opportunity so that all pupils understand that difference is positive and every individual is unique?
- How do we share the values we have in relation to ensuring an inclusive environment for all our pupils?
- What evidence can we draw on that the school culture ensures pupils develop as confident, resilient and knowledgeable individuals?
- How does the culture within the school develop pupils' unique and individual characters and personal traits so that they learn well, are motivated to accept challenge and behave with integrity?

- What strategies do we have in place to keep our pupils well-informed as to the dangers of online and offline risk and inappropriate use of mobile technology and social media?
- What do we have in place to support pupils who may need help in relation to any threats posed by mobile technology or other media?
- What is in place to ensure pupils have the most appropriate and age-related relationships and sex education?
- How robust and enlightening for pupils is our careers information education, advice and guidance?

Relationships, sex and health education (RSHE) is part of the compulsory, statutory curriculum. Ofsted are looking for evidence that schools have specifically addressed issues relating to sexual harassment, online abuse and sexual violence. This is a sensitive area and those involved in the development of the curriculum will need specialist CPD to guide them in what to include, the pedagogy that will best support pupils to understand the significance to their lives, their well-being and their mental health. Here it is often the pastoral team who will be most involved in the development of a sequenced RSHE programme. Their role is critical in alerting others to potential risk factors and safeguarding issues, such as domestic abuse, pupils own mental-health and the potential for exploitation (GOV.UK 2021).

The concepts linked to SMSC should, in my opinion, never be timetabled separately from other subjects. The curriculum is sufficiently crowded already and these specific elements are integral to many aspects of learning across the curriculum (DfE 2014c).

Spirituality does not mean that pupils have to be religious. There are opportunities for pupils to consider their own beliefs and spirituality through their exposure to different kinds of religious education, events in history or wonders of the natural world. All teachers should pay close attention, within their schemes of work, to supporting pupils with their own reflections on belief, religious or otherwise.

Morality should be an integral part of all learning. There are opportunities to teach about the difference between right and wrong, the consequences of poor behaviour and unfortunate actions in literature such as in Shakespeare, Dickens, Woolf or Trollope. History has a wealth of examples and profound opportunities for debate and discussion. The Christian bible has so many stories that could support profound and deep conversations and the passion that arises when something goes awry in a competitive game of sport is fascinating. Morality is also about the pupils themselves; how do they deal with the consequences of their own actions and behaviours and that of their peers?

School is a society and many opportunities exist for pupils to develop their social skills. Creating opportunities for pupils to work as a team will encourage independent learning and enquiry. Pupils should learn how to interact with their peers, to socialise with pupils with different views and ideas, other religions or ethnic groups and varying socio-economic backgrounds. Going beyond school and into the wider community pupils should be encouraged to be a part of their local community and to widen their horizons to look further afield.

Within the social element of SMSC, pupils are expected to understand the fundamentals of democracy, the rule of law, the belief in individual liberty and have respect and demonstrate tolerance of other faiths and beliefs. The teaching of such concepts can easily be accessed through the National Curriculum subjects. For example, how our democracy works in the UK can be viewed through the lens of its inception as part of what happened in the reign of the Stuarts. The fight against communism and the term McCarthyism in the USA in the 1950s or the rise of Nazism in Germany during the 1930s. What has been happening in Ukraine, in the Middle East and in North Africa all demonstrate the issues that require us to question what is right and how opposing factions see things differently. The story of the Suffragettes, the American civil war and the fight to abolish slavery or the rise of the anti-apartheid movement all provide rich opportunities for pupils to look at injustice and how they can live their lives through tolerance and understanding of difference, of opposing views and a deep conviction for right against wrong.

Cultural development is a curriculum area that has huge implications for schools. Exposure to culture differs from pupil to pupil. It depends on their parents and others around them. For some, culture abounds, a house full of books, opportunities to go to the theatre and the cinema, travel to other countries and so on. For others, it is quite different.

Where these cultural influences are not available, there are opportunities for schools to help to close the gap. Pupils from different religions and backgrounds can share their traditions, recipes and stories. Pupils could bring to school traditional dress, share some of the rituals from outside school. They can talk about their country of origin. Field trips, art gallery and museum visits can be enlightening but need to be carefully planned to ensure that all pupils will be guided towards an understanding of why they are there and what they can gain from the visit.

There is so much available online, on television and on the radio to enrich the cultural world for pupils. Watching a film, listening to a podcast, listening to a debate on Question Time or Any Questions. Role play linked to questions that are contentious, difficult to resolve or simply interesting. Bringing the current debates to life can be enlightening and enriching.

SMSC is an essential element of the wider curriculum offer and should be seen as enriching and able to provide pupils with opportunities to deepen their learning and understanding of other elements of the taught curriculum. Leaders and curriculum planners must ensure the following.

- Due regard is given to the statutory guidance on RSHE including having a clear set out policy that has been designed in consultation with parents
- Clear strategies for training staff who will deliver the RSHE curriculum
- Appropriate support for pupils with SEND to have the same access to RSHE
- Pupils have age-appropriate awareness of the nine protected characteristics of, age, gender, race, disability, religion or belief, sexual orientation, gender reassignment, marriage or civil partnership, pregnancy and maternity
- Pupils know how to stay safe, including online
- Profound evidence that pupils SMSC development is sufficiently covered

CAREERS EDUCATION, INFORMATION, ADVICE AND GUIDANCE (CEIAG)

Here we have another statutory element of the curriculum very much to do with a pupil's well-being and future aspirations. Schools are required to provide effective careers education, information, advice and guidance (CEIAG) in line with the internationally recognised Gatsby Benchmarks (Table 10.2). These are:

Table 10.2 The Gatsby Benchmarks – these are amplified in the Gatsby Guidance Document

1	A stable careers programme
2	Learning from career and labour market information
3	Addressing the needs of each pupil
4	Linking curriculum learning to careers
5	Encounters with employers and employees
6	Experience of workplaces
7	Encounters with further and higher education
8	Personal guidance

THE GATSBY BENCHMARKS

In 2022, the statutory guidance relating to careers education (Section 45A of the Education Act 1997) was amended through the Skills and Post 16 Act (2022) to include a specific requirement that pupils be given advice and guidance on the opportunities available to them linked to technical education qualifications and apprenticeships (DfE 2022).

The change is specific in its requirement that pupils have at least 6 encounters between years 8 and 13 with employers, careers advisors, Local Authorities and education and training providers. The DfE have funded The Careers and Enterprise Company (https://www.careersandenterprise.co.uk/) to support schools to develop careers programmes in line with the Gatsby benchmarks and to allow pupils to explore the widest possible range of opportunities including technical qualifications and apprenticeships.

Youth Employment UK, in their Youth Voice survey (7), report that only 4% of young people start an apprenticeship when they leave year 11 Youth Employment UK (2019). The lack of emphasis on vocational routes at 16 is undoubtedly due to the focus on choices linked to the English Baccalaureate that do not encourage vocational learning at key stage 4. It is clear from the research and from the work undertaken by the Gatsby Foundation that all pupils need to have a wider view of what is available to them as they enter post-16 education (Gatsby 2014).

- The Gatsby benchmarks represent good practice.
- Schools should use the Gatsby Benchmarks to develop their plan for careers education from year 7 to year 11 or year 13.
- The Career's Plan should be published on every school website.
- Schools should provide destination data for all pupils for the three years after pupils leave school.
- Schools should have the support of the National Careers Service.
- Careers advisers within schools and from external sources should all have comprehensive training in how to support young people with careers information, advice and guidance.
- There should be more contact and support from employers and their representative organisations.
- There should be an employer representative on every board of school governors who takes a strategic interest in encouraging employer engagement.
- There should be opportunities for young people in schools to encounter young ambassadors from apprenticeships, colleges and universities who have the potential to

motivate and inspire young people because they are closer in age and may have come from similar backgrounds.

- Careers advisors should be drawn from a wide pool of both internal and external advisors who can provide independent and impartial advice.

Creating opportunities for pupils to talk about their own aspirations and dreams for the future will support them in their self-belief and well-being. Pupils could look at enterprise where they learn about finance, marketing, trends, products and services. All pupils should learn about time management, punctuality and reliability. Group work can help pupils develop as team players who work towards clearly defined goals and objectives.

In key stage 3, careers guidance can be embedded into teaching across a range of subjects. Exposure to potential careers in sports, food technology, history, geography and computer science can be applied across these subject areas. The advantage of fluency in a second or third language, the plethora of opportunity in the arts and time to focus on the STEM subjects can all enhance a range of career prospects. Exposure to businesses linked to learning is a part of the whole SMSC and PSHE agenda. Pupils should share their thoughts about the job roles of some of the people they know.

Elements of careers education in key stages 4 and 5 need careful planning and consideration. Pupils must have a careers interview and some exposure to the world of work through work experience. They should be encouraged to talk about their aspirations and ambitions for the future and be given every opportunity to explore what is available for them when they leave school in its widest context, college, university, apprenticeship or into some kind of work.

BUILDING SELF-ESTEEM THROUGH FOSTERING LEARNER VOICE AND POSITIVE AND EFFECTIVE SUPPORT AND FEEDBACK

The elements included in this chapter allow pupils to explore their own aspirations and emotions. It is here that pupils can delve into their own potential and investigate what will help them to make sense of being a teenager in a complex and ever-changing world. Where pupils can explore their feelings and emotions, they can become more self-regulated and recognise when they need to seek help and support.

The pedagogy that supports this must be about learner voice, with the teacher as a facilitator helping pupils to articulate their feelings, ambitions and concerns. Pupils need help to become self-aware, confident and motivated individuals who are prepared to take risks with their learning, find solutions and work together to make decisions, solve problems and discover themselves and their inner talents.

Pupils need to be an integral part of the process of developing as responsible citizens, becoming culturally literate and aware of their growing responsibility for their own bodies and the consequences of misuse or neglect of their own health and well-being. They need to understand the society they belong to, its social norms and the values and attitudes that constrain them. They also need to accept that other cultures may see things differently and learn tolerance and acceptance of difference.

To build a consensus of this across curriculum subjects, there must be professional dialogue. Each subject has a wealth of opportunities to ensure every pupil develops a positive sense of themselves and the skills and abilities to navigate their own goals and aspirations.

Developing learner voice is a powerful driver for school effectiveness. It is for them that the school exists. It is in the interest of the school to see all their pupils flourish. There have been many attempts and initiatives adopted by schools to embrace the creativity of pupils, they come and go because of the constraints of the accountability measures that relate to the EBacc and delivering statutory curriculum content.

Personal, Learning and Thinking Skills were popular in the late 1990s and were creatively framed by the National Strategies a government body set up to support standards in education (QCDA 2019). Carol Dweck's theories around Growth Mindset still have credibility in terms of research and practice (Dweck 2006). Guy Claxton's Building Learning Power and the four Ps of resilience, reflection, resourcefulness and reciprocity still have resonance (Claxton 2002). All have something in common. They stand alone from subject-specific learning and create a powerful framework for discussing how to develop the skills, traits and attributes that pupils will need for the whole of their lives.

It is the 'soft skills' that are at play here and we need to ensure that the pupil's voice is not lost in the clamour of subject knowledge. It is the professional conversations that teachers have that will ensure that these skills can be embedded successfully into subject learning and cross-curricular activities. They are never separate and always the goal for positive learning and achievement.

Finding ways to elicit creative and critical thinking are important in the process of shaping the skills pupils' need for life. The World Economic Forum's 'The Future of Jobs' report (2023) outlines ten skills required that individuals would need for jobs of the future.

1. Analytical thinking
2. Creative thinking
3. Resilience, flexibility and agility
4. Motivation and self-awareness
5. Curiosity and life-long learning
6. Technological literature
7. Dependability and attention to detail
8. Empathy and active listening
9. Leadership and social influence
10. Quality control

Creating the right pedagogy that enables pupils to find their voice and to feel that their learning is enhancing their potential and skills development is crucial. The focus across every subject should be to ensure that pupils can:

- make connections within subjects and across their learning in other subjects to see relevance and meaning;
- answer deep and searching questions that challenge them to find out more, justify their assumptions and their ideas;
- explore and investigate new thinking and different viewpoints and opinions;

- challenge others who may have different views, opinions or ideas;
- be resilient in the face of adversity or difficulties;
- stand out from the crowd and be different;
- be articulate in framing their thoughts and ideas;
- give and receive feedback positively and reflectively;
- work in harmony with others;
- know when it is necessary to practice to achieve;
- accept and embrace change as something that leads to learning;
- be creative and innovative with the academic and the practical;
- show initiative;
- make predictions, take risks and find solutions.

This is difficult for the teenager who has little to build on beyond their experience of primary school and the hidden curriculum that informs their life outside school. Creating conversations where teachers focus on the above list and find ways to engage pupils in how they can develop these soft skills as they learn is powerful professional development. Teachers need to know how to create pedagogy that will allow pupils to think critically about how they learn and what they need to progress and achieve.

Teachers can create the right conditions through focusing on the process that defines critical thinking, teachers need to support pupils to:

find out as much as possible about the subject they are studying or investigating;
comprehend or understand the key points, assumptions, arguments being presented;
analyse how information, ideas and new innovations fit together and relate to each other;
make comparisons with other issues and events and consider how change would have an impact;
synthesise and draw together conclusions to demonstrate understanding;
evaluate how situations arise, how change has had an impact, the consequence of a decision made, whether a cause is worth pursuing;
justify decisions made or arguments for and against and the reasons for choices made.

They are the skills pupils must demonstrate at GCSE and the sooner they can develop them the more likely they are to be adept by the time they reach year 11. Careful steps are needed to ensure these skills can be developed and practised from year 7 onwards.

THE PEDAGOGY OF COACHING IN THE PURSUIT OF LEARNER VOICE, SELF-BELIEF AND REFLECTION

To close this chapter, it is fitting to consider the role of coaching in the pursuit of creating pupils who leave school with a true sense of self-worth and who have had the opportunity to articulate what they want to achieve in life.

One type of coaching is the relationship between elite sports players and those that help them to win. It is through coaching that a relationship of trust and respect is built so that the sportsperson knows they will improve if they take on board the counsel they are given. Even in this context, it is unlikely that the coach will give advice, be directive or judgemental, they will find a way to model good practice so that the recipient is open to trying out something new or different.

The characteristics of coaching in this context are best described by looking at the four Cs of positive youth development (Côté and Gilbert, 2009). These are:

- Competence;
- Confidence;
- Connection;
- Character.

A fifth, that of caring and compassion (Lerner et al. 2005) needs careful consideration as to how coaching goes beyond its use in sport. Coaching is a powerful CPD tool. The teacher is facilitating the learning rather than simply teaching through the didactic imparting of knowledge. It is a process where the teacher must listen actively to pupils, their needs and their aspirations and find ways to immerse them in their own understanding of how they learn (Figure 10.1).

SCOPE is a model designed by the coaching team at Learning Cultures. In the diagram, learning is at the heart of the school vision. This can include for both the pupil and those who plan and deliver the curriculum. It is a useful framework for professional learning communities that define the goals for continuous learning and improvement and translate them into strategies for teaching and learning.

Figure 10.1 The SCOPE model

Where teachers learn to coach, they develop profound skills in active listening and incisive questioning. They learn to be non-judgemental and non-directive. They begin to see how pupils respond positively when encouraged to find their own solutions, work together to share their ideas, build knowledge through enquiry and undertake independent research. Teachers become increasingly aware that they can trust pupils to think for themselves, reflect on their own progress and show resilience in the face of failure or setbacks.

Where pupils learn to coach, they develop a profound skillset:

- Rapport building
- Listening
- Reflecting
- Questioning
- Affirming

(Abdulla 2018, p43)

Teacher-pupil interaction provides a connection and an opportunity for the pupil to feel confident in their endeavours. Teachers need to focus on good eye-contact, being approachable and tolerant and using vocabulary that the pupil can process and comprehend. The relationship here should be respectful and caring and foster a deep understanding of what ensures pupils are ready to learn.

Listening is an integral part of learning. Where both teacher and pupil learn how to listen actively, there is the potential for deeper understanding and a culture of trust and respect. The art of good listening is difficult to learn, it is so easy to be distracted, lose concentration or want to interrupt.

Questioning is a fundamental classroom pedagogy. The right questions help pupils to reflect on their learning, what they are achieving, what they find difficult and where they might find more information. Questioning requires practice to ensure that what is asked challenges and stretches the receiver to think deeply about their answer.

Affirmation comes from strong interaction and partnerships where the use of effective dialogue and questioning are linked to learner autonomy that encourage reflection and self-direction. The following aspects should be an integral part of how to build collaborative interactions linked to powerful coaching skills.

- Both the teacher and the pupil are focusing on achievement of a goal or objective.
- There is a climate of trust and respect on both sides.
- All those involved are entitled to their views and encouraged to be forthright and honest.
- Pupils are confident in their ability to rise to the challenges posed by others.
- Creativity, innovation and risk taking are encouraged.
- Learning is at the heart of every conversation.
- Teachers pursue misunderstanding or misconception without judgement.
- Pupils are actively encouraged to be a part of the decision-making process.

Conversations that lead to learning need structure so that there is a clear pathway to achieving the goal. SCOPE is a good example as is the GROW model (Whitmore 2009). Achieving the goal also requires evaluation of progress and reflection points along the way to help individuals to focus on their successes and where they need to think again. In terms of pupils' well-being and self-esteem.

providing a positive and structured framework for focusing on their own potential, their learning power and their place in school and beyond is helpful. For the teacher, either working with pupils or with other teachers it provides the focus for accountability, shared responsibility and clarity (Sherrington 2017, pp. 210–211).

CONCLUSION

This chapter focuses on elements that are separate but integral to the actual curriculum. Some are statutory and some are important in helping pupils to become culturally, morally and spiritually literate. Included here are two subjects, PE, and food and nutrition, that are not part of the EBacc but are still important.

The potential to weave these elements into most curriculum subjects is evidence that the subject content has depth and a richness that will enhance pupils understanding and create a desire to learn more.

Pupils learn well if they are part of the decision-making process. Where pupils have the chance to express themselves, are challenged in positive ways, given the opportunity to think creatively and know that learning is their passport to a successful future, they are far more likely to progress. It is here that coaching can have a profound influence on their self-esteem and the development of vital life skills.

Ten Top Tips

1 Look closely at the whole school curriculum vision (intent) to ensure it has a deep focus on developing the physically and emotionally secure pupil.
2 Weave through curriculum planning across all subjects how to ensure pupils are ready to learn, feel safe, are healthy and are secure enough to learn.
3 Plan a sequenced curriculum for PE that dovetails what has been taught and developed in key stage 2 with what pupils can build on in key stage 3 and continue to develop in key stage 4.
4 Encourage different subject departments to look at where food and its importance to society, health and well-being are integral to learning across the whole curriculum.
5 Look at the statements for personal development that Ofsted will use to judge schools by and use the questions included in this chapter to start professional conversations about why personal development is essential for learning.
6 Ensure all staff involved in the teaching of RSHE have relevant and rigorous training and ongoing opportunities for help and support.
7 SMSC is not a set of stand-alone elements of the curriculum and can be woven through many other subjects. The elements within SMSC have the potential to enrich learning across a range of subjects.
8 The Gatsby Foundation benchmarks are good practice. Look as widely as possible at how you can support pupils make positive choices about their future through well-planned CEIAG.

9 This chapter is about the pupil, give them a voice and watch them grow.
10 Learn more about the potential of coaching to build powerful relationships between pupils and their peers, pupils and their teachers and teachers supporting other teachers and support staff across the school.

REFERENCES

Abdulla, A. (2018) *Coaching Students in Secondary Schools – Closing the Gap between Performance and Potential.* Abingdon, David Fulton.

Claxton, G. (2002) *Building Learning Power: Helping Young People Become Better Learners.* Bristol, TLO Ltd.

Côté, J. and Gilbert, W. (2009) An Integrative Definition of Coaching Effectiveness and Expertise, *International Journal of Sports Science & Coaching*, 4(3): pp307–323.

DfE (2014a) *National Curriculum Programmes of Study for PE.* London, DfE.

DfE (2014b) *National Curriculum Programmes of Study for Design Technology.* London, DfE.

DfE (2014c) *Promoting Fundamental British Values as Part of SMSC in Schools.* London, DfE.

DfE (2022) *Careers Guidance and Access for Education and Training Providers: Statutory Guidance for Schools and Guidance for Further Education and Sixth Form Colleges.* London, DfE.

Dweck, C.S. (2006) *Mindset: The New Psychology of Success.* New York, Ballantine Books.

Gatsby Foundation (2014) *Good Career Guidance.* London, Gatsby Foundation Charitable Trust.

Lerner, R.M., et al. (2005) Positive Youth Development, Participation in Community Youth Development Programs, and Community Contributions of Fifth Grade Adolescents: Findings from the First Wave of the 4-H Study of Positive Youth Development, *The Journal of Early Adolescence*, 25(1): pp17–71.

Myatt, M. and Tomsett, J. (2021) *Huh Curriculum Conversations between Subject Leaders and Senior Leaders.* Woodbridge: John Catt Educational Ltd. p225.

Oxford, Cambridge & RSA (OCR) GCSE (9-1) (2023) *Physical Education Specification J587 Version 1.4.* Cambridge, OCR.

Ofsted (2023) *Research Review Series: PE.* London, Ofsted.

Ofsted (2024) *Handbook for Schools* London, Ofsted.

Public Health England. (2015) *Food Teaching in Secondary Schools – a Framework of Knowledge and Skills.* London, Department of Education.

Qualification and Curriculum Development Agency (QCDA) (2009) *Personal, Learning and Thinking Skills Framework (2009).* London, QCDA.

Sherrington, T. (2017) *The Learning Rain Forest.* Woodbridge, John Catt Educational.

GOV.UK (2021) *Statutory Guidance on Relationships and Sex Education (RSE) and Health Education.* London, GOV.UK.

The Careers and Enterprise Company, London, DfE. Available online: https://www.careersandenterprise.co.uk/.

Whitmore, J. (2009) *Coaching for Performance: Growing Human Potential and Purpose.* London, Nicholas Brealey Publishing.

World Economic Forum. (2023) *The Future of Jobs Report.* Geneva, World Economic Forum.

Youth Employment UK. (2019) *Youth Voice Survey.* Kettering, Youth Employment UK.

11
CHOICES: VOCATIONAL, TECHNICAL AND ENTERPRISE LEARNING

Contents

VOCATIONAL EDUCATION AS PART OF THE CURRICULUM

Vocational qualifications are designed to allow pupils to develop a range of skills related to a particular profession and that align to the National Occupational Standards (NOS). They can be taken at any stage in life but can be studied as part of a qualification route at key stage 4. They range in achievement grades from Entry Level (pre-GCSE, Level 1(GCSE 1-5_ to Level 7 (master's degree)). The approach to study for vocational learning is through enquiry and learning on the job. Pupils must demonstrate that they have achieved the criteria and have evidence that they have understood the principles and applied them. In this way, they differ from academic GCSEs which measure knowledge and its application mostly through written examinations.

Vocational education had a definitive place in the secondary curriculum until 2010. Emphasis changed with the introduction of the EBacc that came about as a part of curriculum reform. Some vocational subjects remain available as part of the options route. However, the list remains small. Many schools have opted not to pursue vocational learning as an already crowded curriculum makes it difficult to staff and sustain.

There is an increasing awareness that the vocational route is valuable. Post-Brexit skills shortages indicate that young people are leaving school without the relevant skills and experience that fit easily into post-16 vocational routes. Many schools lack the facilities to support vocational learning and are often unable to find the staff with the relevant skills and experience to teach the subjects.

VOCATIONAL QUALIFICATIONS AT KEY STAGE 4

The vocational qualifications fall into these main vocational categories:

- Hospitality
- Travel and tourism
- Sports science or sport activity and fitness
- Childcare, play and development
- Health and social care
- Creative and media
- Engineering or manufacturing
- Construction and the built environment
- Hair and beauty
- Business systems, economics and enterprise
- Digital information technology, graphic design
- Performing arts

This is not a complete list but shows what is on offer for schools brave enough to run these exceptional courses for young people who need a different model to the EBacc.

There is a lot to consider when embarking on a programme of study for a vocational course. Classrooms may need to be equipped with specialist equipment such as for hair and beauty courses, engineering, manufacturing and construction. It may be necessary to timetable longer periods for pupils to complete a practical activity, spend time within a business or work together on a team project.

There are new technical awards for all vocational subjects that became available from September 2022. They follow the same 2 year time frame as other qualification outcomes at key stages 4 and 5.

THE POTENTIAL OF VOCATIONAL EDUCATION TO ENHANCE LEARNING

Not every pupil is suited to a purely academic route where the teacher is the facilitator of knowledge that pupils are expected to absorb and recall in a GCSE examination environment. Vocational qualifications require pupils to demonstrate that they have applied the knowledge they are learning to sector-specific contexts. As part of external assessment, pupils must show that they can do a range of tasks, explain why they are necessary and build a portfolio of evidence linked to the vocational area they are studying.

Qualifications require 120 hours of guided learning time. Schools should timetable approximately four hours a week for teaching and practical work with time set aside for homework and out-of-school activity. Guided learning hours are those that will involve a teacher or tutor supervising, assessing or guiding pupils. There is also the total qualification time of 160 hours which will include private study, preparation for assessment, extra reading, independent research and revision.

Pupils are expected to develop English and maths skills as part of vocational learning. It is often through the practical application of a concept that pupils grasp the mathematics or the reading and writing they are confronted with during their studies.

The objectives of a vocational course aim to:

- offer a high-quality vocational and applied curriculum that engages pupils and allows them to broaden their knowledge and skills;
- create balance and an opportunity to apply knowledge, skills and understanding in the context of their potential future vocations
- provide opportunities to link pupils' learning and the world of work in practical and relevant ways;
- enable pupils to use their English and maths skills in a wide range of contexts that are realistic in the pursuance of a vocational role or job;
- support pupils to develop a range of transferable and interpersonal skills which include working with others, problem-solving and independent study;
- provide progression routes for pupils that may be working towards apprenticeships or further vocational study.

The vocational qualification offers space and time for pupils to use a range of independent learning skills, work together in groups to investigate, create a presentation or a plan, interpret data or design a critical path. Pupils must demonstrate that they have not been told what to write or how to find out or where to look. They must show that they are the facilitator of their own learning and can find ways to record their findings, their thoughts and their results themselves within a portfolio of evidence sustained over time.

The portfolio approach is a powerful tool in documenting an ongoing understanding of how to present work. The portfolio lives with the pupil from day one until it is presented for assessment at the end of year 11. Inevitably the quality of early work is less well presented and often pupils look back and want to change or redo what they have completed. The portfolio is powerful as pupils can see their progress and how they have improved. They are so used to being assessed on stand-alone work that some may struggle to accept that what they have is proof that they are developing their qualification week by week.

The portfolio should encompass all practical learning opportunities and include video material, presentations, pictures of models, diagrams or items they have constructed, diaries of events, role play and discussions, annotated documents and anything else that demonstrates that the pupil has really experienced the sector they are learning about.

The teacher should have a facilitator role guiding the pupil, ensuring all safety rules are followed and asking incisive questions that encourage independent answers. Everything goes into the portfolio and over time mistakes, misunderstandings, misconceptions become the right answer and create a narrative of their learning journey.

PLANNING A VOCATIONAL PROGRAMME OF STUDY AT KEY STAGE 4

There is a clear process that needs to be followed in the set-up of vocational learning that will count in the open category of Progress 8, which means they have points attached in relation to league table performance (DfE 2023). There are three components in most of the level 1 (GCSE 1-4) and 2 (GCSE 5-9) vocational qualifications, one externally assessed element and two that are assessed internally by the school or centre. All three components focus on the assessment of applied knowledge, skills and practices. These are all essential to developing a basis for progression and pupils need to achieve all three to achieve the qualification outcome.

Vocational curriculum planners need to consider how the internal components will be planned, delivered and internally assessed and moderated. Anyone embarking on this process requires training on what the portfolio of evidence should consist of and how they should assess its contents. The awarding bodies will provide set assignments. Following on from internal assessment and moderation, portfolios may be externally assessed by the awarding body.

The internal components require pupils to use sector-specific knowledge they have gained. The design requires that pupils can identify and use an appropriate selection of skills, techniques, concepts, theories and knowledge in an integrated way.

The external assessment comprises 40% of the total guided learning hours. It is taken in examination conditions and can be the obstacle for some pupils who struggle with examinations. However, it is only one component of a three-component qualification and pupils will gain considerable real-life learning and the opportunity to develop essential life skills along the way which can make the external element less daunting.

A clear timetable for how the components will be delivered and assessed needs to be in place prior to embarking on teaching a vocational qualification. The list below provides a potential focus on what needs to be in place to create a streamlined learning and assessment process.

- Decide on the number of hours per week that will be timetabled for actual teaching
- Plan how to integrate extra out of class learning to support classroom learning
- Find out the dates for the externally assessed unit and ensure that sufficient time is set aside to prepare pupils for an examination style assessment
- Create a schedule for how each component will be delivered over what period of time
- Decide who will internally moderate the portfolio of evidence at the end of the two internally assessed components
- Set time aside for internal moderation and appoint an internal verifier who can check the assessment process

All teachers need to understand the assessment objectives. It is important that they know what they are looking for in terms of a pupil's ability to show their own investigation, their own accounts of what they have developed or understood and their own presentations. The work produced cannot be teacher worksheets or answers to questions that the teacher has produced in the classroom. It cannot be work directly lifted from a textbook or online. The secret is in the ability of the assessor to see application in relation to a pupil's understanding of the task they are undertaking.

LINKS WITH BUSINESS, PUBLIC SERVICES AND COMMERCIAL ENTERPRISE

Vocational qualifications require links with businesses that are part of a given sector. For some, this is easier to achieve than others.

- **Travel and tourism** – businesses within the travel and tourism sectors can be accessible for pupils who live in areas of the country that are involved in the tourism industry, London, seaside towns, sites of historical interest and so on.
- **Health and social care** – there are many businesses within any community that can offer support in the health and social care sectors, visiting speakers, visits to care homes, special schools and clinics all provide substance in terms of learning about the sectors that form the overarching health and social care sector.
- **Hair and beauty** – businesses in the hair and beauty sector are often small and may be reluctant to accept teenagers even for a short time, but there are often many establishments within a town where pupils could ask questions, observe and develop case studies.

- **Construction, engineering and manufacturing** - all require some thought in how pupils can see businesses in these sectors in action. There are health and safety considerations and large companies or building sites may be inaccessible. They often have apprenticeship schemes and are looking for students to join them which is often a way in.
- **Creative and media** – there are opportunities for pupils to access the sectors involved as part of the creative world. Local theatres, graphic design businesses, photography and film companies. It is also possible to focus on the media we have at our fingertips, YouTube, television and radio, the school and local productions or art exhibitions.

Universities, colleges and training providers can become ambassadors for the apprenticeship route into the next steps for learning. Take advantage of the fact that many businesses are seeking apprentices and collaborate with the careers education programme at school to find out as much as possible about career routes into the sector being studied.

STEM AND EMPLOYABILITY SKILLS

STEM which stands for Science, Technology, Engineering and Mathematics works in collaboration with government, employers both large and small, organisations and education establishments to deliver positive interactions for teachers and young people in pursuit of information, advice and guidance about future careers in the STEM arena.

Tapping into what STEM can offer to schools in relation to pupils' future options is valuable. The partnership approach and the opportunities for professional development in relation to supporting pupils to consider pursuing further study or an apprenticeship in one of the STEM subjects is invaluable. STEM works with the National Centre for Computing Education who coordinate school-led computer hubs across England. There are nine regional networks for STEM support that cover the whole of England. All have a local representative who is there to create the partnerships that will create a world-leading STEM education for all young people across the UK. All of this is accessible from their website www.stem.org.uk.

STEM provides support on career opportunities for pupils as they consider GCSE (or equivalent) options. They offer a toolkit designed to increase awareness of potential careers across the STEM subjects. There is also a Teacher's Guide that links careers to the STEM curriculum.

ENTERPRISE AND OTHER ROUTES TO PERSONAL DEVELOPMENT IN KEY STAGE 3

Key stage 3 is a time when the introduction of opportunities for enterprise is profoundly worthwhile. The focus of an enterprise project can overlap with other subjects and provides scope for pupils to use their imagination and a range of skills that will be useful in key stage 4 and beyond.

The 2016 Ofsted report 'Getting ready for work' was commissioned to investigate the availability and effectiveness of enterprise education and work-related learning in schools.

It highlighted that few secondary schools had an enterprise and employability strategy. The key findings from this report are summarised here.

- A curriculum for preparing pupils for the world of work is dependent on whether the senior team consider it to be a priority.
- Where schools deliver some kind of enterprise education the impact is unclear.
- Meaningful work-experience is limited at key stage 4.
- Business involvement relies on the personal network of teachers and parents potentially resulting in disadvantaged pupils missing out.
- There is a lack of co-ordination in schools and a lack of strategy by government that has led business leaders to describe the situation as 'chaotic'.
- There is a lack of trust in the quality of apprenticeships and many parents said pupils thought that this route might narrow their options.

The report goes on to recommend that schools:

- ensure there is a coherent programme to develop enterprise education;
- forge stronger links with businesses where there is a clear intent in relation to what these links will do to support pupils;
- make the most of the expertise of specialist teachers and ensure they have good professional development;
- ensure that the delivery of enterprise education develops knowledge, understanding and skills and allows pupils to progress well in their endeavours.

Many things have happened politically and socially since this report was published, all of which may be why the will to include enterprise and employability education into an over-crowded academic curriculum maybe a bridge too far. The demise of the vocational suite of qualifications due to ineligibility for Progress 8 hasn't helped.

The report highlights good practice examples and the need for schools to be made more aware of the resources and expert support that is available around this area of the curriculum. There are many examples of organisations that can support schools to develop this vital element of learning for all secondary pupils, including:

- ASDAN have a superb short course as part of their programmes www.asdan.org.uk/enterprise-short-course/
- Young Enterprise offer several programmes to support schools to work with pupils to develop an enterprising mindset - www.youngenterprise.org.uk
- Barclays Bank has a place on their website called Barclays Life Skills www.barclayslifeskills.com
- School Enterprise Challenge - where schools take a lead in setting up a business www.schoolenterprisechallenge.org

Starting a business is always something that ignites a passion in young people. An idea can become a reality through a module where groups work together to create a business plan. Ideas can be as small as a charity cake sale, a careers fair or a tuckshop. Others may shape ideas around something they do outside school. One of my students, a young lady with a fair degree of attitude rose to the task when she announced she wanted to start a plumbing business. Another saw a piece of wasteland at the bottom of the school playing field as the ideal place to have a skateboarding park that could be a part of the commercial side of school sports.

Enterprise is bigger than thinking about starting a business. It is about personal finance, reliability, resilience, being a good team player, being able to set positive and realistic goals and problem-solving. It is about taking risks and accepting that failure is ok as long as it leads to reflection and learning. A stand-alone entrepreneurship unit that focuses on setting up a business in school can create opportunities to shine outside the confines of specific subjects.

Ideas for enterprise at key stage 3

- A maths module on personal finance linked to calculating interest rates in relation to saving and borrowing, understanding inflation, income and tax, managing one's own money.
- A geography module focusing on settlements and why businesses exist in certain places due to raw materials, proximity of population, terrain, trade routes and transport links.
- A history module looking at the changing value of money, changing shopping habits and the influence of social media on how we now communicate, live and shop. Pupils could also investigate a business that has been a part of the community for some time and how it has changed.
- An art or design technology module looking at marketing and how we are attracted to buy some goods and services.
- A languages module focusing on the cost of living in a different country and how much it would cost to visit or live there.

BUSINESS STUDIES AS A FRESH START FOR MANY AT KEY STAGE 4

Business studies is an optional subject at key stage 4. It provides a rich vein of learning that goes beyond subject teaching and links closely with careers education, cultural literacy, ethics and how businesses deal with change.

It requires pupils to apply their knowledge and understanding to different business contexts ranging from sole traders to multinational conglomerates. The structure of the qualification follows this pattern.

- Knowing what businesses do, their ownership structure, their location, their purpose and their stakeholders
- Being aware of the external influences on businesses such as technology, ethical, environmental and economic constraints

- Understanding the impact of globalisation on business and the effects of the pandemic, artificial intelligence and social media
- Examining the impact of legislation on businesses
- Learning about business operations including quality, finance, marketing and human resources (DfE 2015)

Business studies asks pupils to analyse how businesses operate and provides an opportunity to develop and practise transferrable skills that are useful as part of their future studies and employment prospects. Here are some questions for the business team to discuss as part of creating pathways to deep learning:

- How can we build a vocabulary bank that may be new or have different meaning in the context of business and ensure that pupils can learn and comprehend the knowledge they will be learning?
- What do we have in our locality that will help our pupils to start to understand the concepts that underpin the business curriculum?
- How can we take our pupils out of their comfort zone to look at business in unfamiliar contexts and help them to deepen their knowledge and understanding?
- How do we capture business issues and opportunities that exist around us, on the news and in the press so that we can support our pupils find ways to be investigative, analytical and evaluative in the pursuit of deeper understanding?
- Where do we capture qualitative and quantitative data that will support pupils to be able to select, interpret, analyse and evaluate what is conveyed and be able to justify their choices?

The use of quantitative data is a feature of any business. It is important that pupils have mathematical techniques they can apply to interpreting data in relevant business contexts. Creating partnerships with the maths department can be a positive decision and where maths teachers know that pupils are using quite complex maths techniques in their business studies, they can relate this to concepts taught in maths lessons.

Some of the concepts are listed here:

- Percentages and percentage change
- Mean, median and mode
- Revenue, costs and profit
- Gross profit margin and net profit margin ratios
- Average rate of return
- Cash - flow forecasts, including total costs, total revenue and net cash flow

Pupils must also demonstrate the ability to interpret data and justify findings in a variety of contexts, especially from graphs and charts, ratios, marketing and marketing research data and the interpretation of market share, break - even analysis and changes in pricing structures. Business studies and maths teachers should work together to build confidence and competence in maths concepts to support this aim.

Similarly, pupils need to demonstrate their ability to write fluently, use formal language and read complex documents such as company reports, marketing strategies and business plans. They need to demonstrate that they can make presentations about strategy, marketing, set out their own ideas for business development and articulate how the 4 P's of price, publicity, place and product all combine to create business success. Collaboration with English teachers to strengthen speaking, listening, reading and writing will enhance the potential of pupils in both subjects and across the wider curriculum.

COMPUTING AND DIGITAL TECHNOLOGY IN THE CURRICULUM

Computing comprises three distinct disciplines, computer science, digital literacy and information technology. It is a compulsory National Curriculum subject from key stages 1 to 4. There is no doubt that digital technologies are changing the world we live in. The pace of change impacts every sector including education. It is suggested that computing education across the UK is 'patchy and fragile' (Royal Society 2017).

Schools can struggle to recruit teachers with the skills to teach these three disciplines. There is little in the way of professional development and no cohesive model of how to change this situation (Royal Society 2017). Schools are not equipped or agile enough to meet the pressing demands of the changing landscape for computing in its various forms.

Ofsted's Research Review of Computing (2022) also cites the Royal Society's views of the current secondary computing curriculum and how it is taught, highlighting the lack of time allocated as wholly inadequate. Ofsted conclude that although things have improved since 2017, there are inequalities in provision from school to school. There is also concern about the number of girls taking any form of computing at key stage 4.

Secondary curriculum planners need to be mindful of the computing curriculum that pupils experience in primary school. Year 7 curriculum planners should ask their primary partners:

- What experience do pupils have of designing, writing and debugging programs?
- What examples can you give that show how pupils have used logical reasoning to explain how simple algorithms work?
- How much opportunity have pupils had of computer networks?
- What experience do pupils have of using search technologies?
- What different types of software have pupils used in the creation and use of programs, systems and content to achieve prescribed goals?
- How confident are you that pupils are using technology safely, respectfully and responsibly?

The National Curriculum for computing sets out the aims for what should be taught in both key stages 3 and 4, these are abridged here (DfE 2014b).

- Can understand and apply fundamental principles and concepts of computer science
- Can analyse problems in computational terms and can write computer programs
- Can evaluate and apply information technology
- Can use a variety of information and communication technology

The questions below are important in determining a high-quality curriculum across the computing disciplines:

- Who within your staff can evaluate computational abstractions that model the state and behaviour of real-world problems and physical systems?
- How do you ensure computing teachers can understand algorithms and have the pedagogical skills to help pupils to use logical reasoning?
- What programming languages do staff have and how can they support pupils develop their skills in the use of data structures and develop modular programs?
- How well do computing staff develop pupils' understanding of Boolean logic and how to use it and the importance of binary numbers?
- What potential is there for pupils to have access to a variety of hardware and software components, how they work and how they communicate with each other?
- What are the skills teachers need to explain how instructions are stored and executed and how data are represented and manipulated?
- How does the vision for a creative computing curriculum ensure pupils undertake projects that involve multiple applications to achieve challenging goals?
- What do your staff know about digital artefacts and their use and efficacy?
- What systems exist to ensure the safe and responsible use of digital technology?

Pupils who are not taking computer science as a GCSE should use knowledge learnt in key stage 3 to be creative, analytical, solve problems and be adept at computational thinking and continue to understand how changes in technology affect safety and privacy. In each of the recommendations for key stage 4 computing, there is such potential to strengthen the knowledge and skills pupils have gained in key stage 3 by building computing into other subjects, such as design technology and all the STEM subjects.

There is a comparatively low take-up of GCSE computing. The potential of computing to enhance learning across a range of other subjects suggests that we should encourage more pupils to opt for a qualification outcome. However, there are many constraints that make this unrealistic. Timetabling is an issue, as is staff with the knowledge and expertise. Raising the status of computing and associated qualifications at key stage 4 through high profile links to maths, science and design can ensure that it is timetabled sufficiently well.

Pupils will have been exposed to programming and writing codes to solve problems as early as key stage 1 (DfE 2014a). Secondary curriculum planners need to choose the programming language pupils will learn. There is a prescription that pupils should be taught two languages in key stage 3. A consensus needs to exist to determine how to teach them and ensure pupils develop their knowledge sequentially alongside opportunities for recall and retrieval. The choice of language should be linked to what the computing curriculum is aiming to achieve as well as the ability of pupils and the expertise of staff.

The Ofsted research review findings suggest that pupils are often novice programmers whose knowledge is incomplete with a fragmented model of understanding programs. To address this, it is essential to have well-structured opportunities to build and link knowledge and learning over time so that pupils develop as computational thinkers and are adept at solving problems through computation.

Information technology focuses on how we use computers as the medium for presentations, communication, design, managing data and promotion of products and services. Pupils should have opportunities to create 'digital artifacts' in a variety of contexts. This element of the computing curriculum can be planned beyond the computing classroom. Pupils should be exposed to using the Office suite of software across most subjects and have opportunities to use the software and understand how to ensure presentation, data handling and the manipulation of information is accurate, safe and well-constructed. Pupils also need to understand how computers are essential to our everyday lives and how this was not always the case.

The third element of the concept of computing is digital literacy. Pupils need to have the skills and knowledge to be safe and effective users. Such knowledge and skills do need to be defined sequentially. Schools and those involved in developing pupils' skills and knowledge should not assume that pupils are digital natives because they have grown up with technology.

As with information technology, deepening competence and knowledge in relation to digital literacy can be obtained through other curriculum subjects. The opportunity for cross-curricular collaboration to determine where these skills can be sequenced and strengthened should be mapped and conversations about how they are taught, practised and reinforced are important. Each department should have the opportunity to consider the knowledge and skills that pupils need in relation to information technology and digital literacy and how this can enhance learning across curriculum subjects.

A useful resource for the computer science curriculum is the free magazine *cs4fn*. It is published twice a year and is widely used by over 2,000 schools (Curzon & Brodie 2005).

LANGUAGES AS A PASSPORT TO ENRICHMENT AND EMPLOYABILITY

Where pupils become fluent in another language, they have a passport to future employability and enriched life chances. Hence the subject is included in this chapter. Languages are a part of the EBacc and pupils are expected to have studied a second language in primary school as well as throughout their secondary years. However, language teaching in England is still considered to be poor.

A language curriculum includes three distinct and important elements, phonics, vocabulary and grammar. Pupils learn by making connections between sounds, words, sentences and texts. Language teachers want pupils to be exposed to the target language, learn how to pronounce things properly, read and comprehend texts and write accurately and fluently.

Developing a vision for pupils to learn one or more languages from year 7 requires subject experts to work together to ensure expertise amongst staff and appropriate resources. The first issue is to establish what has been taught in the primary school. There is a statutory obligation to teach a language as part of the key stage 2 curriculum but no stipulation as to which. Where secondary schools draw their year 7 cohort from a wide range of primary schools, there will undoubtedly be a variety of languages studied and to a varying degree of breadth and depth.

At key stage 3, the National Curriculum programme of study emphasises that pupils should continue to build competence in speaking, listening, reading and writing. This should be built on a sound foundation of core grammar and vocabulary. Capturing what has been taught in key stage 2 should not be lost. At key stage 3, the requirements are to study grammar and vocabulary and gain linguistic competence. In terms of grammar, there is an emphasis on tenses, grammatical structures and patterns and deepening vocabulary so that pupils can express an opinion and take part in discussions in the target language (DfE 2014c).

In terms of linguistic competence, at key stage 3, pupils are expected to listen, transcribe, initiate and take part in conversations, express and develop ideas, speak coherently and confidently, read and show comprehension, read literary texts and write prose accurately. The planning of a scheme of work needs to have a progression route for pupils to build their competence and confidence through a sequential focus on the phonics or sounds of a language and how these are set out in written form, a growing vocabulary and becoming increasingly adept at using grammar in the correct form.

Planning a sequential second language curriculum requires the subject leader to focus on how pupils learn and be mindful of the limited capacity of the working memory. Pupils need to learn the basics and build on them over time. As the fundamentals become embedded in the long-term memory, pupils begin to add new learning more easily. The slow introduction of more complex texts, opportunities for deeper conversations and writing for a purpose requires careful sequencing and assessment of how well pupils are absorbing the building blocks of the target language.

In 2016, the Teaching Schools Council conducted a review looking at the pedagogy of modern foreign languages in key stages 3 and 4 (Bauckham 2016). The review provides schools and teachers with responsibility for developing a curriculum for language teaching with a set of recommendations. It then goes on to amplify each with findings from their research. Here I have turned the recommendations into a set of questions for senior and subject leaders to consider as they review and reflect on their languages provision and its effectiveness.

- To what extent is learning a second language accessible to all pupils whatever their ability?
- What evidence can you draw on that the curriculum is sequenced throughout key stage 3 and 4 to ensure pupils gain systematic knowledge of vocabulary, grammar and phonics?
- How do teachers create opportunities for pupils to reinforce and practice their growing knowledge over time whilst maintaining their interest and motivation?
- How does the planning and teaching embrace culture, history and literature of the target language?
- How do you ensure that selected textbooks support the planned approach to teaching vocabulary, grammar and phonics?

- What opportunities ensure there are opportunities for translation of texts and for pupils to extend their vocabulary and understanding through reading short texts and literature?
- How is the target language used in the classroom to support and reinforce learning?
- How do teachers use error to reinforce learning and create the right model that encourages pupils to pay attention to detail?
- What pedagogy is evident in the classroom that ensures speaking, writing, listening and reading are taught in synergy?

Other aspects that need careful consideration are issues such as how much time is allocated to language study, is it best to set pupils linked to their ability or to have mixed ability classes? How is acquisition of vocabulary, accuracy in grammar and improved fluency tested and how much opportunity is there to work with native speakers of the target language?

CONCLUSION

Vocational learning has not been high on the agenda in compulsory schooling over the past decade and a half, but it is now apparent that skills shortages mean that it will need to find a place in a broad and rich curriculum offer for the future that serves pupils well.

The inclusion here of both computing and languages which are compulsory within the National Curriculum is because both offer pupils vital employability skills. There are still shortages of trained staff in both subjects and a low take-up of pupils studying for both at key stage 4. These subjects are compulsory in key stage 2 and creating opportunities to build on what pupils know and can do when they arrive into year 7 is important for both the planning of the key stage 3 curriculum and also so that pupils feel that what they have learnt is valuable and relevant for them.

We also include here is a look at enterprise and its value in strengthening skills and attributes of pupils as well as its links across the wider curriculum. It also provides opportunities for teaching specific topics in key stage 3 that will enhance learning in many subjects such as personal finance and maths or promoting a business idea in design technology.

The curriculum is crowded and some of the elements in this chapter may be a bridge too far for some schools. Optional subjects require extra resources, time and staffing, but in each case, they form profound evidence that the curriculum is rich, deep and learner-centred.

Ten Top Tips

1. Vocational learning at key stage 4 is worth considering for pupils who will struggle with a purely academic curriculum.
2. Delivering a vocational subject requires structured planning for sequenced and interleaved learning as well as an organised plan for assessment, moderation and verification.

(Continued)

3. Tap into STEM Learning, their resources, courses and advice are invaluable and mostly free, funded or affordable.
4. Enterprise at key stage 3 can be a welcome reinforcement of learning across a range of disciplines.
5. Business studies can be a fresh start for some pupils. It is a subject rich in opportunities for developing pupils' life skills and for deep learning of new knowledge.
6. Where business teams develop partnerships with maths and English departments, there are opportunities for pupils to put concepts they learn in both into context through business studies.
7. There is an imperative to increase the opportunities for pupils to develop their skills in all three disciplines of computing.
8. Schools and teachers should not assume that pupils are digital natives because they have grown up with technology.
9. Designing a key stage 3 scheme of work for languages and computing should take account of work pupils have studied in year 6 and the whole of key stage 2.
10. Pupils should study the culture, literature and history of the country of their target language and this can be supported by collaboration with other subject areas.

REFERENCES

Bauckham, I. (2016) *Modern Foreign Languages Pedagogy Review*. London, Teaching Schools Council.

Curzon, P. and Brodie, J. (2005) *CS4FN: Computer Science for Fun*. London, Queen Mary University.

DfE (2014a) *Computing Programmes of Study: Key Stage 1 and 2*. London, DfE.

DfE (2014b) *Computing Programmes of Study: Key Stage 3 and 4*. London, DfE.

DfE (2014c) *Languages Programme of Study: Key Stage 3*. London, DfE.

DfE (2015) *GCSE Business Subject Content*. London, DfE.

DfE (2023) *Performance Points for Qualifications Counting in the 2024 Secondary Performance Tables*. London, DfE.

Ofsted (2016) *Getting Ready for Work*. London, Ofsted.

Ofsted (2022) *Research Review Series: Computing*. London, Ofsted.

Royal Society (2017) *After the Reboot: Computing Education in UK Schools*. London, Royal Society.

STEM Learning, The Career and Enterprise Company. Linking Careers to the STEM Curriculum. PDF York, STEM Learning.

STEM Careers *Toolkit for secondary schools and colleges*. York, STEM Learning. www.stem.org.uk/resources/467467/stem-careers-toolkit-secondary-schools-and-colleges

12

ASSESSING PEDAGOGY AND LEARNING – PROGRESSION AND CHALLENGE FROM YEAR 6 TO GCSE AND BEYOND

Contents

- Assessment and planning the curriculum
- Pedagogy and learning – assessing classroom practice and pupil outcomes
- Adaptive teaching and inclusion – creating parity for all pupils
- Formative and summative assessment
- Planning a continuum of learning at key stage 3
- Assessment at key stage 4 – learning towards summative end-point assessments
- Feedback and coaching for deep learning and progression

ASSESSING AND PLANNING THE CURRICULUM

Assessment is the key that unlocks achievement in every subject. It is a powerful motivator, the more we can affirm that what is being produced is on the right track, the more an individual will strive for better. Praise and appreciation create the drive towards progression. To be told something is 'no good' or falls short of others is deflating and will often dampen enthusiasm that is difficult to rekindle.

The emphasis on the purpose of assessment has changed since 2014. There is a definite shift away from a focus on data towards a more holistic approach. There is a move from assessing what pupils don't know to looking for the knowledge and concepts that pupils are gaining as they progress towards clearly defined end points in their learning. There is also a shift towards pupils being part of the process where they assess their own work and the work of others. Finally, there is a greater emphasis on more descriptive feedback that is motivational and less judgemental.

The *Ofsted School Inspection Handbook* (2024) notes that: 'The school's curriculum is planned and sequenced so that the end points that it is building towards are clear and that pupils develop the knowledge and skills, building on what has been taught before, to be able to reach them'. It is, therefore, essential that assessment is a key factor in planning, the sequencing of knowledge and measuring pupils' skills development. Subject leaders and teams need to plan backwards, knowing the outcome that defines the pathways that pupils follow (Lemov 2015).

Each subject has its own content and knowledge base. The development of schemes of work and their associated assessment criteria are the domain of the subject leader and their team. The aim is that learning, supported by the teaching of sequenced knowledge, is sufficiently reinforced and refocused so that it moves from the short-term to the long-term memory where it will form the foundation for further learning.

Subjects differ in terms of knowledge and skills; however, there is a need for a collaborative approach that focuses on individual pupil's ability to absorb and manipulate knowledge, understand key concepts, comprehend and recall subject vocabulary and develop disciplines to access and retain a growing bank of understanding.

Collaborative professional dialogue, used in assessment planning and shared CPD, gives subject leaders and teams an opportunity to focus on pedagogy that develops confidence and competence in using higher-order taxonomies that underpin mark schemes for GCSE and beyond. These include the ability to explain, to justify, to compare and contrast, to synthesise, analyse and evaluate. Opportunities for teachers to work together on pedagogy and assessment provides excellent training and develops confidence for inexperienced teachers.

Assessing pupils' understanding requires that teachers are aware of the core and wider skills pupils will be developing throughout secondary school. A key indicator for effective curriculum planning is that every subject has a clear focus on reading and how pupils can access and comprehend subject-specific knowledge and vocabulary. Writing is a key element of assessment in key stages 3 and 4 and especially at exam time. Where pupils have the comprehension skills to interpret the knowledge they read and have the grammar skills to manipulate that knowledge, they can develop as higher-level thinkers and responders.

ASSESSING CLASSROOM PRACTICE AND PUPIL OUTCOMES

Ofsted research from 2019 looked at lesson observation and the pupil outcomes their inspectors should be looking for. The research was conducted to validate the consistency and accuracy of their own grading processes. They identified a series of indicators for inspectors to use when observing lessons and for looking at pupil outcomes in books and other media (see Table 12.1).

The prompt phrases replicated below (Table 12.2) are a valuable tool for building a consistent and structured model for assessing pupil output. The phrases below could kickstart teacher discussion on evidencing work that builds on prior learning, has depth and breadth, shows progress is being made and that all pupils have the opportunity for reflection, recall and practice. These statements can be put onto a set of cards to aid professional dialogue.

The lesson observation indicators are also useful as preparation for lesson observation and as feedback prompts. Below (Table 12.3) are the indicators for lesson observation used by Ofsted. Use them to focus on the quality of teaching and learning in the classroom.

ADAPTIVE TEACHING – CREATING PARITY FOR ALL

Ofsted's curriculum indicators for schools (2018) reference the need to 'allow all pupils to access the content and make progress through the curriculum' (indicator 1d - Intent), that 'curriculum delivery is equitable for all groups and appropriate' (indicator 5c -

Table 12.1 Pupil outcome indicators (Ofsted 2019)

Building on previous learning	Depth and breadth of coverage	Pupil's progress	Practice
Pupils' knowledge is consistently, coherently and logically sequenced so that it can develop incrementally over time. There is a progression from the simpler and/or more concrete concepts to more complex and/or abstract ones. Pupils' work shows that they have developed their knowledge and skills over time.	The content if the tasks and pupils' work show that pupils learn a suitably broad range of topics within a subject. Tasks also allow pupils to deepen their knowledge of the subject by requiring thought on their part, understanding of subject-specific concepts and making connections to prior knowledge.	Pupils make strong progress from their starting points. They acquire knowledge and understanding appropriate to their starting points.	Pupils are regularly given opportunities to revisit and practice what they know to deepen their understanding in a discipline. They can recall information effectively, which shows that learning is durable. Any misconceptions are addressed and there is evidence to show that pupils have overcome these in future work.

Table 12.2 Prompt phrases for professional dialogue about pupil outcomes from books and other media

Pupils can link their learning to what they already know	Pupils can make connections with other subjects or in cross-curricular learning	All pupils have access to the same content and knowledge	Pupils have confidence to accept challenge and intervention	Intervention is planned so that all pupils can access the curriculum
Gaps in learning and in skills development are understood and actions taken to support pupils	Progression opportunities are apparent in the way pupils' work is sequenced	Pupils have retained the knowledge from previous learning and know how to use that learning to inform new learning	Pupils can use their previous understanding as a springboard for deeper learning	Pupils can respond to questioning where they can discuss their own understanding of what and how they are learning
Pupils have high self-esteem and are contributors to their own and to others' learning	Pupils know that challenge is a part of learning and that is evidenced in how their work improves over time	Each pupil is using subject matter that will challenge them to extend their capacity	Pupils are studying a broad range of topics within subjects and can understand a range of key concepts	Pupils are given opportunities for recall and reflection and misconceptions are seen as part of learning

Table 12.3 Lesson observation indicators for curriculum and teaching (Ofsted 2019)

Curriculum	**Teaching**
1a Teachers use subject expertise, knowledge and practical skills to provide learning opportunities	2a Teachers demonstrate good communication skills
1b Teachers ensure there is an equality of opportunity for all learners to access every lesson, as building blocks to the wider curriculum	2bTeachers' use of presentation skills allows pupils to build knowledge and make connections
1c Strategies to support reading/vocabulary/ understanding/numeracy are in place for pupils who need it/cannot access the curriculum	2c Teachers use relevant and appropriate resources during presentations to clarify meaning to pupils
1d The content of the lesson is suitably demanding	2d Teachers possess good questioning skills
1e The lesson content is appropriate to the age group and does not lower expectations	2e Teachers give explicit, detailed and constructive feedback in class
1f There is a logical sequence to the learning	2f Teachers effectively check for understanding
1g Teachers provide opportunities for recall and practise previously learnt skills and knowledge	Take each of these indicators and consider the evidence from observation or from discussions with colleagues about evidence you can draw in pursuance of the highest quality pedagogy and learning
1h Assessment provides relevant, clear and helpful information about the current skills and knowledge of learners	

Implementation) and that 'the curriculum provides parity for all groups of pupils' (indicator 9 - Impact). Teaching staff must know their pupils' needs and abilities well so that the planned curriculum can engage every pupil across a spectrum of aptitude. It is my conviction that we should be creating mixed ability classrooms where pupils can work together to access the highest quality knowledge, towards different outcomes linked to capability and growing understanding of a subject.

Teachers learn from each other. There should be professional conversations about modifying classroom strategies so that pupils do not feel they have failed but are given the opportunity to look at the process or the concept differently. This could be through a conscious focus on:

- how different teachers use questioning to support learning;
- analysing the different pedagogies that support intervention;
- using peer support where pupils work together to learn from each other.

Each pupil is different and at some stage will find some learning difficult. A focus on formative assessment as an integral part of lessons will help to ensure that pupils are not left behind because they have not grasped an important concept or forgotten specific knowledge. The SEND Code of Practice (DfE 2015) is clear that differentiated learning is an expectation.

Each cohort has a range of abilities from those who find learning difficult to those who do not. The reasons are many and can be linked to parental involvement, opportunities for learning a hidden curriculum away from school, specific interests and hobbies and other issues to do with well-being and safety. Adapted (or differentiated) learning should be happening in every classroom to challenge those who can go that extra mile, to motivate those who are capable but are coasting and to intervene and support those who are struggling.

There is good evidence to suggest that pupils taught in mixed ability settings have more chance of succeeding and where pupils are taken out of the main classroom for extra help or intervention they can fall further behind. The pupils in the main classroom are forging ahead and learning new knowledge, concepts and skills and those in the intervention group are not.

What does good quality pedagogy look like in the mixed ability classroom where it is differentiated by pupil need?

- Always set the scene and be explicit in what you want pupils to achieve.
- Ensure planning involves an understanding of the vocabulary that will be introduced or revisited and explicitly teach new concepts and words associated with them.
- Use a variety of visual resources as well as textbooks or worksheets, build pupils interest using pictures, videos and diagrams.
- Give pupils opportunities to share what they already know and can do. Teacher talk is complex and requires pupils to listen actively, give them the floor as well as yourself.
- Allow pupils time to work in mixed ability groups to share knowledge and build their own presentations, pupils who have grasped concepts will consolidate their learning, those that haven't may learn from a voice closer to their own level of vocabulary and comprehension.
- Know where pupils may have learnt similar concepts and knowledge in other subjects or where you are building on their prior knowledge in your subject, and build this into the start of the lesson.

- Be mindful of cognitive overload and the limitations of working memory. Give pupils opportunities for recall and revision. Consider small steps over time. Too much content in one go is unlikely to be retained.
- Remain consistent in your approaches especially when introducing new topics or concepts. Pupils learn best when they feel safe with their learning and will respond to familiarity.
- What you want pupils to achieve needs to be carefully defined and the time allocated should be precise and clear so pupils know when they have to finish. Short tasks that are achievable and provide scope for formative assessment are the best.
- Stimulate the memory by reinforcing the learning, asking pupils to share work they have produced and have visual or sensory prompts available to use.
- Know the power of effective questioning and listening skills and use your time in the lesson to probe deeply with incisive questions and make sure you listen to the answers.

Some pupils will have conditions that require specialist help such as mild autism, dyslexia and ADHD. Teachers need to look broadly at the issues that arise out of these conditions and focus on adapting classroom approaches to deal with lack of attention, poor concentration, inability to remember, poor organisational skills and low-level behavioural issues. Teachers should have the opportunity to work closely with the pastoral team, the SENCO and their peers across subjects to share ideas on how to manage these behaviours in the classroom. Finding solutions is elevating, dwelling on the problems is demotivating and stressful.

Ideas that can build adaptive classrooms include:

- **Different outcomes**: Ask pupils to produce different outputs, for some a written piece, for others a picture, for others some oral presentation, etc.
- **Using support staff**: Plan how to use support staff so that pupils with SEND are not singled out, ask teaching assistants or other pupils to work different groups at different times, not just those who are deemed low ability. Ask them to manage group learning, record one-to-one conversations with pupils or supervise the gathering of photographs or pictures for a presentation.
- **Task differentiation**: Give different pupils a variety of tasks that are on the same topic but different approaches so that pupils can share their learning through a variety of outcomes.
- **Topic introductions**: Find different ways to introduce the topic, a recording rather than teacher talk, a set of presentation slides that pupils can use afterwards to annotate or make notes, a picture or set of photographs that explains the topic.
- **Task timings**: Chunking tasks where some pupils can take a little longer.
- **Questioning and feedback**: Ask incisive open questions that stretch even the lowest ability pupil, don't allow them to say yes or no, a full answer is essential in developing and consolidating knowledge.
- **Group work**: Different groups work together to learn from each other, share ideas or make a presentation linked to materials set out for them.

All pupils' needs should be carefully assessed and teachers made aware of issues that might create barriers to learning. There is an imperative to create the right environment that will ensure they can hear, are not overloaded with too much content, visual stimuli or other distractions or cannot understand because they struggle to read the text, comprehend the meaning or vocabulary. Be aware of circumstances outside school, their disabilities or special needs and their interests and hobbies.

FORMATIVE AND SUMMATIVE ASSESSMENT

The goal of summative assessment is to evaluate pupils' learning at the end of a unit of work or topic by comparing it against a standard or benchmark. More specifically, summative assessments:

- take place when a piece of work is complete and unlikely to be reworked except as revision for a final examination;
- are often high stakes and given a points value or grade such as in an exam, coursework, project or presentation;
- generate data that can support next steps in learning.

The goal of formative assessment is to monitor learning and provide ongoing feedback that can be used by teachers to inform teaching and by pupils to improve learning (Wiliam 2011).

More specifically, formative assessments:

- help pupils to identify strengths and gaps in learning and target areas to work on;
- help individual teachers to recognise where pupils are struggling and address problems immediately;
- are often low stakes where the results are not part of accountability measures or set down as benchmarks for performance grades;
- provide an opportunity for teachers to assess prior learning and plan how to develop the next steps.

There remains an emphasis on summative assessment because accountability is linked directly to performance in external examinations at the end of year 11. There is much debate and criticism of this. However, it is the system we have and is unlikely to change any time soon.

Ofsted have made strides in ensuring that the curriculum has greater breadth and depth and will provide pupils with the knowledge and skills they need for their future. In their handbook and recent research, they have placed much greater emphasis on knowledge and what pupils need to learn and be able to do, not just solely to pass an examination. This, however, does not change the fact that for any headteacher and leadership team, their jobs, the reputation of their school and the life chances of their pupils are explicitly linked to the narrow set of indicators that are represented by Progress 8 scores.

CREATING A CONTINUUM OF LEARNING AT KEY STAGE 3

Assessment provides us with a window on how well pupils are developing as critical thinkers, custodians of knowledge and are demonstrating growing competence in a range of skills. Without opportunities to assess, we cannot plan the next steps in learning. Ofsted (2018) sum this up in their curriculum indicators: 'assessment is designed thoughtfully to shape future learning. Assessment is not excessive or onerous. (Indicator 7a) and 'assessments are reliable'. Teachers ensure systems to check reliability of assessments in subjects are fully understood by staff' (Indicator 7b).

The language of progression in each subject's programme of study, across key stages 2 and 3, guides curriculum planning in relation to what will be taught and assessed in terms of creating a sequence of learning that will build the foundations for GCSE study.

Each programme of study is unique to the individual subject, but the principles of assessment are consistent; pupils must show they can use and manipulate knowledge and demonstrate deeper understanding (Figure 12.1).

Subject teams need to examine the concepts that underpin their subject. Concepts create opportunities to make connections that transcend subject divides or have completely different meanings elsewhere. For instance, power in science means something different from power in history. We need to assess how pupils are deepening their conceptual knowledge and how adept are they at demonstrating this within both subject and cross-curricular contexts.

Skills allow pupils to access knowledge and apply learning. Pupils need to use their oral and written skills to analyse and evaluate effectively. They need to deepen their growing body of knowledge through reading increasingly complex texts. Teachers need a planning structure that supports pupils to continually evaluate their learning through their English language skills.

Identifying where maths skills are integral to learning outside of maths can enhance the potential of many pupils. Understanding how a maths concept works in the context of other subjects can be a light bulb moment. How many times have we heard pupils say, 'why am I learning this?' Assessing maths skills alongside other subject content can build confidence and understanding.

Finally, there are the wider thinking, or metacognitive, skills that pupils need to become critical and creative thinkers. Problem-solving is inherent across the curriculum, taking part in group work is an essential skill and helps pupils develop as effective members of a team. Enquiry and investigation create opportunities for pupils to demonstrate growing autonomy in how they think, select relevant information and present findings in imaginative ways. We need positive strategies that assess pupils' growing competence in these skills.

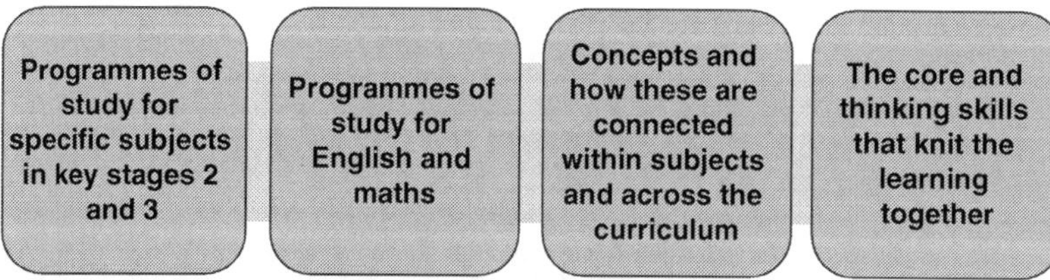

Figure 12.1 Planning for learning and assessing at key stage 3

ASSESSMENT AT KEY STAGE 4 – LEARNING TOWARDS SUMMATIVE END-POINT ASSESSMENTS

All qualifications studied by pupils during key stage 4 form the first tier of the National Qualifications Framework (NQF), an international standard that awarding bodies use to set the level descriptors for assessment of qualifications from Entry Level to PhD. There are three entry levels and eight qualification levels. Included below is a table of the generic level descriptors that should be reached in terms of knowledge and skills.

Table 12.4 is an extract from the Ofqual guide to qualification development and shows the generic level descriptors for entry level to level 3 which is A level. I have not included levels 4–6 (degree level), level 7 (masters) or level 8 (PhD). The descriptors demonstrate what subject leaders need to focus on in determining where pupils are in terms of achieving a qualification outcome. They focus on complexity of task or knowledge, familiarity, increased autonomy and competence in the use of cognitive and practical skills.

Identifying the qualification level a pupil is working towards is important. For some pupils to achieve a grade 4 at the upper end of level 1 is a massive achievement, if they are working towards a level 2 set of grades, they may find this too difficult and fall below their potential of level 4. For pupils with special needs, the three entry-level descriptors are useful. There are many opportunities for pupils identified as working at entry-level. The charity ASDAN specialise in awards for pupils with special needs. Their bronze, silver and gold award schemes form a ladder of achievement which pupils can use towards their next steps in learning and even qualification outcomes. For pupils at the top end of level 2 predicted a grade 8 or 9, it is useful to have an eye on next steps in terms of A level or level 3 vocational courses or apprenticeships.

At the end of key stage 4, there are mark schemes used by awarding bodies to set the questions across all examinations. They are used by external GCSE and A level assessors. They are also used to create assessment grids for vocational courses. The mark schemes all have clearly defined assessment objectives (AO) set out below:

AO1 - Knowledge and understanding - How well do pupils recall and explain the key concepts and ideas in the subject, including knowledge of key terms, theories and concepts.

AO2 - Application of knowledge and understanding - How well do pupils apply their knowledge and understanding to solve problems or answer questions, including the ability to analyse, interpret and evaluate information.

AO3 - Analysis and evaluation - How well do pupils critically analyse and evaluate information, arguments and evidence of subject knowledge, including pupils to make judge, justify and draw conclusions.

AO4 - Synthesis and creativity - How well do pupils synthesise and create new ideas or find solutions linked to their knowledge and understanding of the subject, including pupils' ability to use creativity and imagination to solve problems or answer questions (Ofqual 2017).

The general principles behind these assessment objectives apply across all subjects, but there will be variations tailored to subject-specific requirements. There are also variances in how

Table 12.4 Qualifications and component levels Entry level to Level 3 (Ofqual 2017)

Level	Knowledge descriptor	Skill descriptor
Entry 1	Elementary achievements, beginning to make use of knowledge that relate to the subject or immediate environment.	Progress along a continuum that ranges from the most elementary of achievements to beginning to make use of skills that relate to a subject or immediate environment.
Entry level 2	Basic knowledge or understanding and able to carry out simple, familiar tasks; knows the steps needed to complete simple activities.	Carry out simple, familiar tasks and activities. Follow instructions or use rehearsed steps to complete tasks and activities.
Entry level 3	Basic knowledge to carry out structured tasks in familiar contexts and knows and understand the steps needed to complete structured tasks and activities in familiar contexts.	Carry out structured tasks and activities. Be aware of the consequences of actions for self and others.
Level 1 (GCSE 1 – 4)	Basic factual knowledge of a subject, facts, procedures and ideas to complete well-defined routine tasks and address simple problems and is aware of information relevant to the area of study or work.	Use basic cognitive and practical skills to complete well-defined routine tasks and procedures. Select and use relevant information. Identify whether actions have been effective.
Level 2 (GCSE 5 – 9)	Knowledge and understanding of facts, procedures and ideas in an area of study or field of work to complete well-defined tasks and address straightforward problems. Can interpret relevant information and ideas. Is aware of a range of information that is relevant to the area of study.	Select and use relevant cognitive and practical skills to complete well-defined, generally routine tasks and address straightforward problems. Identify, gather and use relevant information to inform actions. Identify how effective actions have been.
Level 3 (A level)	Has factual, procedural and theoretical knowledge and understanding of a subject or field of work to complete tasks and address problems that while well-defined, may be complex and non-routine. Can interpret and evaluate relevant information and ideas. Is aware of the nature of the area of study or work. Is aware of different perspectives or approaches within the area of study or work.	Identify, select and use appropriate cognitive and practical skills, methods and procedures to address problems that while well-defined, may be complex and non-routine. Use appropriate investigation to inform actions. Review how effective methods and actions have been.

different awarding bodies weight and apply the assessment objectives across subjects. Individual subject leaders and their teachers need to carefully consider assessment objectives when planning the knowledge sequence, the content and how to ensure pupils can demonstrate their skills of recall, application, analysis, evaluation and synthesis.

Shared dialogue within and across subjects can ascertain how to best support pupils to understand what the assessment objectives mean in terms of answering exam questions. This should be linked to their ability to explain, solve problems, analyse a situation, hypothesis or a set of results, to evaluate, synthesise and create. These verbs are part of the mark schemes for all subjects and collaborative dialogue should lead to the strengthening of pupils' ability to answer higher-order questions that support higher grades.

DEVELOPING A WHOLE SCHOOL FORMATIVE ASSESSMENT STRATEGY

A cohesive, whole school assessment policy should ensure all pupils are progressing and can achieve their full potential. Here are ten statements that can support a consistent whole school approach.

So assessment:

- should be an essential element of planning and delivery of the curriculum;
- should be constructive and positive and consider the emotional impact it can have on learner motivation;
- should be motivating and encourage the pupil to want to learn more;
- must be linked to clearly defined outcomes and how they should be assessed;
- works when it focuses on how pupils can improve, gives clear direction about what they do well and focuses sensitively on gaps in learning;
- should include opportunities for pupils to reflect on their own learning as part of self-assessment;
- of learning needs must be a structured element of ongoing professional development;
- should be an integral pedagogy that is central to a learning classroom;
- should consider different starting points, the range of abilities and the need for stretch and challenge.

Learning is complex and the greater the opportunity to ensure pupils are made aware of the skills they are using to access knowledge the deeper will be their capacity to learn.

FEEDBACK AND COACHING FOR DEEP LEARNING AND PROGRESSION

Feedback is so important in ensuring pupils accept the need to do or say more or look again from a different perspective if needed. The EEF have written useful recommendations for embedding the principles of feedback, these are:

- **Lay the foundations for effective feedback** - these foundations are to set learning intentions and deliver high-quality teaching and ongoing formative assessment in the classroom.
- **Feedback focuses on moving learning forward** - it should be timely and target specific learning gaps and self-regulation strategies and not the pupil's personal characteristics.

- **Plan how pupils will receive and use feedback** - pay attention to how pupils receive feedback as it can affect their self-confidence and their trust in the teacher. Teachers should encourage pupils to welcome feedback and use it to support progression.
- **Use purposeful and time efficient written feedback** - only relevant if it is timely and is used by the pupil to further their learning and progression through focusing on the task, subject or self-regulation.
- **Use verbal feedback** - can improve pupil attainment and is more time efficient. However, it has the potential to demotivate if the right approach is not adopted.
- **Create a school feedback policy** - a whole school policy will ensure a cohesive approach. All staff should have the opportunity to have CPD and work with colleagues to develop highly effective strategies that lead to deep learning.

Education Endowment Foundation (2021)

Effective feedback is about supporting pupils to develop higher-level thinking skills that are bound up in the assessment objectives we looked at earlier in this chapter. Active listening and asking incisive questions that lead to deeper thinking are essential (Table 12.5). There are many types of questions that will support learning and progression, here are some with examples:

Closed questions can evoke a yes or no answer - Have you finished? Are you enjoying this approach?

Open questions require a full answer - What else can you add in? How do you think that went?

Probing questions - Where is there more information about this? What more could you do with this?

Leading questions - What can you add in here to finish this piece of work? What are your thoughts?

Loaded questions - How many times have you missed the deadline? What is it that makes you frequently late?

Funnel questions - What was it that particularly interested you? What did you enjoy most about the task?

Table 12.5 Questioning for progression

What .... are the learning outcomes you want to achieve?
.... do you already know that you can build on here?
.... do you need to do now to add to your current understanding?
.... do you need to do to find out more?
So what .... have you learnt so far?
.... are the next steps?
.... else can you contribute?
.... is your new understanding?
Now what .... will you do to build on your current understanding?
.... might learning this skill be useful for in the future?
.... might you do differently now you know about this?
.... might be the consequences of not using your new knowledge and skills?

Recall questions - What do you remember from last lesson? How is this building on your current understanding?

Rhetorical questions - What did the Romans ever do for us? What colour is Monday?

The approach in the Table 12.5 below is a useful way to build a sequence of questions to support progression.

Mark scheme assessment objectives are designed to create opportunities for progression to higher level thinking. We need to challenge pupils to think deeply about their learning and go beyond simple recall. Instead, we need to create a ladder of learning that describes the thinking processes in a scale of increasing difficulty or complexity such as the latest amended Bloom's taxonomy or the SOLO taxonomy (Biggs 1982).

An amended Bloom's taxonomy was part of the changes to assessment of learning in the rationale for assessment of the current curriculum (DfE 2015). The main changes were a listing that moved from nouns to verbs where knowledge and the cognitive processes work together at process level. So, in terms of a taxonomy for progression, we have (Figure 12.2).

To build from lower to higher-order thinking, teachers need to ask questions that challenge pupils towards using higher levels of response. This will give them the ability to answer the questions that lead to higher marks.

Below is a matrix that might help to develop a suite of questions for deeper learning (Table 12.6).

- Remembering – recognising or recalling knowledge for memory
- Understanding – Constructing meaning from different types of interaction for example, written, graphic or spoken and being able to interpret, exemplify, classify, summarise, infer, compare or explain
- Applying – Putting knowledge into practice through the creation of ideas, products, models, presentations, simulations
- Analysing – how knowledge and concepts inter-relate, how to differentiate, organise and attribute cause and effect and being able to distinguish between different elements or component parts
- Evaluating – making judgements, drawing conclusions, critiquing or reviewing, making recommendations and reports
- Creating – putting together the elements into a new pattern or structure. Synthesising or making a new product, project or presentation

Figure 12.2 A taxonomy for progression (after Bloom; DfE 2013)

Table 12.6 Developing deeper learning through questioning

Remember and understand What?	Apply and analyse How?	Evaluate and create Why and what next?
• List the main types of .... • Describe the functions, main points, next steps • Draw a table to illustrate your findings • Choose the method and explain your choice • Illustrate your findings • Complete the task from what you have found out so far • Interpret your ideas of what is happening here • Make predictions of what happens now	• Order the facts to demonstrate your understanding • Summarise your findings • Predict what happens next • From your current understanding construct your arguments for change • Complete the model/diagram/ essay from the information you already have at your disposal • Calculate the answer from the information you have already gathered • Explain the reasons why	• Rank in order of importance the main points and explain why • From your own research what are your conclusions? • Examine the information and how it has helped you make this assessment of the facts • Examine the main reasons that your plan has supported your deeper understanding of the situation • How can you combine the main findings to create your own ideas about this? • What does this mean as a consequence for the future? • Compose your own scenario of what might happen next

CONCLUSION

Assessment is a critical part of planning an effective and progressive curriculum. The process of assessing learning should be considered as part of the whole school vision for excellence. The assessment of learning and pedagogy will generate qualitative and quantitative data. The emphasis in this chapter is on the approaches to pedagogy and learning that will provide the evidence that pupils are making progress and are challenged so that they achieve and exceed their full potential.

Assessment should focus on how pupils can access curricular knowledge and retain it for year 11 examinations. Skilful planning and sequencing create opportunities for recall and reflection where pupils can build on prior learning and add complexity and nuance to their growing repertoire of knowledge and skills. Ongoing formative assessment is essential for ensuring pupils learn well, that inevitable misconceptions are corrected and mistakes can form the basis of future learning. For pupils with SEND, there needs to be a collective and collaborative approach that ensures their needs are met as part of a cross-curricular approach to their development alongside their peers.

Assessment objectives are the bedrock of the grading system across all GCSEs and vocational qualifications. Building reflective, creative and analytical learners is the ultimate aim. Rich continuing professional development is needed so that all those who teach any subject can be involved in supporting our pupils' quest for depth of understanding and a love of learning.

Ten Top Tips

1. Create a consensus so that how pupils work will be assessed is planned alongside what should be taught.
2. Ensure all staff understand the shift in the purpose of assessment in relation to the role of supporting progression.
3. Plan backwards, decide what outcomes in relation to learning objectives and build schemes of work that create opportunities for progression, recall and reflection.
4. Create opportunities for subject leaders and their teams to work together to focus on consistency and validation in relation to assessing learning.
5. Ensure reading is an essential focus for every subject leader and his or her team.
6. Create opportunities for subject leaders and teachers to work together to moderate pupil's work to ensure consistency and accuracy of judgement.
7. Build relationships with the SENCO, tutors and support staff so that all pupil facing staff know the needs of pupils deemed as SEND including their learning, physical and social needs so that planning ensures all pupils can access the full curriculum.
8. Make sure formative assessment is viewed as a pedagogy and is an integral part of every lesson.
9. Create opportunities for teachers and their leaders to focus on the generic level descriptors and NQF level descriptors and to share their approaches to support progression and higher-level thinking.
10. Support teachers and subject leaders to develop a range of coaching skills that will support positive, non-judgemental feedback that motivates and inspires pupils to be creative and deep learners.

REFERENCES

Biggs, J. (1982) *Evaluating the Quality of Learning: The Solo Taxonomy: Structure of the Observed Learning Outcomes*. New York, NY, Academic Press.

DfE (2015) *Final Report on the Commission on Assessment without Levels*. London, DfE.

DfE (2020) *SEND Code of Practice*. London, DfE.

Education Endowment Foundation (2021) *Cognitive Science Approaches in the Classroom: A Review of the Evidence*. London, Education Endowment Foundation.

Education Endowment Foundation (2021) *Teacher Feedback to Improve Pupil Learning*.

Lemov, D. (2015) *Teach Like a Champion*. San Franscisco, Jossey Bass.

Ofqual (2017) *Ofqual Handbook: General Conditions of Recognition, Section E Condition E9 Qualification and Component Levels*. London, Ofqual.

Ofsted (2018) *Research into Curriculum Design*. London, Ofsted.

Ofsted (2019) *Inspecting Education Quality: Workbook Scrutiny*. London, Ofsted.
Ofsted (2024) *School Inspection Handbook*. London, Ofsted.
Wiliam, D. (2011) *Embedded Formative Assessment*. Bloomington, IN, Solution Tree Press.

13
BUILDING A COLLABORATIVE AND SUSTAINABLE FUTURE

Contents

THE CURRICULUM ACROSS THE UK

We are part of four nations and since devolution each separate country has designed their own National Curriculum. In Scotland, Northern Ireland and Wales, the curriculum is designed through the lens of different areas of learning.

The Northern Ireland curriculum defines three key elements relating to each curriculum objective which can be taught through various subjects, developing as an individual, developing as a contributor to society and developing as a contributor to the economy and the environment. There is also a clear emphasis on learning skills and capabilities, through cross-curricular, thinking skills and personal capabilities. In Scotland, there are four overarching contexts of planning and learning, these include, curriculum areas and subjects, interdisciplinary learning, ethos and life of the school and opportunities for personal achievement (Education Scotland 2023). The Curriculum for Wales talks about key purposes for the curriculum in its ambition to create ethical informed citizens of Wales and the world; ambitious capable learners ready to learn throughout their lives; enterprising, creative contributors ready to play a full part in life and work and healthy confident individuals ready to lead fulfilling lives as valued members of society (Gov.Wales 2021).

For each, their curriculum does not divide into separate subjects but into distinct pathways that require inter-disciplinary planning that weaves and connects the learning. Below is how each country has defined their curriculum content (Table 13.1).

It is revealing how England compares. The curriculum documentation for each of the devolved governments in relation to planning and delivery is useful in understanding what works best in a curriculum that will offer a quality education for all pupils (Spielman 2023).

We all want a world class education for those we educate. Whilst the National Curriculum is compulsory in local authority schools, it is not so in schools belonging to academies and I would suggest that as a profoundly useful personal CPD experience, it is useful to look at what our UK partners have developed and are using. The emphasis on the pupil, creating a holistic and connected curriculum and ensuring that pupils develop a range of core and wider learning skills is the mission across all four countries and taking the best from each is very useful (House of Commons Library 2023).

Table 13.1 Curriculum content areas in Scotland, Wales and Northern Ireland

Scotland	Wales	Northern Ireland
• Expressive arts • Health and well-being • Languages • Numeracy and mathematics • Religious and moral studies • Sciences • Social studies • Technologies	• Expressive arts • Health and well-being • Humanities • Language, literacy and communication • Mathematics and numeracy • Science and technology	• Language and literacy • Maths and numeracy • The arts • Learning for life and work • Modern languages • Environment and science • Science and technology • Physical education • Religious education

THE FUTURE OF THE CURRICULUM

The last government White Paper for England came out in 2022 and was ambitious in its aims for what will be achieved by 2030. It set out a proposal that all state schools would be run by a multi-academy trust by 2030. This would mean that the National Curriculum would no longer be compulsory and each school could design a curriculum relevant to their pupils and local and other contexts. Much may change with a new government elected in July 2024 but as w wait for change the last White Paper remains relevant.

The White Paper has some key pledges that will form part of the discussion about the future of the curriculum (DfE 2022: p16).

- A new arms-length curriculum body
- A richer longer, average school week
- Better behaviour and higher attendance

At the time of writing, there are several structural issues that remain outstanding if these are to be achieved. The new arm's length body is an extension of the Oak National Academy, established during the pandemic. It was granted the contract to work with partners to develop curriculum resources designed to reduce teacher workload and guarantee high-quality curriculum planning and delivery. It is now the subject of legal action being pursued by organisations that believe that the plans for the new academy are an 'unprecedented and unevidenced intervention' that risks causing damage to the school sector (TES 2023).

The focus on the school week is controversial and must be investigated as part of the already contentious areas of workload, well-being and teacher retention and recruitment. There is also a need, following the pandemic, to look at blended learning and the greater use of technology in the school system. The potential to create podcasts, video lessons and offer pupils an opportunity to learn in a variety of new ways needs to be integral to rethinking how schools develop the classroom, the school day and the school year.

There does seem to be an issue with behaviour post-pandemic. There may be many reasons for this, but pupils had to adapt to learning independently use technology in a much more involved way and cope with distractions and a lack of peer or teacher interaction for many months. Their world changed and trying to put back what was there before is not the answer. The White Paper answers the problem of behaviour by suggesting that 'better' behaviour can be achieved through more effective data, including an annual behaviour survey and a national data system. Data are a snapshot in time and will not address the underlying problems of poor attendance or disruptive behaviour.

A powerful curriculum, highly confident and well-trained teachers and exceptional resources for inspiring learning will impact on behaviours. What is needed are opportunities for teachers to learn from each other, build self-esteem and self-belief in their pupils and themselves and a create a system that celebrates the potential of every pupil in the school not just high achievers. Where schools value pupil voice, find innovative ways to create learning opportunities and use feedback that encourages reflection, celebrates progress and never dwells on failure the results are profound.

Where we go next will undoubtedly be a political choice. Whether curriculum policy continues to be drawn on traditional knowledge-led lines, or the progressive model where a more skills-oriented approach is preferred is for future debate.

There was certainly a shift towards the curriculum being at the forefront of educational policy when Ofsted revised its framework in 2019. It was clear that Ofsted wanted to change the narrow model that had dominated curriculum planning and the focus on pupils achieving highly in their SATs tests and in GCSE examinations. Their new vision was curriculum breadth and depth, access to the full range of subjects for all pupils including those with SEND, and ensuring reading and maths had cross curricular emphasis as well as in English and maths lessons. Their research that identified three different approaches to curriculum design has been looked at in Chapter 1. The three models are:

- Knowledge-led
- Knowledge-engaged
- Skills-led

The sample study encompassed the early years through to key stage 4. All three approaches have their place. A skills-led curriculum is essential in early years and key stage 1 when pupils are learning through phonics, sounds and simple texts and learning about numbers, number bonds and times tables all through practice, repetition and recall.

In key stages 2 and 3, pupils are perfecting these skills and using them to access knowledge, deepen their understanding and manipulate language and number to describe, explain and analyse the knowledge they are gaining across a range of subjects. This is a knowledge-engaged approach where pupils are using their growing skills in reading increasing complex texts, developing extended writing and presentation skills and learning how to apply maths skills across the curriculum.

Pupils in key stage 4 who have developed their core and metacognitive skills will hopefully have developed their skills and abilities to understand how to answer higher order questions and have the confidence to question knowledge, focus on its validity and look for evidence and are therefore ready for a more knowledge-led approach that will prepare them for GCSE and other year 11 examinations.

Post-pandemic the curriculum must be more pupil-centred. There must be an emphasis on experiential learning that leads to pupils having opportunities to experience life and work. It must consider pupils who have grown up with technology, access knowledge independently and who can shape their own learning and understanding.

SUSTAINABILITY AND CONTEMPORARY LEARNING

Pupils are seeing a rapidly changing world where climate change, the depletion of natural resources and political instability create uncertainty. They will have opportunities to shape their future if they embrace them. As educators we must consider how we create the resilience to shape change and be empowered to work collaboratively to value sustainability over short-term gain (OECD 2018).

Pupils tend to be aware of the issues around sustainability but often only superficially. They hear stories on the news about climate change and its catastrophic consequences in terms of fires, floods, droughts and the displacement of settlements. The curriculum of the future must put sustainability first and embrace the responsibilities and accountabilities that future generations will need. Pupils need to know the causes, the effects and how change might move us all towards a sustainable future. To do this, there must be opportunities for teachers, curriculum designers, inspectors of education systems and the wider business and social community to come together to find a collective and dynamic way forward.

Education plays a vital role in developing these forward-thinking processes. The National Curriculum in England will need to change to offer a greater emphasis on personalised learning linked to what pupils want to achieve as adults. We must double down on our efforts to create independent, passionate learners who are not passive recipients of shallow knowledge but can question the status quo, think critically and be creative with technology, design and science.

To move forward with the curriculum requires reflection on what employers, academics and communities will need to support the radical changes that are essential for all our futures. How can we use curriculum flexibility to ensure pupils are developing as responsible, adaptable and self-aware individuals who will embrace change and challenge?

One answer is to build capacity within the teaching profession to look at how pedagogy fosters reflection and critical thinking; the ability of pupils to question current thinking, consider different perspectives and the consequences of decisions that have shaped our world. The secondary school has an abundance of brilliant subject expertise and opportunities to focus on the big questions about what the future of the curriculum should look like and create the innovators and critical thinkers we will need.

The OECD have defined five common challenges that curriculum policymakers should consider:

1 Confronted with the needs and requests of parents, universities and employers, schools are dealing with curriculum overload. As a result, students often lack sufficient time to master key disciplinary concepts or, in the interests of a balanced life, to nurture friendships, to sleep and to exercise. It is time to shift the focus of our students from 'more hours for learning' to 'quality learning time'.
2 Curricula reforms suffer from time lags between recognition, decision-making, implementation and impact. The gap between the intent of the curriculum and learning outcome is generally too wide.
3 Content must be of high quality if students are to engage in learning and acquire deeper understanding.
4 Curricula should ensure equity while innovating; all students, not just a select few, must benefit from social, economic and technological changes.
5 Careful planning and alignment are critically important for effective implementation of reforms.

These reflect issues we face in the UK, a crowded curriculum, a mismatch between vision and output, the continual quest for understanding quality in planning and implementation, parity for all and a political and sector commitment to reform the system for learning and not for a past ideology.

TECHNOLOGY AND THE FUTURE

We are in the midst of a 'fourth industrial revolution' (Philbeck and Davis 2018) powered by unprecedented technological advancement. Our education system has changed little in a century. The focus on achievement at year 11 with a success rate of just over 50% (pupils achieving above grade 5) demonstrates a system that appears to be failing half of all pupils. We need a system that creates pupils who know how to think and not just what to think. Applied learning matters (Howers 2022) and we need to find ways to marry what employers and communities want. Today's pupils need to be team players, confident enough to accept that mistakes are part of learning, make assumptions and test them, take the initiative and work with others to plan projects and solve problems.

This new revolution includes the impact on society of artificial intelligence and changes in the way we communicate and socialise. Changes in how we educate and learn is largely ignored as we continue to be wedded to a system that tests short-term memory and the resilience to sit and handwrite for several hours over a few weeks. The pursuit of knowledge is key to learning, but we need to rethink how we develop pupils as thinkers and assess their capacity as employees and citizens.

STEM Learning is a powerful driver for curriculum change to enhance the learning in its family of subjects. The potential of an integrated programme of learning that embraces the STEM initiative, alongside the arts STEAM, is a robust curriculum model that has the aim of equipping pupils with the right skills and attributes they will need for their futures (Institute of Arts Integration and STEAM 2023).

ACCOUNTABILITY AND A SELF-SUSTAINING SYSTEM

We all have a responsibility and are accountable for the pupils we educate in the schools we work in. Education is different from any other profession in that every teacher is a leader in their classroom. Observation to test quality of performance and view how well the curriculum is being implemented is infrequent and most of the time teachers are simply there to lead their pupils towards achieving the outcomes and goals that have been planned. School leaders and subject leaders have a difficult job trying to maintain high-quality outcomes when their only means of assessing progression is through data gathered at the end of a given period. Data can only inform next steps, and it cannot undo what has gone before.

Accountability can't be about inspection and data-driven end-of-key-stage results. We need a self-sustaining model of accountability borne out of a deep understanding by every member of staff that they are all working towards a set of parameters linked to structured and timebound quality assurance processes that must include:

- positive leadership;
- knowing the needs of all pupils;
- engaging and empowering all staff;
- defining and achieving successful learning outcomes;
- designing consistent assessment and improvement strategies;
- evidence-based decision-making;
- engaging with the community and all stakeholders.

Where these are broken down into key indicators (Learning Cultures 2020), they can be tracked as progress towards excellence that is realised by every member of staff within the organisation. Quality is about continuous improvement. It is a commitment to reflect on what works well, what can be changed that will enhance learning and how all staff can work together to share strengths and work towards filling any gaps in their own learning.

The most powerful way to ensure that a self-sustaining system of continuous improvement is visible is to embrace a coaching culture where teachers learn from each other, where the power of professional dialogue drives positive change and where there is belief that all staff and pupils can continue to learn and grow their potential over time.

Creating the structure that supports this approach is defined by these guiding principles.

- Matching whole organisation curriculum intent to what is delivered
- Creating a quality assurance process that ensures consistency, coherence and successful outcomes that are consistent across all subjects
- Building a sequential curriculum that builds on prior learning and deepens knowledge
- Ensuring that deepening learners' literacy and numeracy skills are a priority within all subjects and pupils know how these skills support their potential to progress
- Sharing an understanding of key concepts, vocabulary and subject specific knowledge and skills within subjects and across the curriculum
- Unified approaches to assessment that ensure learners deepen their understanding and progress well towards clearly defined end points.

A vision for curriculum excellence requires a learning culture, where skills and knowledge are woven together to foster a deep conviction that we can change and can make a difference for the future for all pupils, for teachers and teaching assistants and for the whole school.

REFERENCES

DfE (2022) *Opportunities for All: Strong Schools With Great Teachers for Your Child.* London, DfE.

Education Scotland (2023) *Curriculum for Excellence.* Edinburgh, Education Scotland.

Frater, G. (2020) *Creating a Culture of Continuous Improvement.* Bridgnorth, Learning Cultures. Available online: https://learningcultures.org/news/quality-of-education/

Gov.Wales (2021) *The Curriculum for Wales – Statements of What Matter Code.* Cardiff, Gov.Wales.

House of Commons Library. (2023) *Comparing the School Curriculum across the UK.* London UK Parliament.

Howers, A. (2022) *What Applied Learning Really Looks Like.* London, The Enterprise Network.
Institute of Arts Integration and STEAM. What Is STEAM Education in K-12 Schools.
Martin, M. and Turner, C. (2023) *Oak National Academy: Judicial Review to Go Ahead.* London, TES.
OECD (2018) *The Future of Education and Skills.* Paris, OECD.
Philbeck, T. and Davis, N. (2018) The Fourth Industrial Revolution: Shaping a New Era. *Journal of International Affairs* 72(1): pp17–22.
Spielman, A. (2023) *Speech to the Festival of Education.* London, Gov.Uk.
STEM Learning: STEM.org.uk.
STEAM. https://artsintegration.com/

INDEX

Zeitfracht Medien GmbH
Ferdinand-Jühlke-Straße 7
99095 Erfurt, Deutschland
produktsicherheit@kolibri360.de